JUN   2003

B MORTON
Reich, H
Jelly's
life, music, and

Jul. 20 '03

WITHDRAWN

JELLY'S BLUES

JELLY'S BLUES

The Life, Music, and Redemption of
JELLY ROLL MORTON

Howard Reich and
William Gaines

DA CAPO PRESS

A Member of the
Perseus Books Group

ALAMEDA FREE LIBRARY
2200-A CENTRAL AVENUE
ALAMEDA, CA 94501

Copyright © 2003 by Howard Reich and William Gaines

All rights reserved. No part of this publication may be reproduced, stored in a retrieval system, or transmitted, in any form or by any means, electronic, mechanical, photocopying, recording, or otherwise, without the prior written permission of the publisher. Printed in the United States of America.

Designed by Trish Wilkinson
Set in 10.5-point Sabon by the Perseus Books Group

Cataloging-in-Publication data for this book is available from the Library of Congress.

ISBN 0–306–81209–6

Published by Da Capo Press
A Member of the Perseus Books Group
http://www.dacapopress.com

Da Capo Press books are available at special discounts for bulk purchases in the U.S. by corporations, institutions, and other organizations. For more information, please contact the Special Markets Department at the Perseus Books Group, 11 Cambridge Center, Cambridge, MA 02142, or call (800) 255-1514 or (617) 252-5298, or e-mail j.mccrary@perseusbooks.com.

1 2 3 4 5 6 7 8 9—07 06 05 04 03

The authors dedicate Jelly's Blues *to the pre-eminent New Orleans jazz historian and collector William Russell, who rescued from sure destruction thousands of pages of documents on the life, times, and music of Jelly Roll Morton.*

ACKNOWLEDGMENTS

The authors thank everyone who helped inspire and create this book, especially Ann Marie Lipinski, Jack Fuller, Jack Davis, Gerould Kern, Geoffrey Brown, Robert Blau, George Papajohn, and Jennifer Fletcher, of the Tribune company; York Eads Nicholson; M. T. Caen, literary agent; John Radziewicz and Ben Schafer, of Da Capo Press; Don and Millie Vappie, of New Orleans; Alfred Lemmon, Mark Cave, and Nancy Ruck, of the Historic New Orleans Collection; Jon Kukla, formerly of the Historic New Orleans Collection; researcher Michael Montgomery; and Professors James Dapogny and Lawrence Gushee.

CONTENTS

PREFACE

At first glance, the petite white building near the crossing of Royal and St. Peter Streets—in New Orleans's age-old French Quarter—looked no different than the other relics on the block. Its hand-painted wooden shutters and wrought-iron latticework evoked the same mystical period in American culture, when the nineteenth century was slipping into the twentieth, and a new music—jazz—was beginning to take shape.

But appearances can be deceiving. The building's classic New Orleans facade might have seemed typical, but its contents, though virtually unknown to the world, were extraordinary. Inside the narrow building and up a creaky flight of stairs, a two-room apartment had been packed from floor to ceiling with used Tulane Shirt Co. boxes, weather-beaten A&P grocery bags, and other cartons, crates, and containers.

The stash all but filled a living space roughly twenty feet wide by thirty-five feet long and twelve feet high, a paper-laden firetrap if ever there were one. Within these walls, an eccentric collector named William Russell had jammed more than half a century's worth of New Orleans memorabilia—the long-forgotten, precious ephemera of

American jazz—with each shirt box and shopping bag meticulously labeled by hand.

Until Russell's death in 1992 at age eighty-seven, no one realized the significance or the value of the precious documents that he had hoarded—in some cases, by seizing them from trash bins just before the garbage collectors did. There were more than sixty-five thousand items in all, including historic correspondence, contracts, photos, and other bits and pieces of music history, most of it pertaining to the man who claimed to have invented jazz, Ferdinand "Jelly Roll" Morton. The collection documented Morton's rise in New Orleans at the dawn of the twentieth century as the first jazz composer, as well as his descent in the 1930s into obscurity and extreme poverty. The authors verified and expanded upon this material by locating and analyzing copyright records, conducting interviews, and examining public documents, including congressional files, civil lawsuits, probate records, corporate filings, and material from the U.S. Department of Justice.

Toward the end of his life, in the late 1930s, Morton was nearly forgotten as a jazz innovator and widely ridiculed as a braggart, pimp, card shark, pool hustler, and, worst of all, has-been. His biographers eagerly retold his colorful stories of life in turn-of-the-century New Orleans but called him a liar when his facts clashed with theirs. More than half a century after his death, in 1941, he was termed a racist by the fanciful Broadway musical *Jelly's Last Jam* (1992), a cliché by the movie *The Legend of 1900* (1999), and a brute and a bully by the Ken Burns TV documentary *Jazz* (2001).

Like uncounted black jazz giants to come, he was caricatured by the white popular press and robbed by the white music industry. But Morton's attempts to claim his rightful place in American music history and to win back the millions he said had been stolen from him were, alas, casually brushed aside by history. Even those who acknowledged Morton's achievements as the first musician to prove that the ephemeral art of jazz could be captured on paper, in the form of complex, contrapuntal scores, blamed his demise on Morton's shortcomings of character or talent. If Morton hadn't rubbed so many people the wrong way, they said, he might have gotten more work when he needed it most. If he hadn't been so hard on musicians, he might have been able to hold a band together. If he hadn't lost touch with the changing musical tastes of the 1930s, he might not have been discarded by the jazz industry he had helped create.

Yet all these well-worn bits of conventional wisdom, recycled and embellished in article after article and book after book, were minted before anyone had studied the full contents of Russell's gloriously overstuffed French Quarter apartment. So only Russell knew that the pulpy myths about Morton were half-truths at best. Only Russell realized that the young man who indeed started out as a New Orleans hustler had reinvented himself as a serious composer who spent every penny on his music. And only Russell knew of Morton's brilliant last scores, the groundbreaking works the composer penned in the last three years of his life but couldn't get anyone to perform or record.

It was nearly sixty years after Morton's death that the composer's epochal last music was heard, and these compositions alone recast his place in history. For even at the end of Morton's life, when he had run out of money and chances, he was writing music more harmonically and structurally advanced than anything else by his more celebrated peers, and he knew it. The man who had made the first great leap in jazz, capturing an improvised art on paper, at the end of his life made yet another: In composing his radical final pieces, Morton pointed the way toward an avant-garde music that still was more than a decade in the offing.

Reconsidered through the avalanche of otherwise forgotten paperwork that Russell rescued from oblivion, as well as newly unearthed documentation from court, probate, and copyright records, Morton emerges as a different character than the prevailing wisdom suggests. He was not the pathological liar of familiar lore but, in his maturity, a focused, if humbled, man whose letters prove verifiably true and honest.

If a Gulf Coast hurricane had blown into the French Quarter before Russell's death, the documents that reveal what really happened in Morton's life might have been swept away forever, leaving the true story of Morton's noble journey unknown and the myths forever in place.

Fortunately for anyone who prefers hard facts to tired tales, no tempest ever disturbed Russell's irreplaceable collection, and as he approached the end of his life, he arranged for his precious papers to be stored in the vaults of a Crescent City archive, the Historic New Orleans Collection. This trove included the heartbreaking correspondence Morton penned in the last three years of his life to his closest remaining friend, Roy Carew. When the archivists at the Historic New Orleans Collection opened Russell's musty grocery bags and unfolded the yellowed shirt boxes, they brought to light hard evidence that could dispel the myths, partial truths, and distortions that long have hovered around Jelly Roll Morton's name.

The composer himself very likely walked past the quaint old building near the corner of Royal and St. Peter Streets many times in his New Orleans youth. But he couldn't have imagined that its contents someday might help vindicate him, showing at last that he wasn't the charlatan that history eventually made him out to be.

one

THE DISTRICT

On a steamy September day in 1904—the Louisiana air far too thick for a Midwesterner's lungs—a soft-spoken twenty-year-old from Grand Rapids, Michigan, showed up for his first day of work and was stunned at what he heard. Though he had spent time in Chicago and New York, the two biggest, noisiest cities he knew, nothing could have prepared him for the bedlam occurring outside the Hibernia Bank and Trust Building, at 313 Carondelet Street, in downtown New Orleans.

Roy Carew, a bespectacled young bookkeeper waiting to meet his new boss in the eighth-floor office of the New Orleans Acid & Fertilizer Company, jumped when he heard an explosion outdoors. Although Carew had been told fabulous tales of the way life was led in New Orleans, no one had mentioned this kind of cacophony.

"There was a sudden burst of music from Carondelet Street, right below the windows of the Hibernia Bank and Trust Company, and everyone went to the windows and looked out," he recalled, viewing the procession from atop a skyscraper that attested to New Orleans's stature as the economic capital of the South. Even before office towers had begun reaching to the clouds up in Chicago, the Hibernia Bank and Trust building soared twelve stories high, a massive, stone-and-mortar marvel as modern as anything in the United States at the time.

From his perch in the building, Carew heard and saw everything.

"Happened to be the Negro Labor Day parade, nineteen hundred and four, and that was my first introduction to New Orleans music. ... They were stepping along in fine shape, down Carondelet Street. There were several bands in the parade, but I don't recollect much about 'em. But inasmuch as the year was nineteen hundred and four and they've talked so much about [cornetist] Buddy Bolden being on the scene then, I feel that possibly he was one of the players, and his band must have been in the parade."

Whether or not New Orleans's most famous, leather-lunged cornetist of the day was contributing to the mayhem on this morning, however, was beside the point. The sonic blasts that rattled the windows of the Hibernia building on this Monday, September 7, were part of the natural order of things in a city where blacks, whites, Creoles, and various mixtures of each bumped up against one another in music, and in the streets.

Their primal meeting ground was the parade, a rough-and-ready civic gathering where roving bands often doubled as street gangs, protecting territory, brandishing blades, and cutting one another before the day was done. But Bolden wasn't the only notorious New Orleans musician who blew a horn as bloody battles played out around him. So did a young musician whose life would become inextricably tied to Carew's several decades later, when the musician would be down and out and nearly forgotten—Ferdinand "Jelly Roll" Morton. As a teenager who had been born in New Orleans, Morton hadn't yet acquired his colorful sobriquet, but by 1904 he already was immersed in the riotous musical culture of his city. Parades, after all, were open to just about anybody willing to bang on a drum or blow on a horn for a dollar or two, and Morton always could use an extra buck.

"Every Sunday there was a parade in New Orleans—[they] would have a great big band, and they would have horses, and they would have big streamers and things that cost plenty of money," Morton remembered. "And one would outdo the other. . . . But the best bands, they all had the streamers and the sashes for things like that. . . . The drums be goin' 'RUMP, RUMP, RUMP, rump, rump.' Then the trumpet would pick it up, they'd be goin' right along. 'RUMP, DUMP,' the trumpet say, 'Voo Doop!' And when it say that, the drums say— 'Rump! Rump!—Rump! Rump! Rum err err BOOM!' And then they'd start, see. Like 'Stars and Stripes Forever,' they play it in this style. Da-da, da, da daa, da-da-daa, da it, da dum, dum. . . . I'm telling you, sometimes it would be a terrible hot and the kids would be jumping up and the boys, like the drummer, would be throwing his sticks up in the air and catching them. Throwing them on the ground, bouncing them up in the air and catching them, and he'd better not miss as the whole bunch would razz him. . . . Any time they walk four or five blocks, why they'd have a keg of beer, sandwiches, whiskey and all kinds of drinks. So they could get drunk and have a good time and of course they called it a ball."

The slightest verbal cue could ignite passions fueled by booze and stoked by the scorching Louisiana sun. One youngster told another to get off his street, the other refused, and, in a flash, a war of words became a battle of the flesh. As the musicians played, a "second line" of locals who marched alongside the band—or behind it—struck the blows. One fellow said, "Get the hell out of here," and another instantly retorted, "If you don't, you black son-of-a-bitch, I'll kick your brains out." Soon blows landed, guns reported and an ambulance rolled up to cart away the casualties, even as the chaos spread. While war raged, the blood turning the dirt in the streets to red-laced mud, the musicians kept blowing, their riffs delivered by bass horn, trombone, trumpet, reeds, bass drum, and snare drum. Ferd relished the music and the money—five dollars for the leader, half that for the rest—while the boys loved the booze.

"I didn't care much for the drinking," Morton explained. "It was a particular kind of fun. There may have been nicer fun, but only in New Orleans could you have fun like that," said Morton, pronouncing the name of his hometown New Orleeeeens. "The first battle of music ever waged was in New Orleans in those parades, I'd wager."

So this was how they lived and died in New Orleans. Roy Carew was startled but intrigued on his first day in this strange city, with its heady music and violent cultural rituals. Carew did not realize that he was witnessing the second of two parades—the "Negroes Ensemble," as the *New Orleans Times-Democrat* put it, in which black labor unions began to march after their white counterparts had finished. Though both pageants began at the same starting point, Elks Place, the one Carew observed took an entirely different route—through the black part of town—progressing from Canal to Carondelet, to Gravier, to Camp, to Poydras, to St. Charles, to Washington, to South Rampart and to St. Philip. After a thirty-minute rest, the 5,000 marchers proceeded to Dryades, to Howard, to South Rampart, to Girod, to Saratoga, to Canal, to Rampart, to Esplanade, and, after another thirty-minute break, back to Rampart, to Frenchman, to Royal, to Canal, and, finally, back to Elks Place. "All the members of the unions who could were in line, and some of the uniforms worn were picturesque," observed the *Times-Democrat*. "Those of the Cotton Yardmen were particularly so. Each member of this union wore a new suit of overalls with a blue jumper, and from his hips to his knees were stretched a stitch of velvet."

Those who witnessed such pomp never forgot it, and for young musicians lucky enough to hear this exultant music as it was being invented, there were precious lessons to be learned from the seeming anarchy of it all. "I remember the time in New Orleans when I was a little youngster—they had the good old street parades, you know, and brass bands, and every one of them was great," recalled Louis Armstrong, who heard horns crying so loudly as to make conversation virtually impossible. "Freddie Keppard, he had a good tone. In the parade, in the early days, I used to notice with [the] second line, he would wrap his fingers with his handkerchief so nobody could catch the runs he was making. . . . Now here's Manuel Perez, one of the trumpeters in the Onward Brass Band, along with Joe Oliver. Just the two of them were back there, and you never heard so much horn blowin' in your life. . . . Now here's an old man—'bout 60-some years old when I was a kid, and he had a big brass band called the

Excelsior Brass Band, his name was old man Moret, he was the leader of that brass band, and I used to notice every time he was gonna get a high note, he would just slightly look up, and there came that note, see? And I admired that so well, 'til I adopted a style myself. . . . Now here's the boss of 'em all, King Oliver, I thought was the greatest of all of them, although he didn't have the tone that Bolden had . . . didn't have the tone that Freddie had . . . but whatever Joe did, I thought he was the greatest creator of them all. . . . I loved the way he used to blow, and I'd stay in the parade by carrying his trumpet."

The most original musicians America had yet produced were dispensing their wares for free, on the streets of New Orleans, to anyone who cared to listen. Though the uninitiated might have thought that these street musicians were randomly hitting odd, discordant notes, artists such as Bolden, Keppard, Perez, Oliver, and Bunk Johnson were forging the rudiments of a rough-and-ready musical language that Armstrong and Morton would refine and Carew would be content simply to savor. Young, on his own, and unschooled in southern ways, Carew wasted no time in exploring the twenty-four-hour carnival spinning around him. He marveled at the street vendors crying out, "Blackberries, blackberries," as if to some ancient blues melody. He took in the minstrel shows at the Crescent and Tulane Theaters, where audiences laughed it up at low, doltish comedy. And he wandered into the District, more formally known as Storyville, a teeming neighborhood of saloons, brothels, shooting galleries, cabarets, and dance halls where desires never discussed publicly back home in Grand Rapids were casually displayed and openly satiated—for a price—practically in public view every night of the year.

"Below Canal street, which split the District in half, was Basin Street, which was noted for its famous and exclusive mansions, operated by such renowned women as Lulu White, [Gypsy] Schaeffer, [Josie] Arlington," recalled New Orleans guitarist and raconteur Danny Barker. "On the other streets that ran parallel to Basin—Liberty, Marais, Villere—the class of the meat market prices descended as low as fifty cents for its entertainment."

As Carew strolled along the already infamous Basin Street, the District's main artery, he marveled to see curbside prostitutes working their cribs, squalid little roomettes barely big enough to hold a bed and a washstand. The half-dressed women reached out to grab him as he hurried by, offering their services for as much as a buck. Carew didn't know it yet, but deeper inside the District, bargain hunters could find gratification of a sort for as little as a dime.

Yet on the next block of Basin Street, where it crossed Customhouse, the price of sex and real estate shot up. On the corner stood Tom Anderson's Annex Café and Chop House, with a hundred electric bulbs lighting up a famously hand-carved, cherry wood bar that stretched half a block. From this opulent saloon, Anderson ruled the District like a king, deciding who came and went, levying fines, settling disputes, and otherwise maintaining a semblance of order. At Tom Anderson's, visitors picked up the infamous Blue Book listing the plush brothels on this block and others close to it, describing the particular charms of each. Armed with this invaluable information, the men—sailors and dock workers with time to kill, businessmen and farmers with money to squander, lads ready to take the plunge— strolled to fancy whorehouses run by infamous madams. The honor roll included women such as Gypsy Schaeffer, who presided over a sprawling, three-story stone edifice at Villere and Customhouse, and Miss Antonia P. Gonzales, who "has the distinction of being the only Singer of Opera and Female Cornetist in the Tenderloin," raved the Blue Book.

There was sex for every taste at every price, the luxuriant brothels notorious for dispensing hedonistic abandon while New Orleans's top piano players unfurled their buoyant ragtime melodies. Music and lust were intertwined here, one almost unimaginable without the other. "I was the first one in New Orleans to employ a jazz pianist in the red-light district," Countess Willie Piazza bragged, having anointed herself "the first lady of Storyville." "In those days jazz was associated principally with dance halls and cabarets . . . it was what most of our customers wanted to hear."

The action in the lowdown cribs, on the other hand, did not unfold to such exquisite accompaniment. On the contrary, the crib prostitutes dispensed fast sex at curbside while a small army of ill-trained piano players pounded away in nearby honky-tonks. At night, there was no escape from their incessant noise, a hundred out-of-tune uprights—thousands of yellowed keys—clattering at once.

"It was always in late evening near dusk or at nightfall when the District woke up, came to life, and its characters went on the prowl for fresh game," remembered Barker. "As night fell, the lights began to flicker on in the hundreds of dens, cribs and traps for the unwary. The joints began to get some action; as if out of nowhere there appeared, going to and fro to their neighborhood hangouts, dozens of whores, pimps, gamblers, hustlers and also all of the local characters who were physically able to move from their beds. When darkness finally settled on the District, it was like an amusement center: Coney Island, Atlantic City, boardwalk, music and laughter."

The noise in this place suggested a neighborhood twice its size, the din of conversation punctuated by any number of bands blowing full tilt inside the saloons or out front, as if trying to drown out one another. The men who played the loudest, the thinking went, stood the best chance of attracting the most customers, and getting the suckers in the door was key. "They used to play [out] on the sidewalk in front of the dance hall before they go inside, about a half hour, see," said Armstrong, who as a child heard Buddy Bolden, Joe "King" Oliver, Bunk Johnson, Frankie Dusen, and Bobby Lyons ragging their rhythms out in the street, where all New Orleans could hear them, their clarion notes on a clear night carrying practically across the Mississippi. While these horns sang, all kinds of vice flourished in the District, which was mandated for its purpose in 1898 and shut down in 1917. In addition to sex on demand, the District offered drugs of practically every sort, including opium, heroin, cocaine, morphine, laudanum, and others available at the nearest pharmacy. Often, the pharmacist dispensed the powder onto a small playing card, which, when folded side to side, could carry the stuff to its destination.

"There were more dope fiends in New Orleans in those days," said Morton, "than any place in the country."

Out on the streets, the sharp stench of lye permeated everything and could make the eyes water. The casual visitor had no idea that the stink came from small, open cans of lye that the street whores half filled with water and stored under their beds or behind a bed stand. This was their only defense when a customer turned violent. The moment some brute got rough, the woman reached down, grabbed the can, and splashed its contents directly into the man's face. Suddenly, the customer "found himself screaming, howling, jumping and frantically trying to wipe the hot lye away from his face, chest, ears, eyes and the upper part of his body," recalled Barker. "These streetwalkers did not like to be beaten and abused and they never missed when they threw that lye. When the victim finally arrived in the hospital, he was in bad shape and burnt up and in pain. The attendants at the emergency ward never rushed to attend the victim because they knew what the scoundrel had done. The lye never caused death, but it scarred a person for life."

Brought to a boil by drugs, alcohol, and desire, life in the District routinely careened into violence, the crimes perpetrated by sadistic pimps, drunken customers, and common thieves. At one point, "a couple of evil men came into the District and went from house to house cutting the girls," said Morton. "With long knives they slashed and hacked the girls across the breasts or face. The uproar was such that after a half dozen girls were cut, the men were caught and a howling mob kicked them to death—a more deserving punishment than being shot."

Amid this vortex of nihilism, sensuality, and hallucination, the place that instantly seized Roy Carew's attention was Hilma Burt's, an upscale brothel at 209 Basin Street, next door to Tom Anderson's (Burt, in fact, was said to be Anderson's wife). Billed in the Blue Book as "a palace second to none," this immense three-story structure towered as the unofficial gateway to the other high-priced brothels on the block. Its front windows looked out on the train tracks that paralleled Basin Street, its huge white awnings serving to block the sun and prurient interests.

Inside, the place was decadence incarnate, its library practically as opulent as its boudoir. For the gentleman inclined to open a book, the reading room conveyed luxury via a collection of rare, hand-bound tomes (including an array of international erotica), oil paintings with frames often more costly than the artworks themselves, and outsized leather chairs that were not easy to escape. In the bedroom, just down the hall, the gentleman observed floor-to-ceiling mirrors bordered with delicate wall stenciling, tassels dangling elegantly from heavy drapes that admitted no light, and a multitude of overstuffed pillows piled all over the bed.

"Miss Burt has been with us but a short time but has won all hearts," observed the Blue Book. "There are no words for her ladies— one can only realize the grandeur of feminine beauty and artistic settings after an hour or so in the palace of Hilma Burt."

It wasn't just feminine beauty and plush accoutrements, however, that seduced Carew. At Hilma Burt's, he heard a piano making a music that danced more sensuously than any of the society quadrilles he had heard in Grand Rapids. It was a music relaxed in tempo but lush in its sheer profusion of notes, its melodies trickling sinuously from the top of the keyboard to the bottom and back again. At times, it sounded as if two or three musicians were playing the instrument, with melody line, bass line, inner voices, and chordal fills rumbling all at once.

This music outshone virtually everything Carew had encountered in a town practically ablaze with hot piano players. Having immersed himself in the city's sounds, Carew learned early to identify piano players after hearing just a chorus or two. He knew all about the virtuosity of Kid Ross, possibly the District's only white "professor," as they called the hot-piano men. He savored the stomps and blues that were Buddy Carter's stock in trade, the keyboard stunts that made Albert Carroll famous, and the back-to-basics ragtime that John the Baptist unfurled at Willie Piazza's house. Carew studied it all—the speed-demon pyrotechnics of Sammy Davis, the deep-down blues of Game Kid, and the weird chords of Mamie Desdoumes, who was missing two fingers in the middle of her right hand and therefore picked odd combinations of notes that no one else did. Frank Amacker, Frank Richards, Trigger Sam Henry, Black Pete, Manuel Manetta—Carew had memorized their keyboard tricks, yet none could be mistaken for the sound he now was hearing for the first time: young Ferdinand Morton at the eighty-eights. Carew had not imagined that a piano could sound as ebullient as it did when Morton was giving the instrument everything he had. After making inquiries, Carew learned that he was hearing one of the city's most skilled young piano men—some would say the best.

"I heard him play at Hilma Burt's," recalled Carew, describing that indelible evening in 1904. "I was passing there one night, and there was some very good Spanish music coming out of there. And I stood out in front and listened as long as that music was. . . . Kid Ross played there most of the time, [but] Ross was not the player that Jelly Roll was. . . . The music was clear cut and very smooth, and of a characteristic Spanish type, and like the well-known brook, it just kept running on. I listened for quite a while, and when the playing stopped, I strolled on," added Carew, who decades later would hear a sick and desperate Jelly Roll Morton playing the same haunting Spanish refrain. "The beat of the music," said Carew, "made an impression on me and kept going through my head."

Morton unspooled his tunes on an upright piano in Hilma Burt's Mirrored Ballroom, the instrument facing the mirrored wall, the pianist's back to the women, who strolled like goddesses for hire through a parlor gilded with crystal light fixtures and glittering gold trim. They wore the most expensive finery, dresses whose layers of material cascaded around them, the hems often lined with silk. Flowers adorned their coiffures and bodices, a garden of vice available to anyone who could afford the costliest champagne and companionship in the South. Everything reeked of elegance, and, each night, a certain ritual played out.

"Nine o'clock the three darkies would start the music in the front parlor, and the piano player would be noodling on the baby grand in the back parlor, which was the parlor for the big muckamucks, the city hall boys, the state capitol gents, the better family folk, out-of-town actors," remembered the madam Nell Kimball.

> The sports didn't start coming in till after a late supper near ten. I'd ring a bell for one of the nigger maids to ask some of the girls to come down. . . . By midnight the place on a good night would have a dozen to twenty men in both parlors, the girls circulating and the maids passing out drinks. . . . By two in the morning the rooms were all occupied and I'd be drinking with the waiting customers, and the girls would sort of slide downstairs again, their faces refreshed and their hair combed.

Despite the lascivious purpose of this place, strict rules of decorum prevailed. The women in their lavish gowns knew what was expected of them by the madam and were reminded sternly whenever they forgot. No swearing, smoking, or heavy drinking by the girls was allowed, and those who ignored these rules paid dearly: five dollars for each cuss word, ten dollars for getting drunk. "No two girls could talk to a man at the same time," explained Rosalind Johnson, one of the few female piano players at Hilma Burt's. "If a man come in, he would sit in a chair, and they had something like velvet footstools, we called them, and the girl sat on that and talked. If the man didn't like that girl she'd leave and another girl would come and talk."

Nor were the girls permitted to speak to one another if the madam was in sight, for fear they might be conspiring against her. The irony must have been inescapable even to the working women, who gave paying customers complete liberty but enjoyed none themselves. "It was really slave trade," noted Morton, with the madam berating the girls if they were caught talking: "'Go on to your room,'" the madam yelled. "'Get away, you bitches—g'wan!'"

Yet in this tautly controlled setting, the piano player enjoyed practically unlimited freedom. The best brothels had several parlors, the piano player scurrying from one to the next, setting a mood and pocketing the cash. In these brothels, Morton began to develop a buoyant music marked by syncopated melodies in the right hand, walking bass lines and bouncing chords in the left, a veritable symphony of New Orleans cakewalks and ragtime at his fingertips.

"Any time I got broke, in a sporting house I would go," said Morton, and the best houses clamored for his services, with Hilma Burt, Josie Arlington, Lulu White, and Gypsy Schaeffer making a fuss whenever Morton strolled in. He even worked for Emma Johnson's Circus House, where naked dances and sex acts were performed, close up, for paying customers—a distinctly New Orleans brand of theatrical entertainment. While the erotic acts progressed, Morton played music to match, both setting the tempo and following it. He usually worked from behind a screen, but to get around this impediment, Morton often cut a hole at eye level with a pocket knife, so he could ogle the action while his fingers stroked the keys.

The ambience inspired a red-hot music, which became still more brilliant and rhythmically free at the Frenchman's, an after-hours saloon nearby, at the corner of Bienville and Villere. After working the brothels or catching cornetist Joe Oliver at the Big 25 (at Franklin and Iberville) or hoisting a few at Billy Phillips's place (around the corner from Tom Anderson's), the New Orleans professors headed for the Frenchman's. They started filtering in at about 4 A.M., ready to blow off steam after a long night's work. This was where they gambled, drank, took turns at the piano, and tried to cut each other with their newest and flashiest keyboard repertoire. More than at the brothels, where the piano men played for money, here they played for each other and, thus, for art. Music lovers, insomniacs, and late-night women swarmed the place, a hothouse for a newly emerging sound that still had no particular name, except for "New Orleans music." In the front room, a bar and nearby piano kept spirits high, while a table in the back room accommodated food, drink, and cards.

Morton went so far as to call this "the place where jazz originated," the birth of an art form attended by whores dripping diamonds and delivered by bone-tired musicians stoking up with a toot of cocaine or winding down with a pinch of heroin.

Yet for all its sordid excess, or perhaps because of it, this scene enticed Morton. To behold its piano players wearing the finest clothes, snorting the most expensive dope, and dallying with wealthy, exotic, independent women was to be transfixed by the possibilities of life as a New Orleans piano player. In this setting, a man who knew his way around a keyboard was admired by his peers, doted upon by the madams, and gifted with bundles of sweet cash.

"The back room would be lighted early in the nights, about the same time the saloon lights would go on, but apparently not used till later," wrote Morton. "New Orleans was credited at that time as the second greatest Tenderloin district in the world, second only to Paris, France. That was before the electric piano days and every house that could afford it would have what they called their professor. Alfred Wilson, Albert [Carroll], Sammy Davis did not care to work, they would prefer to gamble, they all had clothes on top of clothes. Diamonds, studs, Diamond Rings, Diamond Suspenders, Cuff bottoms, Diamond Garters, and etc . . . Money had no value. For instance, Ed Moshay, a very mediocre Pianist and big time ladies man and gambler, died about four years ago. I understand he was broke but left 114 expensive suits of clothes. Well when a A-1 pianist had a $100 night they usually figured they had a terrible night."

That a respectable Creole (a Louisianian of mixed European and African origin) had descended into this forbidden world—embracing it, reveling in it, and earning from it what seemed to him a fortune—proved a source of shame to Morton's censorious middle-class family. So much, in fact, that they would disown him once they realized the kind of musician he was becoming. But for Morton, doubly blessed with at least a rudimentary musical education and an innate ability to play any music by ear that he heard, there was no better way to proceed. The gig was too lucrative, the nightlife too alluring, the music too hot to resist.

The Frenchman's was his conservatory, the District his concert hall, and young Roy Carew his perfervid admirer. Morton did not know that Carew heard him on that summer night in 1904—the two young men did not meet. But Morton's music earned him an unsung champion in Carew, who three decades later would try to break Morton's terrible fall.

The large house where Jelly Roll Morton was born—as Ferdinand Joseph Lamothe—looked regal for its environs, occupying a spacious lot at 1443 Frenchmen Street, downtown in the Seventh Precinct, Seventh Ward. Its brick-and-cement foundation supported a white frame structure stretching so long it obviated the prospect of a backyard. With its porch fully shaded by the second-floor overhang and a second-story dormer that looked out on the rest of the block (which at the time contained only one other house), this "estate," as Morton called it, was enormous among its neighbors. Not as spacious, to be sure, as the mansion brothels that later employed the young man, but big enough to suggest that young Ferd grew up amid comfort.

Louise Monette and Ed Lamothe, a contractor/demolisher, were his parents, but early on Ferd's mother kicked out his father for too much carousing. No marriage certificate is known to exist, nor a birth certificate for Ferd. A posthumously uncovered baptismal citation raises more questions than it answers, and the scholar who found it— thereupon concluding that Morton had lied about his birth date—has since retreated from this claim.

But whether Morton was born on September 20, 1885, as he swore, or October 20, 1890, as the unreliable baptismal citation states, there's no dispute that he spent the late 1890s at the Frenchmen Street address. Christened by his godparents, Paul and Eulalie Hecaut, he lived with an extended family that grew quickly each year. In February 1894, his mother married Willie Mouton, a light-skinned black man who signed the marriage certificate with an "X" and toiled as a porter in hotels and clubs. The arrival of their two daughters, Amede Eugenie Mouton and Frances Mouton, meant that Ferd now basked in the attention of two half sisters, as well as that of his Grandmother Laura Péché and her family, his Uncle Auguste "Gus" Monette and

Aunt Elena Péché—and their relatives. The warmth of this extended Creole family, with Ferd as its first son, was matched only by its inevitable raucousness.

Moreover, in a house where a trombone, zither, guitar, piano, and other instruments were practically strewn about, Ferd couldn't have avoided music if he had wanted to. So far as he was concerned, his life was bound up with rhythm, pitch, and harmony practically from birth. "My godmother, Eulalie, would always take me around, passing me off for her child (I was supposed to be a pretty baby) and one day she loaned me to one of her friends to also make believe," Morton wrote. "Somehow the woman was arrested and refused to relinquish 'her child,' so we both went to jail. It was in jail that my inspiration for music was first noticed. Some of the inmates were singing, and I was supposed to have shown great interest, and would smile along with the singing and weep when they would quit, [so] they sang until I fell to sleep in the cell."

That Ferd's godmother, Eulalie, should consort with the kind of woman who wound up in jail was not so surprising, for Eulalie served the prostitutes of Storyville as a voodoo practitioner. Her repertoire of magical spells, potions, elixirs, and seances made her immensely popular in the District, though her sorcery apparently could not be applied to herself, for none of her nine children survived birth. Perhaps that's why Eulalie, who went by the more mundane name Laura Hunter when she wasn't practicing her craft, developed an intense attachment to her godson, Ferd. It was Eulalie who saw to it that Ferd didn't simply enjoy music but studied it, arranging for him to take lessons on six-string steel guitar at age five.

To hear Ferd tell it, he made plain his keen interest in playing music. He wrote of himself:

Morton's first instrument was made up of two chair rounds and a tin pan. To him, this combination sounded like a Symphony, because in those days, there were only classical selections being played. The next instrument he tried was the Harmonica. He was only 5 years old when he was trying to play these different instru-

ments. After trying to play the Harmonica for two years, he discovered that he was the world's worst, and decided to change to
a Jews-harp. The nearest this instrument would sound like music
was like the humming of a bee. Then he tried Steel Guitar. This
was his first actual lesson in music[,] given to him by an old
friend, a Spanish gentleman.

The unnamed teacher may have given Ferd his first exposure to
the regal habanera rhythms of Spanish music and influenced Ferd's
later belief that jazz required "a Spanish tinge" to be considered authentic. When he wasn't noodling on instruments, Ferd—who spoke
only French in the first few years of his life—regularly attended the
French Opera with his family. Here, he absorbed the European musical tradition of romantic operas such as Gounod's *Faust* and Verdi's *Il
Trovatore,* and harmonic breakthroughs in radical work such as De-
bussy's *Pelléas et Mélisande*. He relished the coloratura lines that sopranos sang in Donizetti's *Lucia di Lammermoor,* their ornate, often
improvised, melodic embellishments sometimes drawing hysterical
ovations from the crowd. Thanks to the French Opera, a broadly popular institution in late-nineteenth-century New Orleans, European
classical music made an imprint on both nascent jazz and Morton's
emerging musical sensibility. Specifically, the Europeans' concepts of
harmony, scale, and melodic ornament inexorably seeped into indige-
nous New Orleans music and into Morton's conception of melody
and phrase.

   Yet even as Ferd was embracing the high art of grand opera, he
also learned music in the traditional New Orleans way, on the streets.
Singing in a cappella quartets at the corner of Jackson and Robertson,
he studied harmony in the best way possible—by making it. "Those
days I belonged to a quartet, and of course we specialized in spiritu-
als," recalled Morton. "The boys had some beautiful harmony they
sang. Of course, we got together and made all kinds of crazy ideas of
harmony which make it beautiful and made it impossible for anyone
to jump in and sing. I tell you, we had such beautiful numbers to sing
at all times."

A few years of guitar lessons made him proficient, but the superior playing of a black friend named Bud Scott, as well as an aesthetic revelation at the age of ten, persuaded Ferd to switch to piano. For though Ferd had been enchanted by the keyboard since seeing a musician play a piano at the French Opera, the man's long and bushy hair suggested to Ferd that pianism might not be a wholly masculine endeavor. "Young Morton did not care for the piano[,] although there was a piano in his home, because there was a saying that it was strictly an instrument for a lady," he wrote. "He did not feel like being embarrassed and laughed at by his associates for playing his instrument. Therefore, he would not touch the piano[,] in spite of it being a home ornament and relic."

But when Ferd witnessed another man—one with properly short-cropped hair—setting off boisterous ragtime rhythms on a piano during a party, he was smitten anew and determined to learn the instrument. Unfortunately, he soon discovered that his piano teacher, Mrs. Rachel D. Moment (of 3231 South Franklin), was a fake: She played every score he put in front of her as if it were essentially the same piece of music, assuming he wouldn't notice. He did, and quit.

As if in protest, Ferd redirected his musical attention, shifting to blues/ragtime piano by studying with a musician named Frank Richards. This radical change of direction did not go over well at home. "In those days, everybody was playing what they called ragtime, and I wanted to play it, too," Morton said. "But my [step]daddy caught me trying one day and took off his belt and tanned me good and proper: He said: 'Son, if you ever play that dirty stuff again, I'll throw you out of here on your ear.' But man, I couldn't no more stop playing it than I could stop eating."

The raunchy blue notes, the relentless rhythms, and the barrelhouse keyboard attacks that Ferd's stepfather deemed vulgar were forbidden in the Mouton home. So Ferd and his instructor headed to Ferd's place of refuge at this time: the home of his godmother Eulalie Hecaut, uptown. Though even at this early date Ferd realized Richards's limitations—particularly Richards's ignorance of music theory—at least the older pianist could correct Ferd's most obvious blunders. "I claim that his contribution was more in the perfection way," explained Morton. "The melodjes were all mine, but I believed he could do much better with it than I could because he made a lot of corrections [in Ferd's music] that probably would have gone maybe haywire."

That Morton should have gravitated from French opera to earthy blues was practically predestined, for this music had become pervasive in New Orleans. Whether voiced informally by street vendors or sung lustily in saloons or transformed toward a higher purpose in church, the searing and rambunctious spirit of the blues—with its expressively flatted melody notes and exquisite clash between major and minor— was the essence of New Orleans music. "I heard blues when I was knee-high to a duck," wrote Morton, late in life.

> When I first started going to school I heard some of the blues pi-
> ano players such as Budd[y] Carter, Josky Adams, Game Kid,
> Sam Henry and many more too numerous to mention. I heard
> blues tunes entitled "Alice Fields," "Isn't It Hard to Love,"
> "Make Me a Pallet on the Floor"—the latter which I played my-
> self on my guitar. In New Orleans the 'ragmen' would take a 10c
> Christmas horn, remove the wooden mouthpiece and play more
> blues than any trumpeter I ever met in the rest of the country.
> The whole world with the exception of New Orleans was igno-
> rant of the fact that blues could be played by an orchestra.

A family doctor announced that the preternaturally thin Ferd was on the verge of consumption and recommended hard physical labor. So Ferd began sweating for pennies after school, first as a dishwasher, then in the backbreaking task of making barrels for the Brooklyn Cooperage Company, at three dollars a week. With each of these steps—the after-school jobs, the blues piano lessons—Ferd slowly was breaking away from the family that had nurtured him. Early in the new century, he spent two years living mostly with his godmother, Eu-lalie, simply to play his music and immerse himself in her voodoo in-cantations. But after the death of Ferd's mother, while Ferd was still in his teens, and the subsequent disappearance of his father, Ferd found himself more profoundly cut off from the family home than he had intended. All he had left of his mother was her memory and of his stepfather, Willie Mouton, a surname Ferd did not like. Mouton, Ferd said, had to be Anglicized to Morton so that no one would call him "Frenchy." And so another tie with his family—its French language and culture—was cut.

But Gallic nicknames were the least of Ferd's problems. Without a mother or a father, Ferd in the first decade of the new century was being pulled in more directions than he could comprehend. His great-grandmother, Felice "Mimi" Baudoin, as well as his grandmother, Laura Péché, insisted he set a good example for his half sisters and hold a steady job. More than once, the subject turned a pleasant family dinner into a battle royal.

"I can remember, when I was about eight years old, my grandmother Laura scolding my brother for staying out all night," recalled Frances Mouton. "I mean she just didn't approve of him playing in those shady places and coming back home where children were. She wanted him to respect a girl, and not come in and tell his experiences of the night before to my uncles. . . . Also, my grandmother was afraid of venereal diseases and thought he might bring them home to the family."

So Ferd's uncle, a barber who served as his legal guardian, took it upon himself to employ Morton at twenty-five cents a week to perform a variety of menial tasks. Yet all the while, Eulalie stirred Ferd's interest in music and voodoo—activities that rendered the barber shop dismal by comparison. It was Eulalie who arranged for Ferd to study with a Professor Nickerson at St. Joseph's School, the last formal music instruction Ferd ever received. Music and Eulalie, forever bound up with each other, became the only constants in Ferd's young life. "The older generations were passing away and friends were vanishing," Morton wistfully recalled. "The estate was being mortgaged, and Grandfather was losing his liquor business . . . and things were generally going bad."

Ferd needed a place of his own, away from his family's dictates and from Laura Péché and Mimi Baudoin's scrutiny, and he found it in the most obvious place, the part of New Orleans where music was everywhere and the spotlight inevitably shone on the man who played piano best. So Ferd veered, inexorably, to the District. At first, the spectacle of so many half-naked women calling out from their cribs, while laughter and hot piano playing rang out from every open window, unnerved a boy of his middle-class Catholic upbringing. Yet he returned again and again, lingering late into the night at the Frenchman's, where he heard the best piano players in the District asserting themselves on the keys.

He recalled:

One night I was at the Frenchman's earlier than usual, and someone in one of the neighboring houses came in looking for a piano player. The boys with me told them I could play and would take the job. I was afraid to but finally agreed to go if the boys would be allowed to go with me. However, the boys were put in another room, and I was put at the piano and told to play. I was so scared that I couldn't play a note and was almost kicked out. My friends came out and insisted that I was all right, and I got my confidence back and played.

As he played, Ferd felt his fears slip away, and the tunes he knew intimately from the parades he had played—surefire crowd pleasers such as "Hot Time in the Old Town Tonight," "Mr. Johnson, Turn Me Loose," and "Bird in a Gilded Cage"—flowed freely from his fingers. The girls began to pull out their bills, tossing twenty dollars his way for barely an hour's work. Ferd protested lightly, then grabbed the cash. Though at first he protested that he couldn't possibly work at such a place full time, the thought of breaking his back at the cooperage for fourteen dollars a week when he could make more than that in an hour—and amid so much youthful femininity—led him to reconsider. It was all so easy. All he had to do was tell his grandmother that he had been moved to the night shift at the cooperage, and the charms of the District were his, at a fantastic rate of pay.

So Ferd unofficially became a citizen of the greatest vice district in the United States, in so doing making the leap from child to adult, from candor to deceit, and from a decent middle-class life to enthralling adventures in music and carnality. If sex was the lure of the District, sensuous New Orleans music was its siren song, seducing with mood and tempo and the dream of romance.

"You'd hear music everywhere you went," recalled Danny Barker, a child during the District's last years.

> You'd hear music in the street—organ grinders pulling their instrument on a two-wheel cart, going from barroom to barroom. And you heard peddlers shouting their wares. You heard music everywhere because everything you did was done musically in New Orleans. New Orleans was a French town and a party town—there was an abundance of entertainment. You could walk down the street and hear a party going on until 11 o'clock the next morning.

Hungry to learn the ways of the District, musically and otherwise, Morton began haunting the twenty-four-hour honky-tonks—noisy, grimy saloons that were just a few blocks from the Storyville mansions that had beckoned him, and several rungs lower on the social ladder. As Ferd put it, they were "the lowest type of dive I have ever seen anywhere, and I've seen all the worst dives." Indeed, they were frequented by women "who had never had a bath in months," Morton said, and by men who would cut your laces to steal your shoes if you nodded off to sleep. "The men, I have personally seen some of them, they were actually lousy. . . . The main revenue for these honky-tonks was the revenue that would come from the little, pitiful gambling games, lot of days waiting for a sucker to come in. But if one really came in, don't worry, he would be really taken."

In these grisly rooms, such as Kaiser's, the biggest of the tonks, at Julia and Rampart Streets, and Spano's, at Franklin and Poydras Streets, Ferd scrutinized the piano players and tried to decipher their techniques. They banged out an up-tempo version of the twelve-bar blues, the rattling bass notes and hammered-out chords later christened boogie-woogie but, at the start of the new century, simply called "playing the horses." No wonder—the two-fisted, galloping piano riffs suggested a stampede gaining momentum every thirty-two bars. Eventually, Morton concluded that all boogie-woogie amounted to was a "non-experienced guy pounding on a piano." Boogie-woogie would never endure, he said presciently, "because there is not enough to it for development—only three or four chords and no other variation. Boogie woogie should be called 'honky-tonk music.'"

Essentially, two classes of musicians jostled each other in this rowdy part of New Orleans. Black players such as Buddy Bolden, Bunk Johnson, and the soon-to-be-famous Louis Armstrong lacked academic musical training and learned to play mostly by ear (though Armstrong in his teens finally learned to read music). These "fake" players, as they called themselves, could not tell the difference between written music and splashes of ink spilled arbitrarily on paper, but they invented a thousand ways to keep a tune interesting, to change it and reshape it according to whim—and to the reaction of the crowd. They lived uptown, above Canal Street, in a neighborhood where music burst forth from joints such as The Big 4 and Big Easy, and under the stars in Lincoln Park and Johnson Park.

Creole musicians like Morton, by contrast, enjoyed the privileges of middle-class life, including formal musical training (to one degree or another), and often could read music on sight. They sprang from a community that thrived downtown, below Canal Street, a neighborhood where music rang out from dance joints such as Economy Hall and Independence Hall. Even in such freewheeling places, it was clear to hear that these Creole artists had embraced the musical values of the European opera and symphony, with their emphasis on precision, accuracy, balance, and refinement.

But in geographically compact New Orleans, unlike anywhere else, the two worlds rubbed up against one another, the high-toned Creole musicians and their self-taught black counterparts playing side by side in parades, funeral marches, curbside bloodbaths, and Storyville brothels and honky-tonks. The clash that ensued when European-influenced Creoles and musically illiterate blacks made music together represented nothing less than a breakthrough in organized sound. It had no formal name, but it opened up expressive possibilities unimagined even by the turn-of-the-century musicians who were inventing it.

"See, the average [black] New Orleans musician developed his own style, because he didn't know how to read music," recalled the Creole trumpeter Percy Humphrey, of the Humphrey dynasty of early jazz musicians. "So he played what he picked up, and he'd catch maybe 18 or 20 different sounds. But the other musicians, like myself and [my brother] Willie, were professionally taught—we knew how to read music because our grandfather taught us how. So whenever you'd hear a band on the street or at a funeral or at a house party, you'd hear these two kinds of musicians trying to get it together."

And there was one more element mixed into this exotic new musical formula: the church, which was paramount in black southern life after the War Between the States. Because newly freed, illiterate blacks were left to fend for themselves, they had nowhere to turn for aid but the Baptist churches, where music held an honored place. "You'd hear the music in church, and when the church Benevolent Societies buried you, they'd do it with music," said Danny Barker. "And everyone wanted to play in the brass bands because it was a good way to get into music. The funeral bands, see, played lots of whole notes," added Barker, referring to the long-held pitches that stretch four beats to the bar. "And that's an easy way to learn how to play."

If music of the church, of French opera, and of the streets inexorably shaped Morton's still nascent art, so did the work of New Orleans's preeminent pianist-singer-songwriter, Tony Jackson, the one man whose dexterous technique and original songwriting left Ferd in awe. Ferd considered Jackson the greatest entertainer that New Orleans ever produced, a man who "could play and sing from opera to blues in its correct formation [and] knew everything that probably was ever printed." Carew, too, fell under Jackson's spell while strolling through the District:

Tony Jackson, I heard him playing at Antonia Gonzales' place, which is on Customhouse and Villere Street. . . . He was tearing it off and in great shape, playing and singing. And I noticed a fellow standing on the curb also listening. So after I listened to a tune or two, I walked over to the fellow, I says, "Who in the world is that?"

He says, "That's Tony Jackson. He knows a thousand songs."

He had a wonderful [singing] voice, and I can't tell you how clear and resonant, you know? He had [a voice] right up into the soprano, you may call it, without any noticeable change. It wasn't what they call falsetto.

Ferd also listened carefully to Tony Jackson, and to Alfred Wilson, Albert Carroll, and dozens more at the Frenchman's, studying their novelty effects and keyboard stunts. The octave tremolos and hand-over-hand figures and shimmering broken chords that were their primary tools intoxicated Ferd, whose classical piano teachers never dared to demonstrate such a loose, bawdy, seemingly uninhibited style of playing. As Ferd mastered this unorthodox lexicon of keyboard tricks, he moved up in rank to junior piano professor, even as his family believed he was dutifully working at the cooperage for fourteen dollars a week.

"By going into the Frenchman's each night I kept getting better and better jobs and soon was making from $80 to $100 a night," he wrote. "I soon learned to play cotch [Spanish poker]. I knew that all I needed to keep was the $14 to take home and that I could borrow from any of the landladies [at the brothels] if necessary. I was playing classics, ragtime and Spanish tunes at these jobs, as well as everything new that was coming out at that time."

With this astonishing windfall, Ferd splurged on custom-made shirts and silk underwear, on high-priced suits and ties of fantastic design. The wardrobe proved so opulent and appealing that Ferd's uncle, who was about his size, began wearing these plush garments behind Ferd's back—until his uncle made a misstep. Recalled Morton:

One night he fell into one of the numerous ditches around New Orleans and ruined one of my best suits. He was very drunk, but I was so angry that I beat him up something terrible. The secret [of Ferd's nocturnal life] was soon out, and I was in disgrace with the family because I had to admit where I was working. My grandmother wouldn't let me stay under the same roof with the rest of the family, and so I was sent out of my home. I was only about sixteen or seventeen at that time, and although I was making lots of money and had been around some, I didn't even know how to go about renting a room.

The dazzling piano player Carew heard while exploring the District was thrust out into the world. His apprenticeship abruptly concluded, Ferd took to the road, bearing the unique musical gifts and singular romantic charms from which he was to fashion his most complex and mysterious creation: Jelly Roll Morton.

two

INVENTING JELLY ROLL

Shunned by his great-grandmother, Mimi, and his grandmother, Laura, for having descended into an indecent place, Ferd was on his own. The stigma of the District, with its drugs and paid-for women and unashamedly earthy music, was not going to pull his half sisters down with him, if Mimi and Laura could help it. "She didn't want to put me out, I guess," recalled Morton, straining to give Laura the benefit of the doubt. Perhaps she did this cruel act, he supposed, "only to curb me so this wouldn't happen again."

Whatever Laura's intent, the result was the same: Ferd's brief dalliance with a lurid but irresistible world had proved catastrophic, forcing him to make his way in the world before he was fully ready. Suddenly rootless, he fell into a nomadic way of living that played out for the rest of his life. Never again did Morton set down in one place for very long or embrace the conventions of the middle-class world that had abruptly banished him.

On his first night alone, Morton wandered the streets of New Orleans until daybreak, mystified as to what his next move could be. As he pondered the events of his youth that had led up to this calamity, he recalled the bitter day his grandmother returned home from a trip carrying a gift for everyone but him. "She told me in French, 'Never mind, when I go again I'll bring you something real nice.' . . . She never did go again, my heart was broken, [and] it was then that I wanted to work for money, and get the things I wanted, and would not have to ask anyone for anything." Now cast out on his own, he was reminded anew: If he wanted anything, he was going to have to find it, make it, or steal it himself. From this moment forth, his existence would depend on how well and how quickly he learned to survive in an alluring but frightening, violent world. When the sun finally came up, he caught an early train to the only place he knew would have him, at least temporarily: his godmother Eulalie Hecaut's country home, in Biloxi, another Gulf Coast party town. The irony probably would have been lost on Mimi and Laura, whose harsh actions had driven Morton simply from one den of sin to another, for Biloxi's tenderloin was every bit as carnal—though not nearly as large or as wealthy—as its New Orleans counterpart. Here, Morton survived in the only way he knew, playing hot piano for the prostitutes, sharpening his skills as a gambler, and otherwise scrambling for cash.

In Biloxi, Morton learned how to cheat at cards, mastering Georgia skin, coon cant, cotch, craps, casino, and five-up. He hustled pool, sported a .38 special, and invented ribald lyrics to sentimental tunes, the revelers roaring at his scandalous rhymes and stuffing his pockets with dollar bills. Clearly, it paid to know more than just how to play a piano. The education of Ferd Morton took him along the breadth of the Gulf Coast, to McHenry, Hattiesburg, Jackson, Vicksburg, Greenwood, and Greenville, where he worked sporting houses and saloons, peddled phony medicine that supposedly cured consumption, learned how to play with rigged dice, trucked cotton in a levee camp, and even ran a tailor shop for a while.

Morton quickly was learning what life was like outside the comfort and care of the Lamothe/Mouton family home, and he was adjusting accordingly. Any way of making money would do, so long as the cash flowed. From here on, New Orleans was little more than a place to go back to, earn some fast money, and head out on the road once more. "Whenever I'd get in trouble," Morton explained, "I'd go back home to New Orleans," where he could regroup. During his periodic returns in the years 1905–1909, he dared to reacquaint himself with old relations, though this time as a man, not a boy. When he showed up at Grandmother Laura's doorstep, he looked leaner and taller than before, his long and slender nose looming over a nearly gaunt face, his golden Creole skin dotted by a mole on the lower right side of his neck. Wearing a narrow-brim cap, a sleekly fitted vest punctuated with the gold chain of a stopwatch, a colorful tie pulled close to the neck, and crisply pleated pants hanging fashionably at the tops of impeccably polished shoes, Morton presented himself as a gentleman of the world. "After my trips, I came either to my god-mother or grandmother," he said, with a degree of satisfaction. "Whatever happens in a family, all you have to do is take some money home, and everything is all right."

So this was the lesson Laura unwittingly taught him: The sordid nightlife was not to be condoned—unless the pay was extravagant and shared with elders. Morton took heed, working tirelessly to make his fortune. "Back in those days I was a wandering boy," he said. "I didn't like to stay too long in one occupation and wanted to see every-thing. I wanted to know all the tricks. I wanted to go to all the towns."

Above all, Morton hungered to learn anything that had to do with music, show business, and hustling, the three fields in which he showed prodigious natural gifts. He tried his hand at the emerging black vaudeville circuit, working practically every two-bit tent show and black theater south of the Mason-Dixon line. "I played road shows," he wrote, rattling off names long since forgotten by history: Kenner & Lewis Stock Company, in Pensacola, Florida; Fred Barasso's troupe in Memphis; Billy Kersands's in Houston; the Ven-dome in Mobile. There were audiences to entertain in stock compa-nies in Kansas City and Oklahoma City. In these hit-and-run appear-ances, Morton sang, danced, joked, played music, and did anything else required.

The locales were not always congenial for a Creole man traveling alone in the Deep South. One evening in 1906, Morton and a troupe appearing with the actor William Benbow played a show in Pine Hill,

Alabama, in a small schoolhouse that sat at the end of a road, over-hanging a steep bluff. "There wasn't no way to get out of that place except along that road," recalled Morton.

> We played to a packed house, and the audience seemed to like our stuff. They insisted that we be held over and wouldn't let us leave town. . . . Next night we pulled the curtain at eight and no one was out there. Nine o'clock, no one had come. Nine-thirty, we began to get worried. I told one of the boys to scout around front and see what was the matter. The guy walked out the front door and ran into a whole nest of men armed with baseball bats, knives, guns and clubs and so forth and so on. They asked him, "Are you with that show?"
>
> "Nawsuh, I come from Scottsborough."
>
> "Well, it's lucky you ain't, because we're gonna kill every one of those black bastards."

The mob swarmed the back of the schoolhouse and began tossing rocks at the windowpanes, the clatter telling Morton that he had to make his move. So he pulled a couple of tattered blankets out of his trunk, cut them into strips, tied them together to make a ragged rope, wrapped one end around a post, and slid down the bluff to safety, the other entertainers scurrying down after him.

Morton had escaped, but not just that time. Throughout his early travels, he heard tales of black men dangling from trees in Greenwood and Biloxi, Mississippi, and more than once he fled town when angry locals presumed him to be fraternizing with a white woman who had paid him a tad too much public attention. These incidents hardly slowed him down, and he tirelessly roamed the South, as if immune to the disasters that befell other men of color in hostile territory. He was strangely unintimidated by these incidents—or perhaps the money was too good, the journey too enthralling, the alternatives nonexistent.

As the cash rolled in, Morton learned how to spend it by watching the vaudevillians around him, including a popular black enter-tainer who went by the stage name String Beans (real name Butler

May). Standing more than six feet tall and wearing outsized floppy shoes, String Beans caught everyone's attention when he opened his mouth, a jewel glittering in his teeth. "He was the first guy I ever saw with a diamond in his mouth, and I guess I got the idea for my diamond from him," Morton later recalled. "I put mine in one time when I had so many diamonds I didn't know what to do with them all, so I said I might as well put one in my mouth. People will do very, very foolish things when they're young and have plenty money."

So Morton paid good cash to have a gold crown inserted in a front tooth and a half-carat diamond set inside it. When he smiled, the rock picked up the glint of the stage lights, as if some pinpoint spotlight were following only him. The Morton persona—a dazzling showman who made sure that he was the focus of an audience's attention and adoration—was beginning to take shape.

In Mobile, Alabama, Morton arrived with enough cash, suits, and jewels to make the other swells look twice. His burgeoning wardrobe became part and parcel of the public image he was cultivating— a flashy, smooth-talking piano player/actor/comedian who looked every whit as good as he sounded.

"I'd gone there to be king of the underworld—a good pool player, good gambler, with all the women after me," recalled Morton.

> The first day I changed to two suits and just walked through the district sharp as a tack, with a big cigar in a holder. The next day with two more; I'd demand plenty of recognition, best of all from the pool players. The second evening, with the fourth suit, a woman called me. The big colored landlady [or madam] in Mobile, Lulu Knowles, had a very beautiful girl, Lila Holliman, in her house. We got stuck on each other, and Lila was making a big play for me.

While Morton eyed her, Lila spoke up. "Where do you get those clothes at?" she asked him. He was ready with an answer before she finished the question: "'If I stay here 10 years, you'll see me in new suits every day."

Lila ate it up. She let on that Johnny King and Skinny Head Pete, two men already on a first-name basis with all the girls in the house, said that Morton knew how to play a piano. Did he? Morton answered without a word, sitting himself down at the keyboard and playing the kind of hot piano that had rarely been heard outside New Orleans. Predictably, the girls gathered around the instrument, watching Morton's slender fingers wend their way around the keys, hitting just the right spots. By the next night, Morton was dining with the girls, regaling them with tales of his adventures along the Gulf Coast, making himself a fixture in this place, and in Lila's affections.

So much, in fact, that when Lila's boyfriend, Billy Mills, showed up and unwisely turned his back to her, Lila dug a knife into him. By stabbing Billy Mills, Lila hoped to liberate herself from a man who presumed to be not only her lover but her pimp. Unfortunately, Lila instantly realized that the blade merely had sliced the loose, boxed-back suit Mills was wearing, not the flesh she had intended to rip. "The coat was split from end to end but the knife didn't cut Billy because of the box back coat," Morton later explained. "The notoriety was in the air that Lila was crazy about me and tried to cut her old boy friend to death."

The next day, Morton showed up at Lila's place again, this time suited up in a striped Oxford gray. He ate dinner, then lay down next to Lila, but with a pistol tucked under his pillow. When he heard a pounding at the front door, he jumped out of bed, threw on his clothes, ran downstairs, and found himself answering to the police, who were following up on a complaint that Morton had hustled some of the locals in a few rounds of Georgia skin.

"You come around here and try to take the town, you big pimp," the cop said to Morton. "We'll show you what we'll do with guys like you. $100 fine and 100 days."

The cop put Morton in shackles, poked a Winchester at his back, and threw him into jail, but Morton didn't blanch or complain. He just bided his time, and after a few days he demurely asked for—and received—an emergency pass to leave the prison grounds briefly. He never looked back. Before the cops knew what had happened, Morton had hopped on L&N train and rode it straight back to New Orleans. Within days, his pockets again were bulging with cash, his wardrobe flush with the latest fashions.

But Morton was not yet finished transforming himself from a frightened Creole boy who once had been afraid to try the piano in a brothel into the opulently dressed, diamond-toothed showman he was attempting to become. He knew that all the great entertainer-hustlers worth talking about had catchy nicknames that enhanced their legends. Listening to the sports talk, he would hear reports of Sheep Eye, the gambler; Game Kid, the blues player; Pensacola Kid, the musician and pool shark; Jack the Bear, the all-around con man; Chicken Dick, the giant brawler; Okey Poke, the bartender; and Willie the Pleaser, the overdressed District glad-hander.

Morton clearly needed a sobriquet, too, to join the ranks of the late-night stars, so he anointed himself "Jelly Roll," a name that several other black vaudevillians already had used with considerable success. Yet he didn't go public with his new identity until one night onstage, while he was playing straight man to the blackface comedian Sandy Burns.

As the sketch proceeded, Burns proclaimed himself Sweet Papa Cream Puff, to which Morton responded, ad lib, that he was Sweet Papa Jelly Roll, "With stove pipes in my hips and all the women in town just dying to turn my damper down." The audience howled, Morton smiled, and the name was now his. But only he knew how elegantly it dovetailed with another, comparably sexual moniker he already had acquired: "Windin' Boy," a reference to a certain pelvic motion at which he had attained particular virtuosity—or at least said he had.

By 1907, the newly rechristened Jelly Roll Morton had made his first foray into Texas, discovering that in this sprawling state—as well as practically everywhere else he went—local piano players were years behind their New Orleans counterparts. The lexicon of barrelhouse, honky-tonk, and brothel piano tricks that were common parlance in New Orleans had not yet been exported, and Morton immediately understood that if he had been formidable back home, he was practically invincible outside the Crescent City:

I made every pig pen from Orange to El Paso—there wasn't a pianist in the state could play doodlee-do. Most every city, town and hamlet had what was known in Texas as a reservation [a tenderloin district]. Gee it sure was easy pickings with no opposition. Every place was heaven. I would jump from town to town. There were no pianists to carve so I just carved all the pool players that showed their heads above water. I kept on through New Mexico, Arizona, California. In the towns where the reservation was not very good, I would usually stay long enough to stage a big dance. The music was by Jelly Roll Morton himself, nothing else. Ducats 25c; if I caught a holiday, Ducats were 50c. When I gave one of my grand dances . . . some stool pigeon had me picked up and jailed; had to stay in for Christmas. I was told I was one of those smart guys and was trying to take all the money out of Texas.

All the world seemed to belong to Jelly Roll, who easily outclassed the two-bit piano men and ham-handed pool players and would-be card sharks who dared to take him on. The kid from New Orleans was too fast, too slick, and too smart for these amateurs. He chortled at the prowess they thought they had, and he embarrassed them more severely than they could comprehend.

The following year, 1908, Morton rolled into Tennessee and met an aspiring musician who called himself Professor Handy. Working as a local bandleader, this was the same man who eventually would acquire fame, power, and prestige as the songwriter and music publisher W. C. Handy. Morton was unimpressed. "I learned that he had not been in Memphis very long from his home town, Henderson, Ky.," recalled Morton. "He was known as Prof. Handy in Memphis," and though the good professor advertised himself as a man of blues and ragtime and jazz syncopation, Morton quickly determined that "Handy could not play either of these types." And when Handy informed Morton that the blues could not be played by a band, Morton almost doubled over with laughter, considering all the blues he himself had played in parades and funeral bands as a boy back home in New Orleans.

Moreover, Morton knew—though Handy could not—that in this very year, 1908, cornetist Freddie Keppard was fronting a hot band in the District that epitomized what New Orleans blues was all about, and doing so in fully orchestrated form. Playing the Tuxedo Dance Hall, on Franklin Street between Customhouse and Iberville, Keppard was raising Cain with a state-of-the-art New Orleans band staffed by trombonist Edward Vincent, clarinetist George Baquet, drummer D. D. Chandler and piano player Bud Christian, each a first-generation jazz man by any measure. Though Handy had no clue that so many players could romp through the blues all at once, Morton was intimately acquainted with this first bona fide "Dixieland" band, as he called it. Their music was so intricately contrapuntal and so rhythmically charged that it very nearly summed up the spirit and fervor of the New Orleans sound. No wonder Handy did not believe that the blues could be played by a band—he hadn't heard what Freddie Keppard and the boys were doing with their horns, laying down a music that pulsed two big beats to the bar, its rhythms so urgent that no one could stand still while it roared. It was this sound—the new New Orleans music—that Morton was reimagining on the piano, his ten nimble fingers articulating the voices of all these instruments as no piano player yet had done.

As a musician, Morton was beginning to feel his strength. The ease with which he devoured second-rate piano players and seduced women of sportive disposition gave him some of the confidence he had once lacked, and he advertised it with his diamond-studded smile, his impeccably tailored wardrobe, and his ebullient brand of pianism. Inexorably, he also was discovering that he was different from the other hustlers on the road, in at least one important regard: Beneath the dash of his attire and the increasing brashness of his manner, something profound was happening to Morton as an artist. For if in the early days in New Orleans he had played tunes as the customers requested them, now he was hearing fresh melodies, rhythms, and chord changes of his own design—a music that came to him unbidden.

The process had begun when he started studying piano with Frank Richards. But the blues idiom that Richards helped Ferd master

did more than just inspire him—the blues somehow unlocked sounds
that young Ferd hadn't realized he had in him. As early as 1902, Ferd
had come up with a series of themes that Richards had helped him
polish and develop, and by 1905 the finished piece was rolling off
Morton's fingers as a bona fide piano composition, albeit one that
wasn't written down. Morton called it "New Orleans Blues" (also
"New Orleans Joys"), and it practically burst from the constraints of
the ragtime era in which it was conceived. It opened with a fairly pre-
dictable introduction, in which both hands played double octaves up
and down the keyboard, but then it slipped into a startling, gently
swaying habanera rhythm. Consciously or not, Morton in "New Orleans Blues" was recalling the "Spanish tinge" he had heard from his
guitar teacher and had early deemed essential to New Orleans music.

From here, "New Orleans Blues" unfurled themes so intricate
that they had to be shared by the two hands. As the piece progressed,
the left hand occasionally fired off a series of driving octaves, recalling
the tailgate trombone that young Ferd had first heard as a youth,
when his father played around the house. Finally, in the most radical
portion of "New Orleans Blues," the right hand burst forth with a series of flying octaves that defied any sense of steady meter or pulse.
Suddenly, the listener was thrown off guard, unsure where the beat
fell or where the piece was going.

Nothing so rhythmically free ever had been heard on a piano—
not from the ragtime piano men of the day (at least judging by their
comparatively more staid published works), nor from the European
masters, whose turn-of-the-century compositions did not approach
this level of rhythmic complexity and sophistication. With the com-
pletion of "New Orleans Blues," the floodgates opened, for Morton
began creating (though not writing) compositions that bristled with
dual themes played at once, harmonies of extraordinary richness and
passing dissonance, and rhythms that surged forward with a ferocity
that foreshadowed the swing era yet to come.

Just as he completed "New Orleans Blues," in 1905, Morton also
was polishing off another work that he had begun three years earlier.
Not even Morton, however, could have imagined that "King Porter

Stomp" would become his calling card in the 1920s, a national hit in the 1930s, and a jazz landmark that composers would perform, re-orchestrate, and reconceive in every generation thereafter.

As Morton developed the piece on the road, trying out snippets of it for paying customers, one listener in particular was beguiled by this music. He was a fellow piano player from Florida named Porter King, and the two musicians struck up a mutual admiration. Morton revered and perhaps envied King's superior musical training, while King—an expert in the music of Scott Joplin—was smitten by the originality of Morton's piano style. So Morton, finally having figured out how to make all the sections of the piece cohere while he was in Mobile, in 1905 named the new work for Porter King, whimsically inverting the title and baptizing the piece "King Porter Stomp."

The composition, which would bring a measure of immortality to both men, was "partially wrote before," said Morton, referring to its three-year genesis. "This was a combination of three or four tunes. These tunes were private material that I kept to shoot at a guy," in piano contests, added Morton, referring to musical duels in which pianists carved each other not with knives but with keyboard virtuosity. Whoever destroyed the competition won the best jobs and therefore the most money, which is why it was imperative for Morton and other piano sports not to publish their tunes. The "private material" had to be protected, lest someone steal the piano players' best tricks.

"King Porter Stomp" quickly became the ace up Morton's sleeve, and it's not difficult to imagine why King was struck by the piece. It opened with a sweet and whimsical introduction played high up on the keyboard, a curtain-raiser elegantly conceived in a manner that Harlem stride pianist James P. Johnson would build upon years later. But after this delicate introduction, Morton startled listeners with a high-flying, bouncing rhythm that made the ragtime music of the era seem practically earthbound by comparison.

With each thematic repetition, the rhythmic tension between the two hands increased, pushing the music forward as only hard-charging, nascent swing rhythm could do. No wonder this piece—written before the term "swing" had been used in a musical context—became the anthem of every decent swing dance band of the 1930s. Its ferocious right-hand syncopations and relentless left-hand rhythms represented one of the first clear-cut distillations of swing rhythm, articulated almost a generation before Louis Armstrong gave this music galvanic new momentum in Chicago, in the mid-1920s.

But the masterstroke of "King Porter Stomp" was yet to come, with the third theme, in which Morton dared to abruptly change keys—from A-flat to D-flat. With this radical gesture, the entire musical landscape of the piece shifted, from the hot, barreling swing pulse of the earlier sections to the sleekly understated rhythmic beat and cooler tone of the finale. In this single composition—a three-minute masterpiece if ever there were one—a composer at the dawn of the twentieth century was pointing the way for at least two decades of musical evolution yet to come. Morton had announced his genius.

Not that he did so consciously. On the contrary, this first burst of creativity was owed to a profound sense of insecurity, at least so far as his musicianship was concerned.

"My reason for trying to adopt something truly different from ragtime was that all my fellow musicians were much faster in manipulations [on the piano], I thought, than I," Morton wrote, years later, to Roy Carew, the man who first had heard him in 1904 outside Hilma Burt's whorehouse.

> And I did not feel as though I was in their class. Of course, they all seem to classify in the No. 1 class, men like Alfred Wilson (won piano playing contest St. Louis exposition, 1904), Tony Jackson (world's greatest single-handed entertainer. Could play and sing from opera to blues in its correct formation, knew everything that probably was ever printed), Albert Carroll (with his so soft, sweet, non-exciting perfect perfection of passing tones and strange harmonies, cool and collective style), Sammy Davis (with his original ragtime idea, four finger bass and speed like the electrified streamliners & etc.). These men set a pace for everyone [who] entered N.O. I have never known anyone to leave N.O. victorious.

This is what Morton was up against, a torrent of keyboard virtuosity that forced him to come up with something different, something of his own, something that would make everyone take notice. He savored this first great rush of creativity, inventing compositions marked by profound innovations in rhythm and intricate variation in melody. These weren't simply tunes of the sort that he played in the parades or the boogie-woogie romps he had learned in the sullen honky-tonks. They were multithemed compositions too complex to sing, with an orchestral array of colors, techniques, and riffs compressed into a universe of eighty-eight black and white keys.

In effect, Morton wasn't just crafting new compositions but helping to invent a musical language that could accommodate them. The music may have had the thematic sophistication of a sonata by Beethoven or Brahms, but its restlessly syncopated rhythms and blue-note colorations had not yet been fully codified into a bona fide musical style by Morton or by anyone else. Ultimately, the young man was advancing an art form while helping to write its underlying syntax—even as he penned some of the emerging genre's first masterworks.

Yet in that same remarkable year of 1905, Morton produced yet another signal piece, "Jelly Roll Blues." In this work, the progress of the music often came to an abrupt halt, so that the right hand alone could play single-line solos running two, three, or four bars. It was as if Morton were foreseeing the early jazz band recordings of the 1920s, when cornetists such as Louis Armstrong and Joe "King" Oliver played their sensational two- and four-bar solo "breaks," while the rest of the band paused and listened, in amazement.

"Jelly Roll Blues" had "breaks" galore, but also other bracingly fresh techniques: ferocious syncopation that defined most of its themes; a tangolike "Spanish tinge" rhythmic pattern in the left hand; and exquisite, long-held trills of the kind that sopranos sang toward the end of arias at the French Opera. In effect, Morton packed much of his musical autobiography into one piece, yet he did so in a fashion that would be easily accessible and pleasantly diverting for brothel customers unconcerned with aesthetics. Art, in other words, was being created in a musical idiom ostensibly designed merely for entertainment, and it was Morton who was beginning to realize that such a revolutionary thing could be achieved in American vernacular music.

And the gems kept coming: "Alabama Bound" (1905), with its lazy, blues-drenched melody; "Animule Dance" (1906), with its radical forearm-on-keyboard roar; "Frog-I-More Rag" (1908, later known as "Froggie Moore"), with its sinuously rising chromatic line as opening theme and leitmotif.

But Morton did not devote all of his waking hours to music. As he created his first signature works, he reveled in the company of the opposite sex. Whores, madams, girlfriends, lovers—all were welcome in his bed, on some occasions more than one at a time. And though he may not consciously have planned it, Morton was fashioning a characteristically complex, two-faceted way of dealing with women. On the one hand, there were the madams and their girls, women like Blanche, an otherwise unnamed prostitute who was "a sporting woman I was living off of" in Memphis, Morton remembered. As New Orleans guitarist Johnny St. Cyr once put it, in speaking of the brothel piano players, they were "all half-way pimps anyway."

But there also was another category of women in Morton's life, the ones he lived with and considered his "wife," though he never bothered with the formality of a marriage certificate. In Biloxi in 1907 and 1908, he courted Bessie Johnson, a buxom, fiery woman with whom he would establish a bona fide relationship years later on the West Coast, when she had renamed herself Anita Gonzalez. The sister of Creole bass player Bill Johnson and piano player Ollie "Dink" Johnson, she was sufficiently fair-skinned to pass for white or Hispanic, when so inclined—which was why she became Anita Gonzalez. Then, from 1912 to 1914, Morton took up with Rosa Brown, an otherwise little-known stage performer with whom he staged a vaudeville act on the road, as Morton & Morton.

To Morton, these and other women were his "wives," and with them Morton established a kind of serial monogamy that became his romantic modus operandi for the rest of his life. Yet he spoke and wrote little about these women, which perhaps reflected their true position in his life, well below his abiding infatuation with the music.

Emboldened by the money he was making, the women he was seducing, and the compositions he was creating, Morton in 1910 dared
to venture further north than he ever had before, to Chicago. This
placed Morton among the first New Orleans musicians to visit the
city, which he found woefully lacking in top-notch piano players. In
Chicago, he played briefly in Armant's Symphony, as well as in
Charles Elgar's orchestra, where he played bass drum, subbing for a
New Orleans friend, Charles Crozet. A year later, Morton traveled as
far as New York, giving the city a taste of an incendiary black music it
barely had encountered before.

"In 1911, when I was still going to school in short pants, I was
taken uptown to Baron Wilkins' place in Harlem," remembered
James P. Johnson, later to become the father figure of the Harlem
stride pianists, referring to the Café Wilkins No. 2, at 134th Street
and Seventh Avenue. "Another boy and I let our short pants down to
look grown up and sneaked in. Who was playing the piano but Jelly
Roll Morton. He had just arrived from the West and he was red hot.
The place was on fire! We heard him play his 'Jelly Roll Blues.' Blues
had not come into popularity at that time—they weren't known or
sung by New York entertainers."

But it wasn't just Morton's sound that struck his young admirers.
His light brown melton overcoat, "with a three-hole hat to match
[and] two girls with him," in Johnson's words, added to the mystique.
As Morton strolled into the Harlem joint, he meticulously "folded up
his overcoat so the expensive plaid lining would show when he put it
on top of the piano," remembered Willie "The Lion" Smith, another
New York keyboard titan in waiting who attended the show.

> You could always tell when a pianist was a pretty popular guy,
> and was making a buck, by his expensive overcoat. . . . Jelly Roll
> had gold teeth, with a diamond in one, wore a twenty-dollar gold
> piece on his watch chain, a fancy colored silk shirt, a vest, a full-
> back (box back) suit with tight pants, short vamp shoes, and a
> Stetson derby. You could always tell a sharpie. He wasn't a stout
> guy; I don't think he weighed more than 120 pounds.

Morton's New York stay was brief, and by 1912 he was back in Chicago, visiting his friend and primary musical role model, Tony Jackson, en route to New Orleans and his vaudeville partner Rosa Brown. Having finessed New York and Chicago without incident, Morton aggressively began exploring the entire middle of the country a year later. In Chicago, he worked the Pompeii, the Little Savoy, the Boston Oyster House, and Colosimo's, the place where Al Capone later launched his career at the bottom end of the nightclub business, as a bouncer. Morton crooned in a vocal trio with Bernard and Cook, in Chicago; played the Elite Theater in Selma, Alabama; and toured with Rosa Johnson in Texas and Oklahoma. At the end of the year, he met the soon-to-be-famous Spikes Brothers—saxophonist Benjamin and piano player Johnny Spikes—nomadic vaudevillians like himself who later became two of the most influential black musical entrepreneurs of the following decade. But they were just scraping by when Morton entered their lives.

"I was managin' a theater in Tulsa, Oklahoma, and he came through there," Benjamin J. "Reb" Spikes remembered, of the Pastime Theater (also known as the People's Theater). "Jelly Roll was the greatest piano player I ever heard. Jelly's the best I ever heard in that Louisiana-style or ragtime or jazz or whatever you want to call it. The first time I heard him in Tulsa, I knew he was great."

Shortly thereafter, the Spikes brothers were performing as members of McCabe's Troubadors, when Reb Spikes suggested that the company hire Morton, who took the job, working the show in blackface. But each night, before the curtain went up, Morton sat down at the keyboard to put the audience in the mood. Spikes said:

> Jelly could play so much piano that after he'd black up—he was much lighter than I am—he'd go out in front and play two or three tunes as an overture before the curtain went up. After they heard him play, they insisted on it. The girl that was playin' on the show was just a strict legit player and would just play note for note. . . . Jelly would go out there and everybody would be

stompin' and goin' on, they liked him so much. Then he'd come back and do his blackface act with the little dark woman.

At about this time, 1914, Morton & Morton were touring widely, playing the Ruby Theater in Louisville, the Pekin in Cincinnati, the Crown Garden in Indianapolis, the Vaudette in Detroit, even Gibson's Standard out in Philadelphia. The flurry of performances earned the first jazz composer his first newspaper review.

"Mr. Morton, 'Jelly Roll' is a slight reminder of 'String Beans,'" an unnamed reviewer shrewdly noted in the *Indianapolis Freeman* on June 13, 1914, perhaps recalling the diamond that also shone in String Beans's mouth. "He does a pianologue in good style. He plays a good piano, classics and rags with equal ease. His one hand stunt, left hand alone, playing a classic selection, is a good one. They do an amusing comedy bit, singing 'That Ain't Got 'Em.' This is sung by both of them in a duo style. They make a hit in this, which is Morton's own composition. In fact he composes most of his own songs and arranges his other work. As a comedian, Morton is grotesque in his makeup," the review continued, referring to Morton's exaggerated white lips and cork-blackened face. "They are a clever pair, giving a pleasing show."

The one-hand piano stunt that the reviewer mentioned, however, wasn't the only novelty Morton dispatched at a keyboard. "I also saw Jelly Roll Morton read a piano manuscript he had never seen, upside down," drummer Jasper Taylor said. "And he played it without hesitating."

Yet in 1914 Morton was doing something considerably more significant than stunt pianism and vaudeville comedy. In that year, he made an intellectual leap forward in jazz: He began to write out the compositions he had been developing thus far exclusively on the keyboard. Though ragtime works by Scott Joplin, Louis Chauvin, and Tom Turpin had been written and published in the late nineteenth century, mostly in St. Louis by Stark & Son, none of these pieces had the jazz-based breaks, stop-time devices, improvisatory feeling, and nas-

cent swing rhythm that already distinguished Morton's work. But
Morton did not begin writing his scores because he wanted to—he was
forced to.

He had come to St. Louis, long famous as a home for innovative
ragtime piano players, to see how he—and they—measured up. But he
quickly earned their ire, for he deceived his competitors, not letting on
that he had been hustling musicians as he had hustled pool players for
nearly a decade.

"When Jelly Roll visited St. Louis, he delighted in showing off his
talent," ragtime piano player Charlie Thompson remembered. "He
would rear himself up to his full height as someone else played. Then
when the performance was over, he would say, 'Now let me show you
how that piece is supposed to go.'"

The St. Louis piano men were startled by Morton's easygoing virtuosity, but they would not yet acknowledge his superiority. Instead,
they tried to tried to test Morton, giving him difficult pieces of music
to play at sight: Dvorak's "Humoresque," the overture from Von Flo-
tow's *Martha,* Von Suppe's "Poet and Peasant Overture," and the
"Miserere" from Verdi's *Il Trovatore.* Morton dispatched them all,
missing nary a note. But he did not let on that he had known these
pieces from memory for years. On the contrary, he feigned to be reading them perfectly the first time through. The St. Louis piano boys
were stunned at such feats. The hustle was under way.

When Morton finally revealed that he had been conning the local
piano players all along, he forever earned their enmity.

They refused to have anything more to do with Morton and rendered him unwelcome in the better circles of St. Louis pianodom, his
name synonymous with musical chicanery. So the only place Morton
could find work was in the German part of town—oom-pah territory,
where the players were not likely to know much about the offbeat
rhythms, blues-tinged harmony, and stop-start techniques that now
defined his music. Morton had no choice but to put pen to paper, hoping that his four-square clarinetist, trumpeter, mandolinist, and drummer could follow him. In so doing, he linked a distinctly African-
American music—which until this moment had been transmitted

wholly through aural methods—to the Western tradition of notation for the first time. This was a milestone in the emergence of jazz, a term that hadn't even appeared in print until that same year, 1914, in San Francisco. With Morton proving that the seemingly chaotic New Orleans music could be captured on paper, he in effect began to unlock the mysteries of a new art form for the rest of the world to see, study, understand, and build upon. By 1915, "Jelly Roll Blues" would be published in Chicago; it was thus the first bona fide jazz composition available in score, a precious document that forever more could be transmitted to musicians and audiences around the world.

Morton had arrived in Chicago the summer before that pivotal event, in August 1914, and made the city his base of operations for the next three years. He quickly felt at home there, not only because he had been to the city before but also because so many New Orleans piano players now were thriving in Chicago. Tony Jackson had come north in 1912 and flourished in the city until his death, in 1921; and Albert Carroll, a piano player revered back in the District, was packing them in at the Pekin Buffet on the South Side.

Morton fit right in. By the end of August he had ascended to the position of music director of the Richelieu Café (formerly the Pompeii Café), and on November 28 he presided over the opening of the Deluxe Café, at 3503 South State Street, in the heart of Chicago's booming South Side nightlife area. He stayed there at least until December 26, leading a "large orchestra" of seven pieces that played his hand-written, still unpublished scores, the gospel according to Jelly Roll Morton.

After the club's premier engagement, Morton took a job as a song plugger in a South State Street music store, demonstrating sheet music but proving a little too good for the job. "I had all kinds of complaints coming back to me," Morton wrote, "for the people who would buy it would say the music was not on the paper as I played it." Indeed, the man never performed a piece of piano music the same way twice, embellishing it as if he still were entertaining the whorehouse patrons back in the District. One only can imagine the disappointment the customers felt when they excitedly brought home their sheet

music, proceeded to play it, and discovered that the full brilliance of
Morton's pianism was not on the page but back in the store, unique to
the composer's touch.

Fortunately, the pianist was rescued from song-plugging with an
offer to manage Chicago's Elite No. 2 cabaret, at Thirty-first and
State, a dressed-up, expanded version of the original Elite, at 3445
South State Street. Jelly Roll Morton and His Incomparables head-
lined, and their signature tune was "Jelly Roll Blues," now played not
as a piano solo but as Morton had originally heard it in his inner ear:
fully orchestrated, its multiple keyboard lines assigned to a glorious
array of instruments, New Orleans style. The trills he once played on
the piano, for instance, now were joyfully articulated on clarinet by
Horace George, while cornetist John Armstrong (no relation to the
great Satchmo) and trombonist Henry Massingill blew riffs specifically tailored for the distinct tone color of their instruments, with
drummer Willie Menns swinging behind them.

Morton exulted in his new status as bandleader–club manager,
posing proudly for a group photo in front of the club. He's easy to
pick out, his lean frame, starched white shirt collar, tightly knotted tie,
and perfectly angled flat-top hat indicating a performer who was
meticulous about visual style. In the background, the facade of the
club is draped with American flags, as well as signs proclaiming,
"Welcome Elks" and "Headquarters for Visiting Elks," a reference to
a convention that the social organization was holding in Chicago that
summer.

Now, at last, Chicago was hearing the kind of music that had
been swinging New Orleans since at least 1908, when Freddie Keppard's Tuxedo Dance Hall band first proved that the innovations of
the brothel piano players and curbside soloists could be transferred to
a working ensemble. Morton's Incomparables made essentially the
same point in Chicago. At the Elite No. 2, Morton was king, playing
the hottest dance band music in the city in what he imagined—incorrectly—was going to be a permanent home. Within months, a variety
of New Orleans bands invaded the town, but Morton's group had
been the first. Chicagoans hardly could get enough of his Crescent

City swing, with Morton racing to keep up with engagements at the Elite Nos. 1 and 2, at the Chateau (at Thirty-fifth Street and Grand Boulevard), the Pompeii, the Richelieu, and even music rooms in far-off, suburban Blue Island.

Meanwhile, Morton's repertoire of piano compositions was expanding each season, a trip to Detroit in 1914 or 1915 inspiring him to write "The Wolverines," a classic ragtime piece observing most of the conventions of the form. With its jaunty rhythms, buoyantly syncopated right hand, and energetic left-hand octaves, it summed up the ragtime craze that still had the country in its spell, but it offered something more as well. Its third theme recalled a sweet chorale, its single-note melodies offering genteel contrast to the energetic ragtime sections. Innovations such as these were making Morton one of the most sought-after musicians in Chicago, which was becoming a bigger, faster, louder version of New Orleans.

"More than one old-timer remembers that the special police were assigned to an opening of the likes of [Tony] Jackson and Morton," said historian John Steiner. "I remember when he and Tony Jackson played all up and down State Street—one here, the other there, along the Stroll," noted theater manager Shep Allen, referring to the stretch of State Street running from Thirty-first to Thirty-fifth. Along these four blocks, music blared from so many nightspots that you could take it all in—admission free—simply by strolling from one end of the strip to the other. "Jelly was a king in those days," recalled Allen. "There was no one better."

Nor had anyone else published the jazz music that was starting to win converts across the country, until Morton did on September 22, 1915, when Will Rossiter released "Jelly Roll Blues" both as a written piano solo and in orchestrated form. Rossiter had been the biggest publisher in town since 1892, the first to publish Zez Confrey, Gus Kahn, and the vaudeville team of Van and Schneck. As early as 1910, he had achieved massive hits with his own corny tune "I'd Love to Live in Loveland with a Girl Like You" (which sold over 2 million copies) and "Meet Me Tonight in Dreamland," by Leo Friedman and Beth Slater Whitson (a million copies).

With "Jelly Roll Blues," Rossiter made history again, publishing the Opus 1 of all jazz compositions at a time when Louis Armstrong was but an aspiring, fourteen-year-old cornetist in New Orleans and three years before bandleader Joe "King" Oliver came to Chicago to unveil his groundbreaking Creole Jazz Band. "Jelly Roll Blues" swept the city, requested so often by listeners that Morton briefly retitled it "The Chicago Blues." Not that it was a cinch to play. Its rhythms proved so tricky and its multiple melody lines so delicately inter- twined that Rossiter advertised it as the "hardest rag on the market."

Even for Morton, however, putting on paper the intricacies of the piece—or, really, any bona fide New Orleans jazz—proved challeng- ing at first. "There's something peculiar to my playing and arrang- ing," he later wrote. "My figurations were impossible at that time, and arguments would arise stating that no one could put this idea on a sheet. It really proved to be a fact for years. Even Will Rossiter's crack arranger, Henry Klickman, was baffled, but I myself figured out the peculiar form of mathematics and harmonics that was strange to all the world but me." Among Morton's various exaggerations, this statement was undeniably true.

Now Morton was everywhere: playing piano in a song-and-dance contest featuring Bill "Bojangles" Robinson, at the Pompeii (on No- vember 6, 1915); fanning out to St. Louis, to work the Fairfax Hotel (in the summer of 1916); joining the musicians' union in Detroit (No- vember 1916).

But in the meantime, New Orleans's best jazz groups had started storming Chicago. In addition to the Original Creole Band's busy per- formance schedule there from 1915 to 1917 (after which Keppard set- tled in the city), Chicago was practically inundated with New Orleans outfits: the Manuel Perez Group, at the Arsonia Café, early in 1915; Tom Brown's Band from Dixieland at the Lamb's Café, in May; Stein's Band from Dixie—headed by cornetist Nick LaRocca, who soon would make the first jazz recording with the Original Dixieland Jazz Band—at Schiller's Café, in March of 1916; the Original Dixieland Jazz Band at Del' Abe's in the Loop, in May of 1916; and a new ver- sion of the ODJB at the Casino Gardens, in September.

As competition heated up, the ever-restless Morton was beginning to conclude that the time had come to move on. The sensational success of the Original Creole Band in Chicago only hastened the decision, for Keppard's startling cornet playing stole Morton's thunder, swiping audiences for his Incomparables at the Elite No. 2 and elsewhere.

So Morton moved on. Though he knew that other musicians might have more musical training, he also realized that few could best him at the keyboard and fewer still could match his flair. Morton had learned from the piano professors, pimps, hustlers, gamblers, and thieves, their methods showing him how to make a buck, how to devastate—or at least unnerve—the competition, how to get by when music jobs were scarce. In essence, Morton had learned how to survive, in the process emerging as the quintessential, self-aggrandizing New Orleans showman.

Now the transformation was complete. The fellow who had been obedient at home, respectful of his elders, and bashful in public to a debilitating degree had created a brilliant alter ego called Jelly Roll Morton. So far as the world was concerned, the new man was loud, brassy, and more than a little overdressed, a cutup, a diamond-laden ladies' man blessed with the peculiar gift of making a piano sing and dance in ways it never had done before. The old Ferd Morton—a sensitive young man shattered by his expulsion from the embrace of his family's home—now hid beneath the gaudy new facade. If Morton were going to survive in the after-dark world of hustlers, gamblers, musicians, and worse, he would beat them at their own game, his clothes flashier, his diamonds bigger, his wad of cash fatter, his attitude sharper, his music more brilliant than anything he had encountered in the District or out on the road. This new invention—Jelly Roll Morton—would make him a fortune to take back to his grandmother and would bring him all the riches and glory his musical genius clearly deserved.

It was a perilous world he had fallen into, and he quickly realized that you had to hustle to survive; you had to slash your competitor before he slashed you; you had to woo an audience faster and harder than the next guy.

"There was keen rivalry and much competition," New Orleans musician Dude Bottley once explained.

> Remember, press agents and magazine spreads were unheard of in those days. You had to outblow, outplay your competitors, like Jelly Roll said, because you had your fans and loyal followers who boasted of your greatness. . . . You had to be sharp in contests or lose your prestige, and with it the future jobs and engagements, for the news would spread like wildfire when a czar was toppled off his throne, and many of the old boys took to their cups after a skirmish.

The piano battles were not refined affairs but bloody brawls in which a cutting contest between pianists might turn literal in a flash. These often thuggish figures—brutal men named Dirty Dog, Steel Arm Johnny, and the deceptively christened Butterfoot—owned rap sheets stretching back years, some with murder in their past. When battling at the keyboard, they didn't simply compete; they played until blood dripped from the cuts on their fingers.

Once triumph had been attained, the victor didn't simply savor the moment—he berated his opponent with "very uncouth descriptions, would humiliate an ex-star and drive him to tears and more alcohol," Bottley explained. And as the former champion's reputation fell, "wherever he went, the ovation was absent, and instead, he was greeted with contemptible facial expressions."

The loser sulked and quietly walked away, having earned the contempt of his betters and of the crowd. In essence, "the feathers had been plucked from the peacock's tail," Morton said, with considerable self-satisfaction, because at this time in his life, it was he who was doing the plucking.

three

THE PROSELYTIZER

Jelly Roll Morton was spoiling to get out of Chicago. Though he always was eager to leave town—any town—when the promise of cash and notoriety presented itself, this was different. Cornetist Freddie Keppard had changed everything when he brought his roaring Original Creole Band to the Grand Theater on Chicago's South Side in the winter of 1915. This ebullient band, each player a veteran of New Orleans street parades, funeral marches, dance halls, and saloons, rendered the rest of Chicago's ensembles obsolete by comparison, Morton's included. For despite his best efforts, Morton could neither teach nor cajole his Chicago musicians into sounding nearly so rhythmically loose, tonally expressive, or melodically creative as their Crescent City counterparts. The Chicago boys could not replicate, let alone absorb, the lazy blues tempos, aggressive stomp style, sensational breaks, and dramatic stop-time rhythms that were at the core of New Orleans music and remained, at least until now, the province of musicians who had come of age in the District.

Once the ample-lunged Freddie Keppard began pointing his horn heavenward, sending his famous high Cs, Fs, and Gs into the stratosphere above Chicago, Morton's Incomparables were history, and he knew it. So did Morton's hand-picked trumpeter, a Memphis man named John Armstrong. When John Armstrong heard those Keppard blasts, he summarily quit Morton's band, simply out of shame.

Morton, who early on had learned the advantages of staying constantly in motion, already had spent three long years in Chicago—notwithstanding quick outings to nearby towns—and that was a couple too many. So in 1917, when impresario Lovey Joe Woodson offered Morton a job at the Cadillac Café, in Los Angeles, deliverance was at hand. Morton packed up his wardrobe of suits and shoes and diamond-studded accoutrements, shipped it off in trunks, and headed west, by train, in July.

He knew he would not be alone in the faraway city of Los Angeles, for as early as 1908—when Morton still was investigating possibilities along the Mississippi Gulf Coast—some of the men from the District had tested the waters in Southern California. They had taken a train through Houston, Dallas, Waco, and Yuma en route to L.A. and played for a month at the Red Feather Tavern, in the black part of town. Their ragtime rhythms had danced from the horn of trumpeter Ernest Coycault, with full-throttle support from bandleader-mandolinist Bill Johnson, bassist Alphonse Ferzand, valve trombonist Albert Paddio, and guitarist Charles Washington. In effect, this was a precursor of the Original Creole Band, the soon-to-be-legendary ensemble that would show the rest of America what music and life in New Orleans were all about. The 1908 tunes may have been stylistically far removed from the hot sounds that a few years hence would be termed jazz, but these Creole players had served up unadulterated New Orleans ensemble ragtime on the West Coast for the first time, probably before it had arrived even in Chicago.

Already, before the first decade of the new century was finished, a black ghetto was rising in Los Angeles along Central Avenue, directly west from Union Station, where various train lines deposited dreamers from across the country. Nurtured by tacit segregation, Central Avenue was becoming the spine of black Los Angeles, an emerging nightlife strip where saloons, restaurants, clubs, and near-brothels entertained thousands of black migrants living on either side of it.

Most of the New Orleans players of 1908 didn't stay out west, but five years later Bill Johnson returned to Los Angeles with another New Orleans band, this one financed by Johnson's sister, Bessie—the same Creole beauty whom Morton had courted several years earlier in Biloxi. Bessie Johnson had entrepreneurial genius in her veins, cash at the ready, and an innate revulsion at being dealt third-class treatment by anyone. That may be why she reinvented herself in Los Angeles, rebaptizing herself Anita Gonzalez, her golden skin allowing her to pass for Spanish, Cuban, Mexican—whichever struck her fancy at any given moment.

As Anita Gonzalez—or "Mama 'Nita," in Morton's endearment—the former Bessie Johnson operated in not one city but two: Los Angeles and a dusty, forlorn desert town called Las Vegas, Nevada, where she ran a saloon. Her younger brother, piano player Ollie "Dink" Johnson, worked there with her, and it was this enterprise that enabled her to underwrite brother Bill Johnson's latest westward venture. By 1914, the newly renamed Original Creole Orchestra was shaking up Los Angeles, the seven-man outfit featuring cornetist Keppard, pioneering clarinetist George Baquet, and the brothers Johnson, among others. They startled Angelenos with an extroverted sound and style that could not have been more authentically New Orleans, but some of the folks who gathered to watch the Leach Cross–Joe Rivers heavyweight fight on August 11, 1915 in L.A. might not have been prepared for it.

"While waiting for Rivers and Cross, some one connected with the management had an unhappy inspiration to allow a company of negroes, perpetrating a vile imitation of music, to enter the ring and insult the audience by very obviously begging for coins," the *Los Angeles Times* witheringly observed. The story's headline underscored the point: "Disgusting Exhibition Marred the Fight."

The boys in the band, however, heard things differently. So far as they were concerned, the place erupted when they let loose a musical force that had been building a head of steam in New Orleans for at least twenty years. "We were there with ringside seats, and this arena takes up a whole square block and was packed," recalled clarinetist Baquet, of the Rivers-Cross matchup. "After every bout we played. And when we played the then popular number 'Mandalay,' Freddie Keppard, our cornetist, stood up with his egg mute and an old Derby hat on the bell of the instrument, the crowd stood up as one man and shouted for us to get up into the ring, and screamed and screamed."

The fight fans were enthralled by the cries emanating from Keppard's horn, and from this moment forth, jazz began to take hold in Southern California. The screams that answered Keppard's blues laments persuaded theater owner Alexander Pantages to hire the Creole band for a national vaudeville tour (with Dink Johnson staying behind in Los Angeles). It was their engagement at the Grand Theater in Chicago, at Thirty-first and State Streets, on February 1, 1915, that not only hastened Morton's departure from the city but established that America's Jazz Age now officially was under way, thanks to a groundbreaking New Orleans band, a shrewd Los Angeles promoter, and a Chicago public hungry for the new music.

Morton knew all this and came to the obvious conclusion: If the West Coast could catapult the Original Creole Orchestra to national fame, surely it could promote him as well, and he was eager to test this idea. His timing could not have been better, for crowds lined up to hear him at the Cadillac Café, at 553 Central Avenue (between Fifth and Sixth Streets), everyday blacks rubbing elbows with movie stars gone slumming. While the girls in the Panama Trio crooned popular tunes of the day, Morton played piano behind them, giving a rhythmic lift to otherwise mundane fare. At closing time, Morton—energized by the change of scene and his soaring popularity—hopped in his car and headed to George Brown's Watts night club to play practically till sunup. Then he came home and wrote music, barely able to jot down fast enough the tunes that were resonating in his head. The man, newly triumphant and reinvigorated, barely slept.

Even so, "he was still trying to figure out what to do with his life," remembered Ada "Bricktop" Smith, who performed with him. "He couldn't decide whether to be a pimp or a piano player. I told him to be both." Morton may have taken her advice, for rumors abounded that he beefed up his income by running a prostitution ring, and puckishly calling it the Pacific Coast Line. More important, Morton worked overtime on music, building a long list of admirers and adversaries. Bricktop was among the first to turn on Morton, when he caught her stealing tips and bluntly confronted her. After an angry war of words between the two entertainers, the boss fired Morton for "getting his Creole up," as the pianist put it.

So he went to work at a roadhouse in rural Watts, several miles south of bustling Central Avenue, but by the end of 1917 Morton was back at the Cadillac. Unfortunately, the house band (probably the Black and Tan Jazz Orchestra) was about as fluent in New Orleans jazz style as their Chicago counterparts had been. Morton tried to lead them through tunes he thought they could handle, from Scott Joplin's already legendary "Maple Leaf Rag" to third-rate pulp such as "Liza Jane" and "Daddy Dear, I'm Crying for You." But he could not deny that he needed reinforcements from the only place on earth where musicians knew how his music ought to sound—New Orleans.

So Morton summoned three of the best from back home: cornetist Buddy Petit, whom Louis Armstrong later cited as a critical influence; trombonist Frankie Dusen, who took over Buddy Bolden's band in 1907; and clarinetist Wade Whaley, who somehow captured the jubilation and radiance of New Orleans melody on his battered instrument, or any other. By calling forth his musician friends from New Orleans, Morton wasn't just turning to reliable pros—he in effect was spreading the sound and flavor of New Orleans music far beyond its birthplace, though not necessarily by design. To Morton, this was business, pleasure, and emerging art fused into one, with the collateral effect of stoking the flames of a new music across America.

Anticipating that his New Orleans cohorts would show up in Los Angeles looking as if they never had set foot outside the District, Morton rushed to meet them at the train station. Sure enough, they were wearing "the antiquated dress habitual to New Orleans musicians, with their instruments all taped up to keep them airtight and Whaley's clarinet in his back pocket," recalled Morton. "We spirited them away so no one could see them in their tight pants and box back

coats, and brought them to a tailor. They wanted to kill us for want-
ing them to change their outmoded clothing for the then-modern
clothes."

It was not a good omen. Though the newly attired District musicians worked with Morton in Watts, at Baron Long's joint, they
proved incorrigible, bringing buckets of red beans and rice to cook
and eat at the show. Morton and Bill Johnson, who rounded out the
band, razzed the threesome as country bumpkins until the New Orleans men could take it no more. They headed back home before the
year was out and swore they would murder Morton if he ever bothered them again.

Even so, Morton was finding his rhythm in Los Angeles, with
work along Central Avenue rapidly picking up as the population of
black California swelled (from 21,645 in 1910 to 38,763 in 1920). He
was becoming known up and down the avenue, for he still looked and
sounded like no one Los Angeles ever had encountered. "I can see him
now with that overcoat on," said Sid LeProtti, who at the time was
leading a band in Los Angeles, the So Different Orchestra. "He was a
kind'a thin-featured fellow and had quite a lot'a gold in his teeth,
which was characteristic in them days. When you first looked at him,
his mouth was twisted like he'd had some kind of a slight stroke, but I
don't think it was that—it was the way he held his mouth," a kind of
puckered-up gesture suggesting that Morton either was deep in
thought or sizing you up. "He'd also always kind'a squint one eye.
. . . He played the blues a hundred and one times and never played it
the same way twice."

Morton noticed LeProtti, too, and made him a tantalizing offer.
"You got a pretty good band," Morton said, referring to the So Different Orchestra, a lavish compliment, considering the source. "I've
got some good numbers; I'm gonn'a let you look them over. Here's
one I want'a give you."

But Morton might as well have handed LeProtti a page of hiero-
glyphics, for LeProtti, like many popular musicians of the day, couldn't
read a piece music if he had been promised a million bucks. Never
mind that Morton took pains to write his scores clearly, with key sig-

nature and meter meticulously notated, the beats lined up so precisely that a crack musician could read this music on the spot. To LeProtti, "The manuscript looked like some kid had dropped ink on it and then the chickens had scratched on it." Embarrassed but undaunted, Le-Protti found a young white piano player to teach him how to decode a series of dots, slurs, and accidentals that contained nothing less than the blueprint to the hitherto ephemeral sound of New Orleans music.

By handing out scores to musicians such as LeProtti, Morton was deepening his transition from sporting-house piano player to bona fide composer. No more was Morton just a whorehouse entertainer playing for well-worn bills—now he was a creator whose work deserved to be played and repeated by others, or at least he so believed. Somewhere along the way, perhaps in St. Louis when he was struggling with the German oom-pah musicians or in Chicago where he had first tried to sell the New Orleans sound, he had come to the conclusion that only written scores would do. If his journeys had taught him anything, it was that most musicians outside the District could not master the complexities and subtleties of his music by simply listening to it. But by capturing on paper, and for all time, his tricky rhythms and blues-tinged melodies and exacting trills and turns and two-bar breaks, he at least stood half a chance of getting players unschooled in New Orleans style to do justice to his music.

Still, these scores were not easy to play, nor were they intended to be, for Morton was uninterested in snappy, easily digested tunes and instantly knowable melodies. He was writing complex, baroque New Orleans counterpoint, and to musicians of Chicago and Los Angeles and other outposts thousands of miles from the District, playing these scores was no easier than negotiating an overture by Verdi or Donizetti.

"We finally figured it out and played out and played it," said Le-Protti, who was confused by the process, in part because he never could get Morton to tell him precisely how the piece was to be performed. "It was 'The Crave.' Jelly played it, but he was pretty cagey; he'd play it one way, then he'd change it and play it again. One day I caught him playin' it and heard him say to a fella, 'Well, this is the way I play it when I'm playin' ad lib,'" added LeProtti, noting Morton's disinclination to perform any of his pieces the same way twice.

So far as anyone else was concerned, however, Morton insisted that LeProtti's musicians play the music precisely as written, nothing more, nothing less. When LeProtti and his men finally got the swing of "The Crave" and mustered the courage to play it in public, they were amazed at the reaction, particularly from the usually jaded Hollywood crowd. "My God, the bunch was just crazy about it, especially Jack Pickford, Mary Pickford's brother, who never got very prominent in the movies, Fatty Arbuckle and Max Schlerman, and they broadcasted it all over Los Angeles," recalled LeProtti. "Everybody was sayin' that you ought'a go out and hear those boys play 'The Crave.' People would walk in there every night and say, 'They tell me you play a number called "The Crave,"' and we'd play it for them."

So Morton, who already had conquered Chicago, albeit briefly, with "Jelly Roll Blues," now was beguiling a new city with another striking original, though he didn't copyright it until two decades later. At this early date, 1917, "The Crave" sounded positively radical, bristling with relentless syncopations, restless key changes, unexpected silences, aria-like melodies, and puckish switches from duple to triple meter. Rather than ride a jaunty, steady rhythmic backbeat—as syncopated compositions of the period typically did—"The Crave" sabotaged listener expectations at least every four bars, and sometimes more often, with one rhythmic surprise after another.

It opened with the usual four-bar intro, though these sixteen beats contained the nucleus of all the musical material yet to come. The habanera/tango rhythm quickly signaled that "The Crave" drew upon Morton's famous "Spanish tinge," the intoxicating rhythmic lilt that drives Iberian dance music. Meanwhile, the piece simultaneously unfurled a haunting, minor-key melody. When Morton played the piece on the piano, he recapped the opening theme by letting loose with a flurry of flying octaves in his right hand, an unusual nine to the bar. This passage, which practically defied the musical notation of the time, recalled a comparable moment in "King Porter Stomp," but here the octaves proceeded more slowly, and with an unmistakable melting lyricism. The most audacious passage was yet to come, however, when "The Crave" pushed into its second theme. Here, Morton wrote a series of "minor seconds," as musicians call them—in effect, the most dissonant combination of two notes possible. Furthermore, Morton articulated these sharp, deep-blue dissonances off the beat, inexorably propelling "The Crave" into an incipient but instantly recognizable swing rhythm.

Listeners were caught utterly off guard by the lushness of these harmonies, the rhapsodic quality of Morton's melodies, the expressive shifts from major to minor, and the irresistible rhythmic momentum that surged through it all. When Morton played the piece on the piano, his shimmering tremolo effects, unconventional rhythms, and haunting, lyric touch disarmed listeners, while the band version of "The Crave" added new colors and textures to a piece already crammed with musical detail. Though Morton sometimes complained about the way LeProtti's men handled the tune, the composer knew that this outfit was helping to put Morton over in Los Angeles. Seizing an opportunity, Morton gave LeProtti another great score, "Jelly Roll Blues," presuming that a tune that had hit hard on Chicago's South Side was bound to make an impact on Central Avenue as well. He was right. Indeed, with each piece that Morton passed along to LeProtti and Los Angeles bandleaders like him, Morton was wriggling out of the straitjacket of piano professor and stepping into a smarter suit of clothes: composer, orchestrator, and champion of his own music. Though still years away from taking the final step in this progression—publishing his scores for mass distribution—he was proceeding headlong in that direction, and at a time when no one else in jazz was even close.

But he had another mission to accomplish in L.A. as well, for he decided to look up Bessie Johnson, whom he had courted in Biloxi seemingly a lifetime ago. By now, she had reimagined herself as Anita Gonzalez, proprietor of a Las Vegas saloon and sponsor of one of the most important ensembles of New Orleans musicians, the L.A.–based Original Creole Orchestra. Gonzalez now was a woman of means,

but Morton had attained a measure of affluence and prominence himself. Now he felt ready to display his wealth—the diamonds and cus-
tom-tailored suits and bulky roll of cash—sure to appeal to a woman
who prized such things. To Morton's consternation, though, Anita's
brother Dink didn't want his sister spending time with a smooth
talker like Morton and wouldn't pass a message to her nor give him
her address, so Morton simply turned to another source—Anita's
mother. Charmed by Los Angeles's new piano king, Anita's mother
promised to get word to Anita that Morton was in town, and in no
time Anita rushed to Los Angeles, rekindled the affair, and invited
Morton to come back to Las Vegas with her. Morton loathed the
place, its weather too cold in winter and too hot in summer for his
New Orleans blood, so the two returned to Los Angeles, where Gonzalez bought a small hotel at Central and Twelfth, dubbing it the
Anita. Many suspected it served as a brothel, with Gonzalez as its
madam.

Now Morton was hitting his stride as pianist, composer, and
small-time businessman, helping open Leak's Lake, a rustic roadhouse
in Watts County. So much money poured in from Leak's Lake and his
other engagements, in fact, that Morton took over a gambling club
next door to the Anita, the couple cornering the market for sin on a
notorious corner of Central Avenue. He drove around town in a late-
model automobile, and when he wasn't counting his fortune, he somehow found time to coach cornetist Ben Albans, Jr., and other young
musicians in the neighborhood.

Composer, bandleader, pianist, teacher, stickler for details, proselytizer for a new kind of written music that sounded freely improvised
but wasn't—Morton was becoming a de facto advocate for a greater
cause, the emerging art of jazz. Everything he did, from playing solo
piano to importing New Orleans musicians to coaching young players
to passing out his hand-written scores had the effect of fanning the
flames of a still flickering new music. The motivation may have been
self-interest, but the effect was to build audiences and train musicians
to play for them. Moreover, because radio and phonograph records
had not yet become powerful cultural forces, Morton was creating an

audience in the only way possible in this pretechnological age—one show, one club, one night at a time. He made Central Avenue his street, working joints such as the Penny Dance Hall at Tenth and Grand Avenue, a mecca for sailors with money and time to burn. There and in a dozen other clubs, some plush, some tawdry, Morton relished the music, the crowds, the admiration, the cash, the jewels, the heady swirl that his life in Los Angeles was becoming.

The cash may have been plentiful or scarce; it didn't really matter, noted Shep Allen, an old friend from Chicago. Morton always had enough to get by and then some, that diamond in his smile suggesting that the man was always riding high. Whenever Morton walked into a Central Avenue club, he didn't simply pass the time or check out a new musician—he announced himself as the best piano player and composer in town and made sure everyone knew it. Typically, he sauntered in, strolled up to the bandstand, and intoned to the unfortunate fellow who happened to be at the keyboard, "Whenever you see me walk in, get up off that piano." The fledgling singer Jimmy Rushing heard Morton speak precisely those words at the Quality Night Club, where Morton—with scant provocation—gave the chump at the keyboard a few pointers, hoping he might learn something.

To those who were savvy enough to understand Morton's solo performances, the man was much more than just another piano man with a few tunes to his name. At times, his right-hand lines evoked the sound of a trumpet, foreshadowing a style that Earl Hines soon would make famous, saxophonist Jerome Don Pasqual observed when hearing Morton in California. Morton's pianism, in other words, conveyed the buoyant, single-note melody lines that made a handful of black and white keys evoke the radiant timbre of a New Orleans horn.

Morton was at the head of the pack, and black Los Angeles knew it.

Morton's style—cocky talk, virtuoso pianism, and a deep well of original music—placed him in high demand along the full stretch of the

North American West Coast. As early as 1918, he played in San Diego as pianist for the Creole Jazz Band, with cornetist Petit, drummer Dink Johnson, trombonist Willie Moorehead, and clarinetist Mack Lewis. Then he returned to Los Angeles to join "a large Chicago contingent," according to a note in the *Chicago Defender*—at the time the leading black newspaper in America—including Bricktop, Lucille Hagamin, and Bessie LaBelle.

But playing an endless series of jobs wasn't going to be the sum total of Morton's musical life, now that he had become a legitimate composer of music, and he proved it in 1918, when he filed a copyright—his first—for his "Frog-I-More-Rag." He had created the piece fully a decade earlier, toward the end of his first great creative blossoming on the Gulf Coast, and he had entertained listeners with it ever since. Never before, however, had he gone to the trouble of sending the score—in his own hand—as well as the requisite fee to the U.S. Copyright Office in Washington, D.C. Through this gesture, Morton officially proclaimed that his work was singularly his own and merited protection of the federal government. Few, if any, piano players from the District ever had done such a thing, but then, few had Morton's ambition and intellectual reach.

Yet precisely as Morton's musical life was gathering momentum, his personal life was starting to career out of control, for Anita Gonzalez—mercurial in her moods and steely in her resolve—was not easy to romance. On a whim, she accused Morton of cheating on her, abruptly stopped talking to him, packed her bags, and prepared to leave Los Angeles without telling him. When Morton discovered her departure in progress, she announced that she was moving to Arizona whether he liked it or not—then added that he was welcome to tag along. He did, but after Gonzalez's Arizona restaurant failed, the two headed back to California, this time to San Francisco, in 1919, at the onset of Prohibition.

They opened a doomed club called the Jupiter, in the city's notorious Barbary Coast, a waterfront bastion of vice that San Francisco authorities had been trying to shut down for years. As early as 1913, the city's Board of Police Commissioners had decreed that "no dancing shall be permitted in any café, restaurant or saloon where liquor is sold" in the area, and that "no women patrons or women employees shall be permitted in any saloon in the said district." Police regularly hovered at the Jupiter's front door, urging patrons to stay away and occasionally raiding the joint.

For a while, The Jupiter survived on the strength of Morton's fame alone.

"Jelly Roll Fred [*sic*] Morton is now mayor of Frisco—that is, neighborhood mayor—and is driving a 12 cylinder touring car that makes the natives sit up and take notice," noted the *Chicago Defender* on February 22, 1919. Morton, the item continued, "has organized a Jazz band at San Francisco, Calif. where he is making his home. He sends regards to all friends and would like to have them write." The newspaper published Morton's new address, 3119 Broderick Street, an indication not only that Morton had planted the item but, more important, that he wanted to maintain his links to Chicago—in case he ever needed to go back there again.

In San Francisco, he toiled constantly, working to keep the Jupiter afloat, writing scores for his ten-man band, trying to teach his players how to perform his music, and striving to keep Anita interested. It was not a light load, nor was it made easier by the unfortunate location of the club in the cellar of a building on Columbus Avenue, away from the action on Pacific Street. Worse, once again the local musicians had no idea how New Orleans music was to be played, its limber swing rhythms and bent-note expressions being well beyond their comprehension. To hear his music massacred by men who called themselves musicians sometimes was more than Morton could bear.

"The clarinet would be playin' a solo—and didn't play to suit Jelly—and he'd holler for him to quit," said LeProtti, who often dropped in on Morton's rehearsals. "If you didn't play it accordin' to Jelly's idea, he was just liable to bawl you out right there. My boys and me, we always played like a family together, and it was what you call Dixieland-style today. We had our rehearsals together, and I'd take a chorus, another guy would take two choruses, you take a chorus, and that's the way it went on."

But Morton did not regard making music as merely a convivial affair. To the contrary, it was hard work, and every note he wrote was to be played precisely as he had penned it, at the right instant and with the correct intonation. He would not suffer violations of New Orleans vernacular, he would not accept wrong pitches, wobbly vibrato, or sloppy articulation. His music would not be treated that way. Nor were improvised solos allowed, except by himself or by another bona fide New Orleans musician who understood his techniques—and the old District players still were scarce in San Francisco.

The way things were going at the Jupiter, however, Morton did not have to worry very along about dealing with the hacks who played in his band. The police raids slowed business to a crawl, prompting Gonzalez one day simply to wash her hands of the whole mess. She was fed up and skipped town without a word to Morton.

"She run off and left him one night," recalled musician Reb Spikes, who happened to be in the club the night Morton got the bad news. "She sent him a telegram and told him not to follow; she said when you get this telegram I'll be movin'. Anyway, that was about nine or ten o'clock at night, and that guy quit right then and left to follow her."

Didn't he always? This was simply the way it was between Morton and Gonzalez—she ran, he followed; she erupted, he consoled. Morton is not known to have told anyone what it was about Gonzalez that kept him coming back for more. Was it her Creole beauty, her buxom sensuality, her shrewd business sense, her embrace of vice as a way of life? Probably all held appeal for Morton, who, like Gonzalez, had learned how to make a comfortable living off the illicit goings-on in brothels, gambling dens, and the like. Here was a woman unafraid of sin but determined to get her share of its profits, a proud and fiery Creole who insisted on living like royalty, with all the attendant comforts and freedoms—just as Morton himself did. But Jelly Roll Morton, the brash piano player who lectured musicians and dazzled admirers, was merely a diversion to Anita, who depended on no man for money or love.

The telegram that caused Morton to bolt from the Jupiter said more than Reb Spikes realized. In this dispatch, Gonzalez wrote that she was heading to Seattle en route to Alaska—and if Morton wanted to see her before she vanished into that frigid place, he had better move quickly. He obliged, ditching the Jupiter and everything he had invested in it. When Morton arrived in Seattle, however, Anita informed him that she had never had any intention of going to Alaska, of all places. She just wanted to see him, immediately, and figured the Alaska story would get him moving.

So it went with these two, a part-time pimp now chasing a woman only half interested in him. Anita's bait-and-switch game took the battling duo to Vancouver in September of 1919, and to Portland and Seattle in 1920. At some points during this sojourn, Morton was studded with diamonds, literally pinning them to his underwear for safekeeping. At other times, however, Morton didn't have five dollars, his money squandered on cards, pool, and other forms of wagering. The sharp turns in his fortunes could not have helped his relations with Anita, who in a drunken rage one night shattered a large steak platter over Morton's head, then lunged at him before several men dragged her off. As Anita's outbursts became increasingly violent, Morton drew back from her, and by 1921 they had split up, Morton's tempestuous lover returning to Los Angeles while he worked jobs in Casper, Wyoming, and Denver.

Yet once again, Anita resurfaced—this time sending Morton a telegram that implored him to drop everything: "NAN AND DAD BOTH AT POINT OF DEATH," Anita cabled, hysterically, referring to her parents. "MUST UNDERGO OPERATION IMMEDIATELY. COME HOME. ANITA."

Morton leaped once more, traveling back to Los Angeles, only to find that no one in Anita's family had so much as the sniffles. Morton threw a fit, raving and hollering, as he put it, then simply went back to work. The jobs still were fast and furious in those days, so Morton had no trouble getting back into the tempo and glamour of late-night L.A. "YOU'LL SEE THE MOVIE STARS FACE TO FACE," trumpeted an ad for Morton's engagement at the Paradise Gardens, 1007 South Central Avenue, on June 25, 1921, advertising celebrity appearances, wrestling exhibitions, and an acknowledged jazz master: "MUSIC BY JELLY ROLL JAZZ BAND."

By the fall, Morton was itching to get out on the road again, having spent more time in one city and with one woman than he cared to. He landed at the Kansas City Bar, across the Mexican border in Tijuana, an increasingly popular place for Southern Californians unhappy with the strictures of Prohibition. Briefly distanced here from Anita's tempestuousness, Morton finally could focus again on writing music and created two of his most important works.

He conceived "The Pearls" as a valentine to an attractive though unnamed waitress at the Kansas City Bar, and judging by its unflagging lyricism, he was smitten. The title refers to the way the piece is laid out, with each of several sections designed as an exquisite miniature unto itself, the sum glistening like perfect beads on a necklace. "The Pearls" was an ineffably poetic work, its phrases shaped as if they were short sentences with brief pauses set between them. Each time Morton restated a theme, he transformed it, uninterested in merely recapitulating familiar material. The filigree with which he embellished each of the three main themes might be called operatic, except that no soprano could possibly articulate the runs, arpeggios, and other flourishes that the five nimble fingers on Morton's right hand could spin on the piano. With its meticulously composed jazz "breaks" recalling New Orleans trumpet solos and its long-held coloratura trills marking the end of particular sections, "The Pearls" again drew upon New Orleans street music and European opera, the two primary sources of musical inspiration in Morton's youth.

If "Kansas City Stomp," written at the same time, didn't show quite the emotional depth of "The Pearls," it was a colorful work of a sort that one might expect to hear in a Tijuana saloon when spirits were running particularly high. Yet for all its romping rhythms, fat chords, and speedy double octaves, the piece contained charming details, including a choralelike motif and a series of chromatic chord changes that were daring for this early date in American music.

With "The Pearls" and "Kansas City Stomp," Morton expanded his lexicon of pianistic devices, the sheer originality of the new works keeping him constantly in demand. Returned to Los Angeles in January 1922, Morton still was on the ascent. In March, the same Pantages circuit that had presented the Original Creole Orchestra coast to coast in 1914 sent Jelly Roll Morton and his Jazz Band on tour to play "everything from grand opera to jazz," reported the *Chicago Defender*. And in April, Morton took over as manager of the Wayside Amusement Park, the newly expanded venue in Watts County he had helped create years earlier when it was known as Leak's Lake. Here, Morton not only led a band that played six nights a week but presented Joe "King" Oliver—New Orleans's most famous cornetist of the day—to the West Coast for the first time. Angelenos, who until now had believed that Freddie Keppard was the last word in cornet virtuosity, had not anticipated the degree of sound and fury that rushed out of King Oliver's horn. "King Oliver set Los Angeles on fire," reported the *Chicago Defender*. "He was offered all kinds of inducements to stay, and the highest salary ever offered anyone. All Los Angeles says he's the greatest, and some hot babies have been here the past year." Indeed, Oliver's band, which had not yet recorded, became a sensation during this run, in part on the strength of a Morton tune Oliver picked up at this time, "Froggie Moore" (which Morton had copyrighted as "Frog-I-More-Rag").

Yet as the Roaring Twenties took shape, Morton could no longer suppress his need to keep moving and to get away from Anita's hysterics. As relations with her turned sour and as the scene in Los Angeles grew all too familiar, the road started to look more appealing to Morton. After five years on the West Coast, after earning and gambling away more money than even he could keep track of, after chasing Anita across thousands of miles and enduring the cycle of breakups and makeups that she savored and he detested, Morton was ready to exit once more. Anita agreed, perhaps imagining simply another exciting twist or turn in their love affair, another opportunity for a dramatic reunion.

But Morton was well beyond that, and in the spring of 1923 he left, perhaps echoing again the night when his grandmother and great-grandmother had thrown him out of the house, forcing him to find something better somewhere else. He returned briefly to New Orleans but soon realized that many of the best musicians had long since left town, scattering to cities across the country. Storyville, after all, had been shuttered by legal mandate in 1917, and though many fine players still made New Orleans swing, the heady nights and outsized paydays were over. Even Roy Carew, the fellow who, standing outside Hilma Burt's house in 1904, had been enchanted by Morton's pianism, had moved on, hitting the road as a traveling salesman for the Remington Typewriter Company before World War I and dropping in on Tony Jackson in Chicago whenever possible.

With the old New Orleans scene diminished, Morton needed someplace else to go, some new refuge, some reason to move on, and he got it—directly between the eyes—from two old acquaintances of vaudeville days, the brothers Reb and Johnny Spikes. Three years earlier, in December 1919, Morton's former vaudeville partners had opened the Spikes Brothers Music Store in Los Angeles, at Twelfth and Central, and the fledgling operation had quickly evolved into a focal point for black music on the West Coast. Everyone had converged there, including Morton, but he had never anticipated the chicanery that early on had become the Spikes brothers' method of operation. On the surface, Reb and Johnny Spikes appeared to be running a wholly legitimate business. "Back in those days—this was about 1919—there was no place in town where one could purchase recordings by Negro artists," said Reb Spikes. "As a result we did a huge record business. Wealthy Hollywood people would drive up in long limousines and send their chauffeurs in to ask for 'dirty records.' When the local Columbia distributor received a shipment of Bessie Smith records, we'd take the entire lot . . . a few hours later they'd be gone!"

The entrepreneurial Spikes brothers ran various clubs around town, among them the famous Dreamland Café at Fourth Street near

Central Avenue, and they commissioned the first recording session by a black jazz ensemble from New Orleans, Kid Ory's Creole Jazz Band, in 1921. Through grit, brains, and hard work, these dirt-poor vaudevillians became affluent, powerful black businessmen, among the first in music to control the money in the cash register rather than supply it. They started the Negro musicians' union in their store, and they booked bands for parties and films.

But in 1922 they branched out, launching a fledgling publishing business that took full advantage of the often illiterate musicians it served. With so many itinerant players coming into the store humming new tunes they did not know how to write, the Spikes brothers hit upon a new source of revenue. "Fellas would come in, would have an idea, would want a song, my brother [would] write it, and we'd put our name on it, you know, with them, and that way we . . . ah, you know, work together on it," said Reb Spikes. Then the Spikes brothers copyrighted and published the piece, listing themselves as co-songwriters, alongside the illiterate musician who had actually created the tune. If the piece generated interest along Central Avenue, the Spikes brothers sold the copyright to a white publisher looking for a surefire hit, which is how they put one over on Morton.

At the time, Morton became acquainted with a song by a sharp-dressing San Diego man called Kid North (real name Robert North), who could play only one tune on the piano, the bawdy "Tricks Ain't Walkin' No More." Knowing that Morton was a real musician who could play anything, Kid North recommended the tune to Morton, who, in turn, refashioned part of it with Reb Spikes as a new song titled "Someday Sweetheart"—a considerable thematic switch.

"Someday Sweetheart" became an instant hit for Alberta Hunter, who recorded it on the Black Swan label, and the tune accrued additional fame from recordings by artists as far-flung as Eddie Condon and Bill Crosby. Unfortunately, when the Spikes brothers published it, they conspicuously left Morton's name off the sheet music and its copyright. Morton shrugged off this loss—he hadn't really written the piece anyway, so he said he hoped the Spikes boys would enjoy more hits like it. At most, the Spikes brothers' ham-handed maneuver made him laugh.

But Morton raged when the Spikes brothers two-timed him on another tune, "The Wolverines," which was entirely his own creation. An exuberant ragtime work that Morton recalled creating nearly a decade earlier in Detroit (though Johnny St. Cyr remembered hearing Morton and others play it in New Orleans in 1906), by 1923 "The Wolverines" had become one of the most hotly requested tunes in Chicago. King Oliver's band played it across the South Side, perhaps having picked it up when Morton presented Oliver at Wayside Amusement Park, in Los Angeles, the year before. But "The Wolverines" had not yet been published, which was why two white farm boys new to Chicago's music business became interested in the piece. Brothers Walter and Lester Melrose didn't know much about music, but that hadn't stopped them from opening a music store on Chicago's South Side, where virtually every nightclub was featuring "The Wolverines." Itching to get into the publishing side of the business, the Melrose brothers decided that they couldn't miss by printing a song that quickly was becoming a hit across Chicago's South Side.

When Walter and Lester Melrose learned that the Spikes brothers already had published "The Wolverines" in Los Angeles, they mailed a proposal to the Spikes Brothers Music Store offering three thousand dollars to buy the copyright, which the Spikes boys happily sold. Unfortunately for Morton, the Spikes brothers added lyrics to the tune and made themselves co-songwriters, just as they had been doing all along with lesser, illiterate songwriters. Now the Spikes brothers were listed as Morton's songwriting partners on "The Wolverines" and could collect half the songwriter royalties on a tune they had had no hand in writing.

Morton was outraged—not because he was going to lose songwriting profits but because he was given second billing, with the authorship of the tune listed as "Spikes-Morton-Spikes." This set him off and, more important, finally gave him all the reason he needed to leave Los Angeles and head to Chicago.

He knew that he needed to straighten out this copyright business immediately, because "The Wolverines" was beginning to take on a life without him. On February 14, 1923, the Melrose brothers copyrighted the tune under a new name, "Wolverine Blues," presumably to help it sell, even though this up-tempo romp was anything but a blues. Or perhaps the Melrose brothers didn't yet know the difference between bona fide blues and exuberant ragtime. The renaming of the piece was bad enough, but the Melrose brothers also had rebaptized its composer "Fred" Morton. Within a month, on March 13, the New Orleans Rhythm Kings—a white group of Crescent City expatriates working in Chicago—had recorded the newly retitled "Wolverine Blues," and a few weeks later, in April, King Oliver's Creole Jazz Band headed to Richmond, Indiana, to cut a large part of its repertoire for Gennett Records, starting with "Wolverine Blues."

The tune was everywhere, but its composer was painfully aware that he wasn't getting proper credit for it. So in April 1923, he ventured to Chicago, intent on telling the Melrose brothers exactly what they had done to his work.

Yet even as Morton was preparing to leave L.A., the Spikes brothers swindled him once more, though he didn't realize it. On April 16, 1923, Reb and Johnny Spikes filed a copyright on a tune titled "Froggie Moore," with words by Benjamin Spikes and John C. Spikes, music by Ferd Morton. And though the copyright version used just two of Morton's three themes, the music was wholly by Morton, who intended no lyrics and no songwriting partners.

If Morton had known what the Spikes brothers had done with the "Froggie Moore" copyright, his anger would have swelled. But this was the least of his problems, for Morton did not realize—and could not have anticipated—that the Spikes brothers' swindle was child's play compared to the shell game that the Melrose boys had in mind.

four

CHICAGO HUSTLE

No one—not even Walter and Lester Melrose themselves—imagined that two white farm boys from southeastern Illinois would ascend as kingpins of black music in Roaring Twenties Chicago. A lifetime in the cornfields seemed more like it.

Born ten miles from a speck on the map called Olney, the Melrose boys knew more about horses and cows than they did about jazz or blues. As a fifteen-year-old, in fact, Lester toiled in his father's livery stable in nearby Sumner, Illinois, where the family had moved in 1906. But what the Melrose brothers lacked in musical knowledge they overcame with ambition and cunning.

Walter—the eldest of a brood that included two other brothers (Franklyn and Lee) and three sisters (Mamie, Merle, and Belle)—was the first to flee the farm, landing a job in Marshall Field's sprawling department store, near the epicenter of Chicago's Loop, at State and Randolph. Born on the midwestern prairie in 1889, Walter never had seen a place of such grandeur, its high-priced merchandise stacked ten floors high, a magnificent stone tower in a city that already was reaching for the sky.

There may have been little glory in peddling sheet music at Field's, but to Walter this was merely a fifteen-dollar-a-week stepping-stone to the more glamorous future he envisioned. Though he possessed neither musical talent nor training, Walter aspired to become a great songwriter, spending his spare time penning sentimental lyrics. Alas, they were written to melodies that only he heard, since he could neither read nor write a note of music.

Lester, born two years later than Walter, nourished outsized dreams as well: He was going to become a major league baseball player, to him a clear-cut trajectory from his spot as catcher on the bush league team of Henderson, Kentucky. But Lester saw his future crumble after his first season, when the K&T League folded. The only work he could find in the aftermath of this debacle was a backbreaking job shoveling coal into train engines, and he lost even that when the boss discovered that Lester wasn't yet twenty-one years old. Running out of possibilities, Lester packed up in 1912 and followed his brother to Chicago, quixotically trying out as a catcher for the White Sox, then settling for a nine-dollar-a-week job at Maurice Rothchild's department store at State and Jackson, just down the street from Field's. Within two years, Lester had scraped together enough money to open a grocery store on the South Side, at Thirty-seventh and Vincennes. If baseball wasn't going to toss him a fortune, something else would have to do.

So the Melrose brothers were on the make, looking to get ahead in a booming metropolis that had taken scant notice of their arrival. But the big money would have to wait still longer, for Uncle Sam snatched them up in the last year of World War I, 1918. Forced to sell his grocery store because he was being shipped out to war, Lester lost everything, and when the brothers returned to Chicago the following year, prospects didn't look much better than when they had left.

Their ambitions thwarted at every turn, the Melrose brothers decided to pool their still unproven talents. By combining Walter's experience pushing sheet music with Lester's brief run at the grocery store, the brothers supposed they might have a shot operating a music shop, which they opened in 1920 in rented space at 6311 South Cottage Grove Avenue.

Again, they floundered.

"The music business was very slow at the time," recalled Lester. "We carried a full stock of pop sheet music, piano rolls and small musical instruments and records. Emerson and Gennett were the only records we could [afford to] purchase at that time, so the going was pretty rough."

Meanwhile, Walter hacked away at his songs, in May 1920 copyrighting his words and music for a maudlin tune he titled "Since I Lost You," and in July "My Old Home of Yesterday." The latter was practically a carbon copy of George Gershwin and Irving Caesar's enormous hit of the year before, "Swanee," which had triggered an avalanche of back-home-in-the-South knockoffs. Like most of them, Walter's version went nowhere.

But at 5:45 P.M. on February 16, 1921, the Melrose boys finally lucked out, with the opening of the ornate Tivoli Theatre, a $2-million entertainment palace at Cottage Grove and Sixty-third Street, just a few doors south of the brothers' music store. Loosely modeled after the Chapel at Versailles, the towering Balaban & Katz edifice seated fully forty-five hundred, at the time the largest such theater in Chicago. The Melrose brothers watched eagerly as throngs swarmed the very block on which they coincidentally had staked their future.

In newspaper ads, Balaban & Katz proclaimed the Tivoli opening "The Greatest Amusement Event Since The World's Fair," referring to the celebrated World's Columbian Exposition of 1893. "As a Chicagoan, you'll be proud of the Tivoli. You'll boast of its magnificence; of its magnitude; of its many marvelous features; its cozy coves and picturesque recesses."

The prose may have been purple, but the place truly reeked of money, its sunburst-dome ceiling, neo-Gothic architecture, cut-stone proscenium, twenty-eight-foot-wide stage, and multiple balconies and boxes more gilded than anything even the Loop had seen. So what if everything about this place was fake, its stone walls actually a facade plastered onto cement, its accoutrements cheap facsimiles? It looked genuine enough, with 11,438 Chicagoans ogling the inside of the

Tivoli on opening night and thousands more left waiting outdoors, denied a chance to witness a faux architectural wonder, at least on this night.

The souls lucky enough to get inside marveled at a stained-glass window stretching sixty-five feet high, crystal chandeliers that looked as if they had been commissioned by Louis XVI, seemingly endless rows of plush seats piled six stories high, and oil paintings reported to have cost an inconceivable forty thousand dollars. The *Chicago American* dubbed the theater "a sanctuary of entertainment which is nothing less than an art museum," and curiosity seekers from across Chicago—and from other cities, too—packed the place.

"Our Sincere Regrets to the Disappointed Ones," noted the ad in the next day's paper. "It seemed as if the whole world came to see this wonder theater and to witness its superior performance. From Pullman and West Pullman, from Indiana Harbor and Hammond, from South Chicago and Gary, from Englewood and Cicero and from other adjacent points came men, women and children to mingle with citizens of Chicago, Evanston, Oak Park and other sections of the north shore, the north side, south side and the west."

The masses may have come to savor the plush new theater that the ads touted as "A Sensational Spectacle—Blend of Stage and Screen Novelties," but they also swarmed to nearby shops—including the Melrose store. Still whistling and humming tunes that the Tivoli bands had played between movie screenings, the crowds voraciously snapped up the latest sheet music and records, as well as flyers, posters, publicity photos—practically anything the Melrose brothers could put on the shelves.

"Business boomed and word got around to the record pub.[lishing] companies that we were doing a tremendous business," recalled Lester Melrose, who, with his older brother, Walter, at last was vindicated. A couple of farm boys really could hold their own in a brawling city like Chicago. "Our store was too small to handle our business," added Lester, "so we moved across the street to 6318 Cottage Grove Ave.," in February 1923.

Now the Melrose brothers were precisely where they needed to be, at the nexus of commerce and musical culture on the South Side of Chicago. The moviegoers who streamed out of the Tivoli morning, noon, and night could not avoid seeing the Melrose Brothers Music storefront, which directly faced the theater, on the west side of Cottage Grove.

Unfortunately, the Melrose brothers' landlord threw a monkey wrench into the proceedings, jacking up the rent from $40 a month to a staggering $350. So even though money was rolling in, it was rolling right back out, keeping the Melrose brothers perpetually in the red. In essence, all they had were the outward appearances of success, a facade as phony as the Tivoli's across the street. Yet here, in a storefront space twenty feet wide by eighty feet deep—spacious for the era—the Melrose brothers were gaining stature if not profit. Though at first Victor, Columbia, and Brunswick wouldn't sell them records, preferring to work with their own agencies in Chicago, the big New York labels quickly came to their senses. Within three months of the Melrose brothers' arrival on the new premises, in fact, the store carried a full line of Victor, Columbia, and Brunswick disks, as well as Gennett, Emerson, Okeh, and, not long after, Paramount.

But it wasn't just the general public that made the Melrose Brothers Music store practically a round-the-clock destination. Black musicians from across the South Side started to converge there, much as their Los Angeles counterparts had done at the Spikes brothers' shop in Los Angeles. Suddenly, and through no planning of their own, Walter and Lester Melrose found themselves at the center of a revolution in American music. With more than sixty-five thousand blacks having arrived in Chicago from Louisiana, Mississippi, Alabama, Arkansas, and Texas between 1910 and 1920, and with nearly a million more pouring into the urban north throughout the decade that followed, a new audience was emerging. Raised in the South but working where the decent-paying jobs were, up North, the newly anointed Chicagoans were hungry for down-home, blues-driven music and thereby were redefining the sound of the city's South Side.

Moreover, Chicago's fierce and unyielding brand of segregation kept migrant blacks confined to an increasingly overcrowded ghetto, bounded by Twenty-sixth Street on the north, Fifty-first Street on the south, Cottage Grove Avenue on the east, and State Street on the west—a captive audience just a streetcar ride from the Tivoli Theatre and the Melrose brothers' wares. Word quickly spread among musicians who played the South Side's black theaters and saloons that the Melrose brothers were looking for talent.

"We were getting inquiries from various composers, including colored, about publishing or getting their selections recorded on phono records," remembered Lester, who, with his brother, shrewdly realized that selling records and sheet music was chump change. The real money, the Melrose boys concluded, was in owning copyrights and publishing the material. And if the big New York publishing houses and record companies had the mainstream pop and theatrical material all sewn up, the Melrose brothers at least could clean up the leftovers—the South Side black music that the big-time firms back East wouldn't touch. "It was [financially] impossible for us to publish pop tunes at that time, so we decided to take a whirl at the blues," recalled Lester, who at the time was sharing an apartment with Walter nearby, at 6031 South Calumet Avenue. "The blues selections started coming in, and we soon had ten or twelve selections we thought were good material."

Yet none matched the hit Walter and Lester found one evening in 1923, when they wandered into the Lincoln Gardens dance club—at Thirty-first Street near Cottage Grove—to hear Joe "King" Oliver's Creole Jazz Band unleashing hot, homegrown New Orleans dance music. Oliver had come to Chicago in 1918, at first playing cornet in bands led by two old friends from New Orleans, mandolinist Bill Johnson's outfit at the Royal Gardens and clarinetist Lawrence Duhe's ensemble at the Dreamland Café. But considering Oliver's charismatic solo style and unassailable musicianship, it surprised no one that he soon was leading the Dreamland group, which he rechristened the Creole Jazz Band and took out to California in 1922. Jelly Roll Morton presented Oliver's Creole ensemble at Wayside Amusement Park that year, and when Oliver and the band returned to Chicago in the middle of 1922, they were received as conquering heroes, trumpeted as the marquee attraction at the Lincoln Gardens (formerly the Royal Gardens).

Determined to live up to his billing, Oliver sent for his young New Orleans protégé, cornetist Louis Armstrong, to join his Creole Jazz Band, but even Oliver did not anticipate the force he had unleashed by bringing the incomparable Satchmo north. The glorious two-cornet dialogues that Oliver and Armstrong played at the Lincoln Gardens caused a sensation on the South Side of Chicago, attracting overflow throngs that never had heard such sonic firepower. Backed by Johnny Dodds on clarinet and Honore Dutrey on trombone (both veterans of New Orleans saloons and street parades), the Creole Jazz Band played undiluted, blues-drenched, nascent swing style for a southern black audience starved to hear it.

Oliver and his men, reported the *Chicago Defender*,

> startled white musicians. From all over the city they would gather to hear King Joe blow those weird, soulful tunes. . . . Later on, he brought Louis Armstrong, a green-looking country boy with big forehead, thin lips and robust physique. This newcomer brought us an entirely different style of playing than King Joe had given us. He was younger, had more power of delivery and could send his stuff out with a knack.

The music making was so freewheeling, aggressive, and technically alert that even Satchmo, heading straight to the Lincoln Gardens from Chicago's Twelfth Street Station (where the Illinois Central train from New Orleans had dropped him off), was overwhelmed by what he was hearing. "When they opened that door for me to go in the cabaret, them guys was wailing so great I started to get back in the cab and go home," recalled Armstrong. "I said, 'I can't play in that band.'"

It was in Chicago that he "got good," said Armstrong, the level of playing across the South Side setting new technical and artistic standards for the still swiftly evolving art of jazz. Nowhere else came close, as Memphis trumpeter Johnny Dunn discovered after playing with W. C. Handy's band in New York in 1917 (Handy by then had recognized that a band *could* play the blues). When Dunn came to Chicago to stake a claim—bringing with him an outsized horn vaguely resembling a cannon—Morton warned him that he was entering treacherous waters. "I saw him right after he got off the train," remembered Morton, who told him, "You better take that long thing and go right back to New York—these Chicago boys'll cut you to death."

One night a week, the Lincoln Gardens opened for whites only, and on just such an evening the Melrose brothers heard King Oliver and the band play one smoldering tune after another, showing the brothers where their future lay. One hit above all others jolted the crowds, and it was Jelly Roll Morton's "The Wolverines," which Oliver may have picked up from the composer a few months earlier, at Wayside Amusement Park in California. The tune was becoming the band's signature hit at the Lincoln Gardens, so the Melrose brothers seized their chance: If they could obtain the copyright and arrange for Oliver to record the tune, they might make a small fortune in royalties on the sales of sheet music and records.

Thus the Melrose brothers bought the copyright to the tune from the Spikes brothers, who added lyrics as well as their names as cosongwriters of "The Wolverines." Then the Melrose brothers quickly began circulating their hot new number, which on February 14 they renamed "Wolverine Blues." They arranged for Albert Short and his Tivoli Syncopators, who regularly played the piece across the street for Tivoli audiences, to record it in March for Vocalion. But that was just the beginning. On March 13, five members of the New Orleans Rhythm Kings—white musicians who had grown up in the Crescent City but now were in residence at the Friars Inn nightclub in Chicago—recorded "Wolverine Blues" at the Gennett studio in Richmond, Indiana, with the estimable clarinetist Leon Roppolo, trombonist George Brunis, and cornetist-leader Paul Mares cutting a version that became one of the band's most popular disks. A couple of weeks later, Frank Westphal and his orchestra recorded the piece again for Columbia in Chicago. On April 6, 1923, King Oliver and his band headed to the Gennett studio in Richmond, Indiana. And a few weeks later, Oliver's first recording—featuring Morton's renamed "Wolverine Blues" on one side and "Dipper Mouth Blues" on the other—hit the street.

On the strength of these recordings, as well as live performances every night of the week in Chicago's theaters and saloons, a seminal jazz hit was born, with the Melrose brothers cranking out at least two new published versions: a piano-vocal sheet music version and a larger instrumental-ensemble arrangement. Everyone involved was ecstatic, with one notable exception: the New Orleans musician who had written "The Wolverines" and received second billing for it, Jelly Roll Morton.

So on the warm day in May when Jelly Roll Morton walked into Melrose Brothers Music, he was out for blood.

The Melrose brothers finally had proved to themselves and to the world that they could engineer a bona fide hit, and they relished the sweet fact that "Wolverine Blues" was theirs. "Columbia & Victor stores were getting plenty of calls for a record by King Oliver," remembered Lester Melrose, who gloated that he had a hit that Columbia and Victor did not. If anyone wanted to own the record of "Wolverine Blues," he would have to hurry over to the Melrose brothers' store to pick one up, while they lasted. Walter and Lester Melrose reveled in this coup, plastering an enormous banner out front to exult in it: "Wolverine Blues Sold Here."

As Jelly Roll Morton approached the Melrose brothers' shop, he couldn't miss the enormous sign and instantly realized that his fame had preceded him. Anger began to melt into pride. And though the street noise practically was deafening, with streetcars rattling along Cottage Grove and crowds raising a ruckus outside the Tivoli, Morton gradually began to pick up the faint strains of his "Wolverines" played—atrociously—on a piano. Nearing Melrose Brothers Music, Morton peered inside to determine exactly who was mauling his "Wolverines." The culprit hammering the defenseless instrument proved to be Walter Melrose, who deserved credit for bravado in the face of keyboard incompetence, if nothing else. Like most self-taught pianists, Melrose tried to peck out the tune on just the black keys but never could get the melody and harmony to line up quite right.

Yet Melrose barreled ahead, as if oblivious of his blunders. With these discordant sounds as a backdrop, Jelly Roll Morton made his entrance.

"One day a man wearing a Western style hat with a red bandana around his neck walked into our store and announced that he was Jelly Roll Morton, the greatest stomp & blues player this side of New Orleans. Cassius Clay had nothing on Jelly Roll," Lester Melrose said years later, referring, of course, to Muhammad Ali, another loquacious black man whose physical prowess and mental celerity made good most of his boasts. Like Ali, Morton knew his worth and detailed it for all to hear. As Morton launched into his soliloquy, so well rehearsed from a lifetime of retellings, Walter Melrose mercifully stopped badgering the piano and listened. For more than an hour, Morton unreeled tales of life in New Orleans, describing the honky-tonks and brothels he had played in Storyville at the turn of the century, the vaudeville theaters he had worked thereafter and the long list of cabarets, nightclubs, and dives from Tijuana to Vancouver that had featured him. He recalled creating the first bona fide jazz tunes as far back as 1905 and 1906, he revisited his triumphs in uncounted piano contests, and then he sat down at one of the several pianos in the store to establish his pre-eminence.

"He had a flock of numbers," said Lester, and as Morton's long fingers manipulated the keyboard, musicians and store employees and passers-by began to gather around him, just as they had when Morton played in New Orleans's brothels nearly two decades earlier. The first tune, of course, was "The Wolverines," and as Morton ticked off its most difficult passages, customers and sales clerks dropped what they were doing to savor the way the New Orleans piano man was making the keys sing and dance.

Morton played fragments of a tune later known as "Milenberg Joys," Lester Melrose remembered, and one can only guess at the other gems he might have displayed on this historic afternoon. The impromptu audience would have been disarmed by the habanera rhythms of "New Orleans Blues," the meteoric octaves and surging swing rhythms of "King Porter Stomp," and the nimble solo breaks and operatic trills of "Jelly Roll Blues." Every piece sounded utterly unlike the rest, each a singular mixture of New Orleans rhythm, southern blues, and European harmony somehow compressed into three minutes (or less) of extraordinarily picturesque music making. Though Chicago already had heard such estimable New Orleans piano men as Tony Jackson and Albert Carroll, Morton was different, playing fully developed compositions in which themes and counterthemes were ingeniously structured, developed, and recapitulated. Every note mattered when Morton played, every change in key and tempo and texture signifying a dramatic turn in the progress of the music.

Finally, having made his point in melody and rhythm, Morton removed his hands from the keyboard and informed the Melrose brothers that he was not going to tolerate second billing to the Spikes brothers on "The Wolverines." The tune had borne his musical fingerprint since his days in the District in New Orleans, and there was no room for negotiation.

The young Melrose brothers, flummoxed by this extraordinary man's orgy of music making and storytelling, rushed to say they were only too happy to oblige their unexpected visitor. Here, sitting before them, was the man who had penned their first bona fide hit, a song so rhythmically alluring as to give both King Oliver's Creole Jazz Band and the white New Orleans Rhythm Kings, among others, big-selling records.

So the Melrose brothers immediately resubmitted the copyright, giving Morton top billing over the Spikes brothers, though all three would share credit and royalties forevermore. Morton didn't make a penny on the correction, though he gained something that apparently was more important to him at this point than mere cash: his artistic due.

Moreover, Morton liked what he saw in Walter and Lester Melrose, for these two hicks sitting on a potential gold mine in front of the glittering Tivoli showed energy, ambition, big plans, and the right skin color for doing business in Chicago's emerging music industry. Yet even before Morton plunged into a partnership with the Melrose brothers, he began to stake out the opportunities that Chicago could afford him.

Though the Melrose brothers later took credit for bringing Morton to the attention of the world by arranging for him to record for Gennett in Richmond, in fact Morton began recording for Paramount in Chicago in June 1923—just weeks after arriving in the city. The man who had once taken pride in keeping his best material secret—the better to surprise and thus carve competitors in piano contests—now plunged wholeheartedly into making recordings. This marked a major conceptual advance for Morton, who realized that money and fame no longer were to be found in cutting contests and fancy brothels. That was the past. Recordings now afforded a new path to riches and glory, and Morton—armed with a bulging repertoire of painstakingly and uniquely constructed jazz tunes—took off in hot pursuit.

So Morton organized a band that Paramount, unfortunately, misspelled as Jelly-Roll Marton and His Orchestra. Nevertheless, their versions of Morton's "Big Fat Ham" and "Muddy Water Blues"—recorded in June, one month after he had arrived in Chicago—stand as his first known recordings. Granted, these were not exactly major breakthroughs in modern music. Jasper Taylor played woodblocks as if they were lead weights, thereby mitigating any real sense of swing, while the other musicians—including no-names such as alto saxophonist Charles Harris and clarinetists Bernie Young and Wilson Towne—rounded out what amounted to a novelty.

Yet for Morton these sessions were critical, for they showed him that he could bring crucial elements of his bandleading style to the recording studio, documenting for all time the composed solo "breaks" and the instrumental counterpoint that drove so much of his ensemble music. Equally important, these sessions introduced Morton to the rigors of making records. From this moment forth, he increasingly focused his talents and energies on composing, arranging, and rehearsing for the recording studio, at the expense of his pimping, card sharking, and pool hustling. In essence, Morton was refashioning himself as a complete musician, driven to commit his deeply autobiographical tunes to the new technology suddenly available to him in Chicago. At this late date, nearly two decades after he had been tossed out of the family home in New Orleans and left to survive by his wits, Morton finally was assuming the full responsibility for his talent. To Morton, music was becoming not just a trade but an art, to be pursued vigorously and promoted tirelessly.

Meanwhile, the fame of Morton's "Wolverine Blues" was spreading quickly beyond Chicago, with Gene Rodemich and his orchestra recording it for Brunswick in New York on June 21. This recording signaled to bands along the East Coast that a new sound was blowing out of Chicago, and in short order Morton's New York counterparts took notice.

By the next month, on July 17, Morton was recording piano solos for the first time, not surprisingly starting with his earliest compositions: "King Porter Stomp"—which Gennett incorrectly labeled "King Portor (A Stomp)"—and "New Orleans (Blues) Joys." These were the two early compositions Morton had completed in New Orleans in 1905 and, not surprisingly, were the pieces he felt most comfortable recording. Apparently unfazed by the large microphone that loomed over the piano, Morton produced not only a note-perfect "King Porter" (in an era when stops and starts and postsession editing did not exist) but added seductive new musical details. As he arrived at the second bar of "King Porter Stomp," for instance, he played a startling dissonant blue note, as if to update the jazz flavor of a piece that had first emerged in the ragtime era. In "New Orleans Joys," the gen-

tly swaying Spanish-tinge rhythms attested to the originality and ex-
oticism of the music Morton had developed in New Orleans and on
the road.

But Morton wasn't done for the day: He recorded "Sobbin'
Blues" and "Mr. Jelly Lord" with the New Orleans Rhythm Kings,
the white Chicago band that had been drawn from the ranks of the
Friars [Inn] Society Orchestra in Chicago and which earlier in the year
had released a recording of "Wolverine Blues." And on the next day,
Morton and friends recorded his "London Blues" and "Milenberg
Joys." Now Morton was making history, shattering the color barrier
in jazz recording for the first time, more than a decade before Benny
Goodman received credit for doing so with Lionel Hampton and
Teddy Wilson. Still, the idea of white musicians collaborating with a
black man—even one as light-skinned as the Creole Morton—posed
problems for all involved, particularly when it came to hotel accom-
modations in provincial Richmond. So Morton was asked to pass, the
boys in the band saying he was Cuban.

Morton's effect on the New Orleans Rhythm Kings was dramatic,
turning a rinky-dink ensemble into something closer to a bona fide jazz
band. The Morton–Rhythm Kings recordings of "Mr. Jelly Lord" on
July 17 and "London Blues" and "Milenberg Joys" on July 18 did not
fully capture the blues-swing feeling and orchestral counterpoint that
Morton would achieve on recordings a couple of years later. But they
evoked authentic New Orleans ensemble music more closely than anything the Rhythm Kings yet had created on their own.

The composer-pianist went before the microphone again that day,
July 18, cutting additional solos from his enormous repertoire. The
list included the ebullient, stomping rhythms of "Grandpa's Spells,"
with its brilliantly ascending staccato chords, tailgate-style bass lines,
and innovative laying of the forearm on the keyboard, and "Kansas
City Stomp," energized by its syncopated left-hand lines and tricky
stop-time rhythms. In "Wolverine Blues," Morton underscored his
jazz credentials by reinventing each theme with every statement—the
essence of jazz solo improvisation. And in "The Pearls," he proved
that a piece in which every section or theme sounds utterly unlike the

others can be made to cohere as a single work, a tour de force of performance as well as composition.

The technicians, instrumentalists, and hangers-on at Gennett were amazed to encounter such a profusion of far-flung musical ideas emanating from one man's hands. Yet none of the music sounded virtuosic for its own sake, for Morton had designed these pieces as musical statements rather than as bravura pianistic displays. Some, such as "Milenberg Joys" and "New Orleans Blues," painted pictorial scenes of life in or near Morton's hometown. Others, such as "King Porter Stomp" and "Jelly Roll Blues," were more abstract, expanding the ways in which swing rhythm, blues scales, and extended chords could be applied in a jazz setting.

But Morton was just getting started.

On October 30, Jelly-Roll Morton's Jazz Band, as it was listed, recorded for the Okeh label (the new "race records" division of Columbia) "Someday, Sweetheart" and "London Blues," which, though rhythmically a bit plodding, captured more of the ripe blues spirit that Morton was after. With New Orleans veterans such as cornetist Natty Dominique, trombonist Zue Robertson, and clarinetist Horace Eubanks in the band, Morton at last could strive to achieve the distinctly Crescent City sound he had heard growing up.

The Melrose brothers, meanwhile, were discovering that when Morton had strolled into the store on that lucky day in May, he carried with him a seemingly bottomless satchel of composed music ready for the selling. In just the first months of their collaboration with Morton, in 1923, the Melrose lads published "Grandpa's Spells," "Kansas City Stomp," "London Blues," "Mr. Jelly Lord," and "The Pearls," as well as the already released "Wolverine Blues"— in effect, the first great canon of jazz compositions. To the Melrose brothers, Morton wasn't just the author of "Wolverine Blues": He was a one-man band who could write tunes faster than they could print them, then dazzle customers with his meticulously conceived recordings and dramatically improvised performances.

No one in jazz was writing, publishing, and recording his own music as prolifically as Morton, and no one was benefiting more than

the Melrose brothers. Thanks to Morton, the days that Walter and
Lester had spent toiling in department stores and grocery markets
quickly were slipping into an unlamented past.

The honeymoon between the Melrose brothers and their resident
New Orleans piano genius was on, and Morton believed he had
walked into a dream—or at least an ideal setting in which to write,
record, and promulgate his music. The proselytizer no longer had to
win over audiences show by show, night after night. Now his records
could do the work for him, carrying the sounds that he heard in his
head across Chicago, and beyond.

The Melrose Brothers Music store became practically his second
home. "Often he [Morton] and I used to rehearse together at the Melrose office," remembered the reedist Volley de Faut. "Morton was a
tremendous worker. If he was working on something, he would sit
there for four or five hours at a stretch." As Morton wrote and rehearsed at the Melrose store, the pandemonium of Sixty-third and
Cottage Grove roaring outside, the composer simply tuned out the
distractions and created. It was a skill he had developed in the brothels of New Orleans, where brawls and bodacious sex and gunplay had
to be taken in stride if a piano player meant to keep the gig.

But as Morton rehearsed and composed in the Melrose shop, others watched, listened and learned. A teenage clarinetist named Benny
Goodman whiled away his hours at the store, absorbing concepts of
New Orleans music that were not offered to him at Jane Addams's
Hull-House, where he had been taught the rudiments of the instrument. As Morton and his New Orleans sidemen (most notably the
clarinetist Johnny Dodds) worked up their performances, the young
Goodman took a front row seat, learning at close range the inner
workings of jazz—from its first great architect.

The Melrose brothers, meanwhile, were stunned by their good
fortune in latching onto Morton and wanted everyone to know it.
They issued a news release bragging about their coup, the *Phonograph and Talking Machine Weekly* picking it up verbatim on November 7, 1923. "'Jelly Roll' Morton, Record Artist, Joins Writing Staff of
Melrose Bros.", the headline noted.

The initial release of the Gennett recording "Kansas City Stomps" and "Grandpa's Spells" is already out and judging from dealers' reports is enjoying a big sale. . . . The following numbers have been accepted by the Melrose Bros. Music Co. of Chicago for immediate publication: Kansas City Stomp, Grandpa's Spells, The Pearls, King Porter, Chicago Breakdown, New Orleans Blues, Deuces Wild, Shreveport Stomps, Any Ox, Stratford Rag, Mamanita, London Blues, Southern Town and Mr. Jelly Lord. These numbers will be published under the title of 'Jelly Roll' Morton's Famous Blues and Rag Series. . . . His latest hit, Wolverine Blues, is considered by musicians a noteworthy contribution to music and is one of the popular numbers now on the market.

Morton's growing roster of hit songs was yielding new profits for the Melrose brothers from sales of sheet music and records, as well as publisher's royalties for each. At long last, the Melrose brothers were making money. "He helped a great deal in pulling us out of the red," conceded Lester Melrose. Morton may have carried on incessantly about his talent, but "damned, if he didn't prove it." Walter Melrose concurred: "I'll have to hand it to him, that guy was prolific. He could go home and produce overnight."

More than that, Morton became a walking advertisement for the Melrose brothers, who watched as Morton's friends—the most important black jazz artists in Chicago—streamed into their store, bringing hand-written tunes under their arms. Though Walter Melrose couldn't read music, he also realized that he didn't need to, for Morton was on hand to pan for gold from amid the stream of manuscripts that poured into the shop. "Melrose knew nothing about music," Morton later recalled. "Through my advice, lots of successful things were done, purchases like 'Some of These Days,' 'Some Day Sweetheart,' publishing 'St. Louis Blues' and 'Beale St. Blues,' my piano book of Stomps and Blues, 'Louis Armstrong's Books of Chorus[es] and Hot Breaks.'" As resident pianist, composer, arranger, and musical jack-of-all-trades in the Melrose store, Morton routinely lent his talents to artists struggling over a tune. In the summer of 1923, for instance, clarinetist Leon Rappolo and cornetist Paul Mares (members of the New Orleans Rhythm Kings) had been noodling with a couple riffs in need of a main theme. "Walter asked Jelly if he could fill it in," reported *Down Beat* writer George Hoefer, who had been told the story by Walter Melrose. "Jelly said, 'Sure,' and sat down at the piano. Ten minutes later they had a new tune that the New Orleans boys told Walter to call 'Milenberg Joys.'"

Morton's name was becoming legendary in Chicago, not only for his tunes but also for his keyboard virtuosity. The very sight of Morton approaching a piano unnerved even the most accomplished players. Pianist Lil Hardin, a songwriter at the Jones Music Store before she married Louis Armstrong in 1924, crushed all challengers, until Morton showed up. "I had never heard such playing before," said Hardin.

> Jelly Roll sat down, the piano rocked, the floor shivered and the people swayed as he attacked the keyboard with his long, skinny fingers, beating out a double rhythm with his feet on the loud pedal—I was amazed and thrilled. Finally, he got up from the piano, grinned and looked at me as if to say, "Let that be a lesson to you." It certainly was a lesson, so much so that I didn't want to play while Jelly Roll was there, but the people insisted that he hear me play and I finally gave in. I figured there was no need for me to try to compete with him on popular music, so I laid the "Witches Dance" and Rachmaninoff's Prelude in C-Sharp Minor on him. The way people applauded when I was through, one would think that I had won the contest, but I know I could never beat Jelly Roll and, from that day on, I put all my 85 pounds to work trying to sound like him.

But no one could, because the man drew upon a personal repertoire custom-made for the contours of his hands, honed in saloons across the country, and reinvented every time he sat at a piano. In effect, Morton was the personification of a new American archetype—

the perpetually roving jazz musician. Unlike his highbrow European counterpart, the American jazz man reeled off fresh, original music and openly idiosyncratic improvisations every time he sat down to play. He was no mere interpreter, dispatching a Brahms sonata for the thousandth time, but rather a creator equal in stature to the composer, inventing tunes to suit his moods and excite his audience. His songs were his own, and even if the tune was familiar, as "Wolverine Blues" and "King Porter Stomp" rapidly were becoming, the jazz musician sabotaged listener expectations with the new twists and turns he applied to each performance.

Jelly Roll Morton in 1923 at last was asserting himself as composer, pianist, bandleader, and recording artist, taking his place at the forefront of an art form that he had been the first to capture in ink on paper. But what Morton didn't know—what he had no reason even to suspect—was that just as he was ascending in Chicago, the Melrose brothers were beginning to swindle the black jazz musicians whose hits they published, none more than Morton. Walter Melrose, who worked hard to keep Morton's tunes in print and on record, also hustled his way onto Morton's copyrights, a move that would make Melrose rich and Morton anything but.

Walter Melrose yearned to write hit songs, but lacking any discernible artistic musical gifts or the barest musical education, he was bound to fail. Perhaps even he wasn't surprised that the songs he wrote and copyrighted, starting in 1920, courted oblivion.

But if he didn't know whether he was looking at a piece of music right side up or upside down, he quickly came to understand his power as the publisher of songs created by oft-illiterate black musicians in a virtually unregulated business. It was the publisher, after all, who filed the paperwork with the U.S. Office of Copyrights in Washington, D.C., and it was these filings that indicated who would receive royalties on published and recorded works of music. As early as April 25, 1923—before Morton even had set foot in the Melrose Brothers Music store—Walter Melrose filed a copyright for "Tin Roof Blues," by the New Orleans Rhythm Kings. Nearly two months later, on June 7, 1923, Melrose filed a new copyright on the instrumental composition, adding his name to the paperwork as lyricist. In so doing, he could double-dip, collecting the publisher's traditional 50 percent of royalties, as well as an additional 50 percent of the songwriter royalties.

Walter Melrose was exultant when he made this discovery, for in a single stroke he not only increased his profit margin as publisher but emerged as a self-styled songwriter, at long last credited with coauthorship of famous tunes—though, in truth, they had been created entirely by instrumentalists such as the New Orleans Rhythm Kings, Louis Armstrong, Joe "King" Oliver, Jelly Roll Morton, and others who were playing them across the country. This strategy was particularly egregious in precisely the jazz idiom that was the specialty of Melrose Brothers Music, for these complex and intricately structured compositions generally lent themselves to instrumental performances, not vocals.

Having succeeded in making himself coauthor of "Tin Roof Blues," Walter Melrose pressed ahead, adding his name to Charlie Davis's "Copenhagen" a week after filing the original copyright. He did the same with Joe Oliver and Louis Armstrong's "Sugar Foot Stomp," anointing himself lyricist and partaking in the songwriter royalties.

Then he moved on to Morton's music, making himself cocreator of "Milenberg Joys," "Sidewalk Blues," "Dixie Knows," "Sweetheart O'Mine" (a blatant reworking of part of Morton's "Frog-I-More" recopyrighted under the new name by Melrose), and possibly others. In each case, he took the publisher's traditional 50 percent of royalties, plus half of Morton's composer's royalties. Morton had no way of knowing that Melrose did this, because the copyrights were filed a thousand miles away, in Washington, D.C. But even if he had, he might not have objected, so long as he got top billing. It was acclaim that mattered most to Morton at this stage of his life, not cash, for he was rolling in it, touring the Midwest—through Illinois, Ohio, Kentucky, and beyond—when he wasn't recording. Indeed, money, gigs, and women rolled as never before.

"He talked to me about making some records with him, so one day I went over to see him about this at his room at 35th and Grand Boulevard," remembered trumpeter Lee Collins, who was working at the Lincoln Gardens. "There he was—in bed with two women, one sitting on each side of him. I tell you, he was some character."

When it came to cash, Morton doled it out almost as easily as he made it, paying his New Orleans sidemen the kind of money they never had seen before. At the end of an evening, generally around 1:30 A.M., Morton summoned his men, then showed them what real money looked like. "When he got through playing I remember Jelly called me and said, 'All right, Albert, let me pay you off,' and Jelly went into his pocket and took out a roll of bills and started peeling off fives until he got $50, which he handed me," recalled New Orleans clarinetist Albert Nicholas, who had moved to Chicago in 1924.

> Coming from New Orleans, where the little gigs paid three or four dollars a night, it was a big deal. So when this cat gave me this $50, I'm thinking it was to split up. So I put it in my pocket, and before I opened my mouth he said, "Hey Barney [Bigard]," and he paid him, and then he called Paul [Barbarin]. So we got our heads together, and I whispered, "How much did you get?" Barney said, "I got 50." I said, "Me too." Jelly was looking at us and said, "I know what you all are talkin' about. I know you never made that much money in your life before. . . . You see, if you all'd be playing with me you'd be making money."

By the end of 1923, Melrose Brothers Music also was hauling in cash, its catalog listing fully forty songs, all blues and stomps, most penned by Morton. On the success of Morton's originals, Walter Melrose moved the music publishing end of the business downtown, to Cohan's Grand Opera House, on 119 North Clark Street, in the Loop—just a few months after Morton had sauntered into the Mel-

rose brothers' lives. Enticed by the fortune that could be made publishing music and swindling songwriters, Walter sold his interest in the
store to Lester, who agreed to give his brother regular payments until
the note was paid off.

For the Melrose brothers, business never was so good.

"The unprecedented demand for 'Kansas City Stomps,' by 'Jelly
Roll' Morton, published by Melrose Bros., has caused the firm to
bring all the hits of this popular rag writer into one folio, soon to be
placed on the market," reported *The Music Trades,* an industry publication for dealers of records and sheet music, on February 2, 1924.

> The demand for the Gennett records of all Mr. Morton's hits has
> exceeded the supply of some of these popular records. They are,
> it is reported, among the best selling numbers of the Gennett list.
> "Jelly Roll" Morton will be remembered as the man who wrote
> "Wolverine Blues," "Grandpa's Spells," "London Blues," "New
> Orleans Blues," "Chicago Breakdown," "Stratford Rag,"
> "Shreveport Blues," and the popular "Kansas City Stomp." Espe-
> cially does the last number seem destined to be a popular and
> standard rag. People hearing it buy it, and after playing it for
> some time lay it aside, only to come back to it later. "Grandpa's
> Spells," "The Pearls," "Chicago Breakdown" and "Stratford
> Rag" . . . if there is such a thing as standard rags, these numbers,
> by their popularity, can be said to be in that class.

After all those years working odd jobs and getting nowhere, the
Melrose brothers finally were in the money, and they shrewdly plowed
their profits right back into the business, taking out costly, quarter-
page ads in the trades promoting sheet music of Morton's "Someday,
Sweetheart" and "Mobile Blues" in 1924 and opening a New York
office in March of that year, at 1547 Broadway. But they could afford
it, thanks to the pervasiveness of Morton hits such as "Someday,
Sweetheart," which crossed the great divide separating black Chicago
on the South Side and white Chicago on the North Side. No less than
the "Million Dollar" Rainbo Gardens—an opulent North Side dance

hall at Clark Street and Lawrence Avenue with a stage that extended from inside the ballroom outside to the gardens—built an entire production number around "Someday, Sweetheart," sending thousands of Chicagoans home each humming the tune. Any songwriter would have been thrilled with this kind of exposure. "The honor is a signal one," noted *The Music Trades*.

Morton was as inspired by this success as the publishers he considered his business partners and wasted no time in building on his triumphs. In April and May 1924, he headed back into the studios in Chicago, recording solo piano versions of his old "Frog-I-More Rag" and "London Blues" for the Rialto label and leading Jelly-Roll Morton's Steamboat Four in "Mr. Jelly Lord" and Jelly Roll Morton's Stomp Kings in "Steady Roll" for Paramount. At the same time, he was positioning himself as the most recorded solo pianist in jazz, cutting "Thirty-fifth Street Blues," "Mamanita," "Froggie Moore," and "London Blues" for Paramount; then returning to Richmond to document "Tia Juana," "Shreveport Stomps," "Mamanita," "Jelly Roll Blues," "Big Foot Ham," "Bucktown Blues," "Tom Cat Blues," "Stratford Hunch," and "Perfect Rag" for Gennett.

Willing and eager to try anything to get his music heard and make a few bucks, Morton sat down in June and July to record thirteen piano rolls, a fairly newfangled technology that enabled customers to put the rolls into their own player pianos and watch the keys jump as if Morton himself were at work. Once again, Morton played the best material available—his own—letting his seemingly airborne left hand and his dexterous right produce evocative versions of "Mr. Jelly Lord," "Mamanita Blues," "London Blues," "King Portor Stomp" [*sic*] and "The 'Jelly Roll' Blues" for Autograph in Chicago. This swirl of activity made Morton the most talked-about jazz musician in a city crowded with them, the trade publications writing him up as the hit maker of the year. With Melrose arranging for nationwide broadcasts of Morton tunes such as "Someday, Sweetheart" by the Terrace Orchestra and Bucktown Five Orchestra, among others, Morton's moment clearly had come. "Of late 'Jelly Roll' has jumped into national prominence because of the life and color he injects into all his offer-

ings," noted *The Music Trades*. "He is being hailed as the 'blue' artist
of the decade."

Even W. C. Handy, the newly famous songwriter-publisher whom
Morton had first encountered when Handy was still toiling as a cornetist in Memphis in 1908, made his way into Morton's circle, albeit in-
directly. W. C. Handy used Jelly Roll's Incomparables for a radio broadcast out of Chicago in 1924, said Harrison Smith, a would-be publisher
who briefly would do business with Morton later in New York. "Ladies
and Gentlemen, you have just heard W. C. Handy and his famous
Memphis band," the announcer said. Morton, thinking the microphone
had been switched off, yelled out in disgust, "Like hell you have!"

Morton's notoriety, paired with his gifts as a composer, produced
lavish sums for the Melrose brothers, who ordered up a complete
overhaul of the shop at 6318 South Cottage Grove in the summer of
1924, making it "one of the most complete neighborhood music
stores in Chicago," according to *The Music Trades*. Chicagoans pouring out of the Tivoli could not miss its two huge new display windows, and as they neared the store, they marveled at a sprawling inventory of Steger & Sons pianos, C. G. Conn horns, and the complete
line of Frank Holton & Co. musical instruments inside. The brightly
buffed saxophones and trumpets gleamed under state-of-the-art indi-
rect lighting, the display framed by walls newly painted robin's-egg
blue. A large sheet music counter served up the latest pop hits, and
nearby an inventory of new phonograph records and the "talking machines" that played them were moving quickly.

Walter Melrose was practically beside himself, the scent of money
getting stronger with each passing month. "I think we are going to
have a real big year in music," he boasted in December of 1924, pre-
dicting high times ahead. "Everyone else in the music industry is enjoying excellent business, which naturally helps increase the sales of
sheet music. The sale of sheet music, in a great measure, depends on
the way the public feels. If the public is happy, it buys sheet music; if
the reverse, it doesn't. At present the average man is happy and has
the money to buy what he wishes. This wish, I might add, is shown
everywhere in the sale of things musical."

There was much more than mere commerce at play here, however, for Morton was making recording history in a new American genre. Though the results of his sessions with his Kings of Jazz in September 1924—a less than top-flight pickup group including trumpeter Lee Collins—were undistinguished, Morton and King Oliver created one of the first electrical recordings with their duets on "King Porter" and "Tom Cat" in December 1924 (using a microphone twelve inches in diameter). And when Jelly Roll Morton and his Jazz Trio recorded "My Gal" in May 1925, with the white clarinetist Voltaire "Volly" De Faut, Morton's integrated trio foreshadowed the interracial sessions that Benny Goodman's trio would play a decade later.

But Morton had been working feverishly and without pause for two solid years since returning to Chicago in 1923, and the pace of his life, as well as the breadth of his artistic activity, finally caught up with him late in May 1925. Suddenly sick, exhausted, and approaching a nervous breakdown, he needed someone to help him through it and called for his younger half sister, Frances Mouton, to come to Chicago to help. She traveled north immediately, never having lost her affection for her colorful older brother, and stayed through October. She was struck by how tired he looked—and by how concerned he had become that he was getting old in a young man's racket.

"I never really got to know my brother until 1925, when I visited him in Chicago," she recalled. "Soon after he met me at the station, he said, 'Now remember, sister, I am not but 28 years old, [and] I don't know how old you are.'

"I said, '28? Jelly!' But he didn't give me a chance to say more than that. And he knew he was so much older. Men don't want to show their age, not any more than women. He would take tweezers and pull his gray hair out. He wanted to be young, as young as me. I wasn't quite 25 when I went to Chicago."

Morton was not only plucking the silver from his temples but also was shaving years from his true age, the result being later confusion over his real birth date. Even in sickness, however, appearances meant everything to Morton, which was why he ditched his old Marmon sedan while Frances was in town and drove a friend's sleek new roadster, trying to pass it off as his own. Frances saw right through her brother's bluff but, out of affection, said nothing.

As Morton gradually recovered, Frances asked to meet his friends and business associates, but Morton introduced her to only one. With pride, Morton brought her to see Walter Melrose, the man who in less than two years Morton had transformed from struggling neighborhood shopkeeper to big-time, downtown publisher, the man who had prospered from Morton's genius and benefited from the long line of New Orleans giants who came into Melrose's store simply because Morton was there, the list including Louis Armstrong, Baby Dodds, Johnny Dodds, and Omer Simeon. To Morton, Melrose wasn't just a music publisher—he was a business partner, a close friend, and a man worthy of introducing to his kin, up from New Orleans.

But Walter Melrose harbored no such feelings toward Morton or anyone else. In fact, Walter was starting to dislike the very black music he was publishing and the black musicians his brother Lester befriended at the store. Walter Melrose was a downtown publisher now, a man of stature who moved among the best businessmen and entertainers in the Loop, where the faces onstage and in the office towers were white, like Walter's. The whole world of black music and black saloons and black life was becoming repugnant to Walter Melrose, who decided that the time had come to rid himself of the South Side ghetto sound, and he started by destroying the store that had launched the Melrose boys just a couple of years earlier. When Lester fell behind on his payments—having overextended himself with his huge inventory—Walter sued him, shut the place down, and left Lester to fend for himself. It took Lester Melrose more than a decade to start to get back on his feet with a fledgling publishing company of his own, Wabash Music. But that wasn't Walter's problem. He had places to go and deals to cut.

This was the kind of man Morton had placed his faith in, believing that Walter Melrose would make a fortune for both of them.

He was half right.

five

THIRTY-FIFTH AND CALUMET

The honking car horns and screaming cornets and laughing, shouting crowds signaled to everyone that the party was on. You could hear it blocks away, the roar of so many voices clamoring at once, the sirens wailing as squad cars rushed by, the occasional pistol going off—sometimes by accident, often by design—the music pouring out of jazz joints every time someone swung the doors open.

A crush of bodies gathered here, on the South Side of Chicago, obliterating any distinction between streets and sidewalks, jamming up traffic beyond belief. And the whole heady spectacle—the anything-goes nightlife, the revelers swilling too much bootleg hootch, the cops packing the paddy wagons—unfolded as if in daytime, under the white-hot beams of electric street lamps that bathed the place in light.

Black Chicago converged here, in Bronzeville, as everyone called the overcrowded tenement area, informally named for the skin color of its residents, some packed seven or eight to a two-room flat. White revelers showed up, too, some looking for vice a safe distance from home, others—particularly the youngsters—hoping to cop a tune or two from the New Orleans musicians, who swung spirits ever higher till daybreak. As the New Orleans jazz men played, teenage white

musicians from the West Side of Chicago got as close to the stage as
they could, trying to decipher the deep-blue chords and decode the
mysterious swing rhythms that rendered this music freer and more
airborne than anything they had heard before. Eventually, the white
kids became jazz stars in their own right, but before they did, each—
from future "King of Swing" Benny Goodman and cornetist Jimmy
McPartland to guitarist Eddie Condon and piano ace Art Hodes—
studied the artistic breakthroughs happening in Bronzeville. And it
wasn't just the kids who were lifting ideas whole from the black jazz
men. The handsomely paid pros who played for Paul Whiteman (the
self-anointed "King of Jazz") double-timed to Bronzeville with pens
at the ready, scribbling notes on the white cuffs of their tuxedo
blouses.

Meanwhile, the pimps, card sharks, pool hustlers, and drug dealers welcomed customers of every skin tone, for thrill seekers of all
tints spent freely, their appetites whetted by homemeade booze on tap
till dawn. All the pleasures of the sporting life, in fact, flowed abun-
dantly, dispensed right out on the street—or indoors for the more de-
mure. At the Pleasures Inn, visitors could watch, in near disbelief,
while a man who called himself Gloria Swanson hit falsetto high notes
more piercing than anything Mary Garden was producing at the
Chicago Opera in the Loop. Or they could visit boxer Jack Johnson's
Cabaret D'Champion, where the spittoons notoriously were made of
gold.

Not even the Loop, with its swank showrooms and gargantuan
movie palaces, compared with the carnival that overran Thirty-fifth
and Calumet, on the South Side, 365 nights a year. But it was the music—more incendiary than anything the legit musicians were playing
for polite society downtown—that took Jelly Roll Morton by surprise. In sheer volume, this music dwarfed the sounds of the bordellos
where he had first learned his craft, if only because so many bands
were playing so many clubs at once. In musical sophistication and
polish, the South Side combos easily outstripped the rough-and-tum-
ble outfits Morton had heard along the West Coast, when he first began handing out his scores for others to play. And in its nearly sym-

phonic grandeur, with several instruments wailing at once—while a rhythm section churned out propulsive but easy-to-dance-to back-beats—it towered over the ragtime-tinged tunes that had danced across the keyboards in Harlem, where he had dazzled youngsters James P. Johnson and Fats Waller as early as 1911, seemingly ages ago.

Now, in 1925, Morton had placed himself at the vortex of a new music that New Orleans musicians were re-creating and redefining on Chicago's South Side, though often at a brisker tempo and with a raunchier fervor reflecting the noisy big-city setting. The southern blacks who had come up north and were herded into this slum—with its decaying buildings and clattering "el" trains rattling by every hour of the day and night—needed this music and the exultation it inspired. Working twelve-hour shifts butchering cattle at the Union Stockyards or sweating on assembly lines in a thousand grimy factories, they had earned their moments of release, and then some.

Not surprisingly, they had little use for Chicago's homegrown musicians, who still clung to their stiff, old-time rhythms and four-square dance tunes, clueless on how to get an audience to bump and grind. The Crescent City players, on the other hand, practically had written the book of swing, so they monopolized the best club and theater gigs, recording dates, radio broadcasts, and avenues of glory.

"Jelly would not use musicians unless they was born in Louisiana," said New Orleans trombonist Preston Jackson, who had moved to Chicago in 1917, the year they shut down Storyville.

I say Louisiana because there was a lot of musicians that was not born in New Orleans but in the small towns in Louisiana, such as Ory, the Hall Brothers [clarinetists Edmond and Herb], and others. There was strained relations between the Chicago musicians and the Louisiana musicians. If Jelly had any work, he's going to get somebody from New Orleans. So did Joe Oliver and all of them. . . . The New Orleans musicians, they had the stuff. The two drummers Jelly Roll used was Baby Dodds and Andrew Hilaire. He said the Chicago musicians just didn't know how to

ALAMEDA FREE LIBRARY

drum. The drummer, you see, is the heart of the music. That's
what it was, *rhythm*! And the Chicago drummers didn't have
that rhythm.

On this glorious, dangerous, and sometimes bloody corner, where
South Calumet Avenue dead-ended at East Thirty-fifth Street, before
picking up again a few hundred feet to the east, the chief conceptual-
izers of New Orleans jazz were transforming a once casually improvised music into a rigorous art form, though for no other reason than
to make the crowds move, the booze flow, and the money pour in. Yet
by polishing their tunes every night in the saloons around Thirty-fifth
and Calumet, then documenting this music in Chicago's proliferating
recording studios and sending the news across the country on platters
and over the airwaves, the New Orleans jazz men were showing
everyone else how to play. It was as if they were saying that Bach,
Beethoven, and Brahms were fine for the longhairs in Orchestra Hall,
on swanky Michigan Avenue downtown, but this was music for other,
decidedly corporal pleasures.

Before long, as 1925 turned into 1926, this corner would make
history, with cornetist Louis Armstrong and piano virtuoso Earl Hines
teaching violinist Carroll Dickerson's orchestra how to swing at the
Sunset Café, 315 East Thirty-fifth Street. Kitty-corner from the Sunset,
King Oliver—backed by New Orleans pioneers such as clarinetists Albert Nicholas and Barney Bigard—was igniting stomps and blues at
the Plantation Café, 338 East Thirty-fifth Street. Next door, New Orleans clarinetist Jimmy Noone was wailing at the Nest, an upstairs
club on East Thirty-fifth that didn't open its doors until three in the
morning and convulsed well past dawn. And in a dozen joints up and
down the street, hot musicians famous and obscure were either
spreading the gospel of New Orleans jazz or learning it.

"Thirty-fifth and Calumet was jacked up every night, with Louis
and Oliver and Jimmie all playing within a hundred feet of each
other," recalled Eddie Condon, one of the white Chicago teens learning the trade from the black and Creole New Orleans musicians who
invented it. He might also have mentioned Bix Beiderbecke, the jazz

genius from Davenport, Iowa, whose ineffably expressive cornet represented a sublimely muted response to Armstrong's soaring high notes; Sidney Bechet, his arabesques on soprano saxophone as piercingly lyrical as anything coming out of Satchmo's horn; the brothers Johnny and Baby Dodds, the latter playing New Orleans street beats on his drums, the former producing the hottest clarinet lines this side of Jimmy Noone. "Unless it happened in New Orleans," added Condon, "I don't think so much good jazz was ever concentrated in so small an area. Around midnight you could hold an instrument in the middle of the street and the air would play it."

Midnight looked practically like high noon, for "35th and Calumet was lit up like Paris," remembered Earl Hines, who had arrived in town the year before, in 1924, to find out if a Pittsburgh piano player could survive in a town practically repopulated by the best musicians in America, direct from Louisiana. The notorious intersection might just as well have been called the corner of Sunset and Plantation, for these two spectacular rooms were the mob-run engines that kept the street humming. With dozens of chorus girls, screaming house bands, mob-supplied liquor, and even an occasional cameo by Al Capone, whose men provided copious beverage service, the two clubs were temples of hedonism and vice, serving blacks and whites, men and women, adults and kids, rich and poor, sober and drunk.

"The Sunset had the cream of the black-and-tan shows, and there wasn't a big name in colored show business that didn't work for me at one time or another," said its manager, Joe Glaser, who soon took over Armstrong's career until Glaser's death in 1971. "I spent more money on my shows than the Cotton Club. . . . We had a high-class trade—not like some of the other joints—the best people." Roughly six hundred crowded around the Sunset's puny café tables, and they were served drugs, booze, and girls practically out in the open, while Armstrong—whose name Glaser plastered across the facade of the joint—blew his horn.

On the other side of the intersection stood the Plantation, a cabaret that took its name to heart, with fake red fruit made of tissue paper scattered everywhere. "You could just see the vines all over the walls, and the ceiling was decorated with watermelons," recalled Frances Mouton, Morton's half sister, who had seen nothing like it back home in New Orleans. Though King Oliver's band was firing up stomps and blues—his stable of New Orleans all-stars including drummer Paul Barbarin and clarinetists Barney Bigard and Albert Nicholas—it was the look of this room that left Frances Mouton speechless. "I didn't hear the music played by King Oliver and Albert Nicholas for looking up all the time," she said.

Even from the musicians' point of view, the proceedings seemed nearly overwhelming, an orgy of rhythm pulsing within four walls.

"When the people came we'd be playing, and the hat check girl would move in rhythm to pick up your hat," remembered Nicholas.

When you get in, the waiters met you at the tables swinging with their trays and asked, "What are you having?" It was Prohibition time and they didn't sell liquor, only the set up and so on. You came with your own jug. When they put their trays down they're swinging. Everything was in rhythm. Even Sam, the owner, he was a great big guy, weighed over 200 pounds. He was behind the cash register, and when he hit that register—bam—you know it was rhythmic. The shoe shine boy . . . the washroom attendant, who would brush you down . . . when he'd take the whisk broom he'd brush you in rhythm and hit behind your pockets and jingle that change, you know. It was all in rhythm.

Jelly Roll Morton roomed within earshot of the mayhem, at Thirty-fifth and Wabash, a block west of Thirty-fifth and State, the heart of Chicago's black commercial district, its banks and businesses attesting to Bronzeville's inexorably growing economic muscle. From Morton's apartment, where he kept a bed, a baby grand, and a wardrobe that might comfortably outfit three men, he could stroll to Calumet in five minutes, and he came prepared for battle in one of the roughest districts in the city. Armed with a small pearl-handled pistol nosing out of his vest pocket and a sharp tongue ever at the ready, Morton intimidated anyone who might have intended to harm him. He subscribed to the

philosophy that pianist Hines put into words in describing this place
and time: "You had to act bad whether you were bad or not." If anyone
tried to get the better of Morton, he was ready with a line: "I've got
more suits than you've got handkerchiefs," or "I've been further
around the world than you've been around a teacup."

Morton, whom Hines considered the "most popular underworld pianist around," made the corner of Thirty-fifth and Calumet
his place of business, talking with the boys from New Orleans when
he wasn't playing a date in town or taking a pickup band out on the
road. To amuse himself during the day, Morton bet on the White
Sox games that were played a few blocks away, at Comiskey Park,
boasted about his latest achievements at the keyboard, and, in so
doing, let everyone know he was around, taking bets and engagements. Because he was pulling in an average of fifteen hundred dollars a night on the road, Morton deduced that he was on his way toward millionaire status and wanted everyone to know it. As he
walked down the street, he conspicuously stopped to chat with
friends or acquaintances, gave a sigh, and said, "I'm tired, and I
want to sit down, man." Then, as he prepared to sit, he pulled up
his pants leg a bit, so that everyone could see the diamond glistening
from his leg garter. A beat or two later, he smiled wide, with
supreme self-satisfaction, revealing the half-carat rock that shone
from his mouth. Once Morton started talking, an audience inevitably swelled around him, and he held forth on the meaning and
origins of jazz, delivering curbside discourses beyond the ken of
conservatories and universities. In Morton, the new music had not
only a distinctive pianist and innovative composer but a man who
kept practically the entire history and prehistory of jazz in his head
and shared it with anyone who wanted to listen. If Morton had been
present at the creation, he reasoned, why shouldn't he be the one to
lay down the gospel?

"Why, that man, you could talk to him for hours," said Arm-
strong, who had traveled from his hometown, New Orleans, to
Chicago in 1922, a year before Morton returned to the city from the
West Coast.

He'd always have a crowd around him. And some cat that was standing there says, after Jelly run his mouth so long, he says, "Well, Jelly, you must be the best piano player in town."

He says, "In town? In the world."

You know, he'd always give you a big laugh like that.

Most days, Morton dropped in on the music store of Clarence Williams, an acquaintance from New Orleans days who had moved to Chicago, like everyone else, and opened a music shop on the east side of State Street, near Thirty-first, across from the Grand Theatre. (Like Morton, Williams was perpetually on the move, playing recording dates in New York with his Blue Five band when he wasn't minding the store back home in Chicago.) Or Morton sauntered into Ed Victor's Barber Shop, on the east side of State Street, between Thirty-fourth and Thirty-fifth, where the New Orleans pimps and gamblers congregated, just as they had when Victor's Shop still was back in New Orleans on Toledano Street. Between the New Orleans gamblers and the Chicago workingmen who walked in from the Mecca Flats—a sprawling apartment complex occupying a city block across the street—Victor's Barber Shop offered a smooth-talker a soapbox, a crowd, and a plethora of financial opportunities.

Or Morton strolled over to the black musicians' union, a few blocks south at 3934 South State Street, and soliloquized, while the boys from New Orleans played cards, guzzled booze, and swapped stories. When Morton saw a gang of musicians standing out front, he launched into his patter, just to see if anyone would dare to take him on. "You fellows just can't play anything," he said, then tried to teach them a few things. If the audience was too small, he told the secretary to ring up all the piano players in town: "I want to give them all a lesson."

Occasionally, one of the men—irritated by Morton's verbal riffs—foolishly tried to shoot down Morton's big talk, presuming that anyone who humiliated the great Jelly Roll would inherit his stature and prominence. But this was not easily done, as pianist Dave Peyton discovered the night he dared to say—in front of everyone—that Morton couldn't read music. Morton smiled at that one, then asked Peyton if he had the nerve to take him on at the piano, with all the musicians invited to watch. Peyton couldn't back down now, so Morton announced that the showdown would be held the next morning at the Grand Theatre, the very place where Peyton led the house band. With these words, Morton had upped the stakes considerably, for Peyton now ran the risk of being humbled in his own house, with the men in his band all watching.

The next morning, Peyton and Morton showed up at the Grand a couple of hours before it opened to the public, and a small crowd of musicians gathered around to place bets and watch the battle. Without saying a word, Morton "sat down at the piano and played one of his own compositions, 'The Pearls,'" remembered trombonist Preston Jackson, who witnessed the confrontation. "Dave listened, and when Jelly finished put the piano part to 'Poet and Peasant' in front of him and said, 'Jelly, you so good, play that!'"

Morton didn't make a sound, though on the inside he was chortling, for he had been hustling musicians with precisely this piece of music practically from childhood and could have played "Poet and Peasant" in his sleep. Nevertheless, he squinted at the score, as if it were more difficult than he had anticipated, placed his fingers on the keys, and started making music, with every chord, every melody, every bass note played exactly as written, not a phrase or trill out of place. "Jelly played it right through," recalled Jackson. "Then Jelly removed the sheet music and said, 'Now I'm going to show you how well I memorized 'Poet and Peasant.' Then he proceeded to play the piece again," but this time, without the music. Peyton recoiled, aghast at how wrong he had been, awestruck by Morton's prowess at the keyboard. He had been had.

For a kid who had been kicked out of his family's house, Morton had reached a zenith in his life and his art. He crushed anyone who doubted his preeminence; he carried a roll of two thousand dollars or more in his pocket; and, most important, his tunes—the work of years plying the brothels of New Orleans and hoboeing about the Gulf Coast—helped form the sonic backdrop for life in big-city U.S.A. "King Porter Stomp," a number he had labored over from 1902 to

1905, now was being recorded from coast to coast. Fletcher Hender-
son and his orchestra cut a version for Vocalion in New York, as did
Johnny Sylvester and his orchestra for Pathe Actuelle, Lanin's Red
Heads for Columbia, and the Tennessee Tooters for Vocalion. Out in
St. Louis, trumpeter Charlie Creath's Jazz-O-Maniacs put out a "King
Porter Stomp" for Okeh.

Meanwhile, Morton's "Milenberg Joys" was generating almost as
much heat, with New York relishing newly minted versions by Ted
Lewis and his band on Columbia, the Tennessee Tooters on Vocalion,
the Seven Missing Links on Pathe Actuelle/Banner, the Cotton Pickers
on Brunswick, Bob Fuller on Banner, Busse's Buzzards on Victor, the
Varsity Eight on Cameo, and so on. In Chicago, Boyd Senter waxed
"Milenberg Joys" for Pathe Actuelle, Joseph Gish and his orchestra
for New Flexo, and Jimmy O'Bryant's Famous Original Washboard
Band for Paramount. As far away as Los Angeles, Carlyle Stevenson's
El Patio Orchestra recorded "Milenberg Joys" for Sunset. On the
other side of the Atlantic, in Middlesex, England, Jack Hylton's Kit-
Cat Band immortalized the piece for His Master's Voice.

With his health restored, Morton was ready to send Frances back
home to New Orleans. On her last day in town, he drove to the house
where she was staying, stepped inside, and waited for her at the spinet
piano in the living room. As Frances walked down the stairs, she
heard Morton serenading her with an Irving Berlin hit, "Always."
"I'll be loving you, always," he sang, as Frances's eyes became moist.
"Not for just a year, but always."

Morton drove Frances to the train station and bid her farewell,
not imagining that they never would see each other again. He simply
resumed his touring life with vigor, fanning out across the Midwest
and into the South, leading a variety of bands, rarely alighting in one
place for very long. But one stop—Spring Valley, Illinois—stood out
from the blur of the rest, thanks to a piece of information that happened to come Morton's way. Playing a couple hundred miles outside
Chicago, Morton heard for the first time about ASCAP—the American Society of Composers, Authors and Publishers—a New
York–based organization that collected broadcast and performance

royalties from radio stations and theaters and distributed the proceeds among its members. Formed in 1909, the organization was becoming increasingly important to composers, who had previously
had no way to benefit financially from the broadcast of their music
over the airwaves and the performance of their tunes in auditoriums
and saloons across the country. ASCAP changed that, negotiating
with broadcasters, theater owners, and the like for a percentage of
their gross profits, then divvying up the money among the ASCAP
members.

There was just one catch—you had to be an ASCAP member to
get your cut.

"My first knowledge of ASCAP was in the year of 1925, whilst
playing a date at Spring Valley, Ill.," Morton recalled. "A man walked
up to me & ask me to join ASCAP. I agreed that I would but would
speak to my publisher on it, Walter Melrose, which I did. He enticed
me not to bother with it, & spoke ill of ASCAP. I knew Melrose was
my publisher and did not want to offend him, so I passed it by."

Morton did not know, however, that Melrose himself was preparing to join ASCAP and soon would start collecting royalties from the
organization. Nor did Morton foresee at this early date that radio
would pervade America, providing music for free to the public and
handing over millions in advertising revenue to ASCAP, which in turn
distributed the largesse among its members.

For the moment, Morton was in the money and didn't want to offend his publisher, partner, and friend, Walter Melrose, so the composer took what he believed was the tactful course and made no application to ASCAP. Even if he had, he quite likely would not have
been admitted, for jazz and blues men as yet had no place in ASCAP.
Morton quickly put the ASCAP matter out of his mind, savoring instead the cash already rolling in from a relentless schedule of performances in Chicago and on the road. With Melrose eagerly hawking
Morton's newest tunes, venues across the Midwest looking to book
him, and musicians black, white, and Creole standing in awe of his pianism and his hit-making prowess, Morton had ascended to the pinnacle of the music business.

Not that he had Chicago entirely sewn up, for no single artist really dominated in a city as vast, populous, and hot as Chicago was becoming. In fact, by 1926, a younger man from New Orleans was coming up from behind, threatening to take a measure of the spotlight from the eminence grise of hot piano. Most everyone called the twenty-five-year-old cornetist Satchmo—a shortened version of his New Orleans nickname, "Satchelmouth," for the huge expanse of his smile. He had begun playing and recording as a Chicago sideman in King Oliver's Creole Jazz Band in March 1923, even then announcing himself as an original in American music. The rounded, golden tone that young Louis Armstrong produced on "Chimes Blues," his first recorded solo, the talking-horns duets he played with Oliver on "Snake Rag," and the phenomenal technique he showed on "Tears" in 1923 heralded the arrival of the first great improvising soloist in jazz, as he soon would be known. Here was a New Orleans cornetist whose sound, style, phrasing, and stratospheric high notes were so indelibly fresh as to redirect a still fledgling art form, jazz, into a music for and about the soloist—or at least to begin that process.

The sheer size of Armstrong's sound and the combustibility of his attacks practically blew out the microphones at the same Gennett studios where Morton had been recording. "When they recorded Louis," remembered pianist Hodes, one of the young white Chicagoans who studied at the feet of the black and Creole masters, "they had to put the mike five feet away from him so he wouldn't blow it out of business."

Though Armstrong had married the college-educated Chicago pianist Lil Hardin in 1924 and then—on her advice—had moved to Manhattan in the fall to join Fletcher Henderson and his orchestra, the New Yorkers proved too rigid in rhythm and sloppy in delivery to hold the interest of the ascending Satchmo. Worse, Henderson berated Armstrong, telling him, "You'd be very good if you'd go take some lessons." So Armstrong left New York after fourteen months that yielded at least a few important recordings (collaborating with piano player Clarence Williams's Blue Five) and arrived in Chicago as the star he was born to be. Outside the Dreamland Café, at Thirty-fifth and State, Armstrong's wife had placed an enormous sign announcing the Second Coming of "The World's Greatest Trumpet Player," a reference not to the once unrivaled Oliver but now to his unstoppable protégé, Armstrong.

"I first heard Louis just when he came back to Chicago from New York, and I swear I hadn't heard anything like that music," recalled trumpeter Doc Cheatham, newly arrived in the city from Tennessee. "Actually, it was his wife, Lillian, who had advised him to come back to Chicago. And when he came back, I never have seen so much publicity in all my life. Trucks and loudspeakers announcing 'Armstrong this' and 'Armstrong that.' When he went to play at the Vendome Theater," the vaudeville palace at Thirty-second and State, where Erskine Tate's Vendome Theater Symphony Orchestra had been ensconced since 1919, "you couldn't even get standing room in the place when Armstrong was there."

Armstrong went into the studio in Chicago for Okeh to record the first of his Hot Five sessions in 1925, not considering himself the leader of the band or presuming that he was redefining the sound of American music. But when the first of the recordings reached the streets, early in 1926, Chicago devoured them, never having heard such soloistic brilliance captured on record. The extraordinary ripeness of Armstrong's tone in "Gut Bucket Blues," the haunting, minor-key solo flights in "King of the Zulus," and the exuberant singing on "Heebie Jeebies"—the first record to document the nonsensical syllables and made-up words that eventually were termed "scat"—inexorably changed the course of jazz. It was as if some unprecedented force had been unleashed through the man's horn, through his instantly identifiable, gravelly voice, and through his ability to shape solos that sounded at once spontaneous and inevitable.

Not surprisingly, Armstrong's sidemen—New Orleans pros such as trombonist Kid Ory, clarinetist Johnny Dodds, and banjo player Johnny St. Cyr—were overshadowed by Satchmo in the Hot Five sessions. With these recordings, the fundamental assumptions of the still emerging art of jazz already were beginning to shift. For if the music in its New Orleans beginnings had been built on the premise of several instrumentalists playing at once, a noisy democracy in which everyone had his say, Armstrong radically altered the equation, putting his brilliant horn forever out front. With these recordings, jazz started to become an arena for incendiary solo improvisation, all of it to some degree or another owing to Armstrong's model. The piercing sound of Armstrong's horn—bold, brilliant, and spilling over with the spirit of the blues—cried out above the din of music and life on the South Side of Chicago.

Not even the formidable Jelly Roll Morton, who had left New Orleans while Armstrong still was in knickers, could compete with this. Nor did he try. For all Morton's eminence as a pianist, his bouncing left hand the marvel of piano players across the South Side, no one sitting at a keyboard could make a noise half as thrilling as Armstrong could simply by putting a brass mouthpiece to his lips.

Morton recognized Armstrong's genius and embraced it. The two men—each in his own way forging the basic musical grammar by which jazz musicians communicated forevermore—immediately hit it off, shooting the breeze at the Melrose music store and encountering one another all along Thirty-fifth Street. Morton, for his part, regularly stopped by the apartment where Satchmo lived with his bride, at 421 East Forty-fourth Street, but Morton wasn't lured there by the Armstrongs' hospitality alone. He also admired the smart new baby grand the trumpeter had bought his new wife, Lil Hardin, the same woman whom Morton had dazzled two years earlier, in 1924, when he had walked into the Jones Music Store and showed her what hot piano playing was all about. Now, with Hardin and Armstrong married, Morton still had a few more lessons to impart.

"We all went to Louis' place and Jelly sat down at that piano and really gave us a serenade," remembered drummer Zutty Singleton of a gathering in the Armstrong apartment.

But Morton did not merely play the piano—he traced the birth and evolution of jazz, as he had witnessed it, reminding Singleton and Armstrong of age-old tunes and obscure players and salty lyrics that they thought they had long forgotten. Taking nary a breath, Morton rhapsodized on the groundbreaking players, describing in detail the sound and style of Creole greats such as clarinetists Alphonse Picou and "Big Eye" Nelson and trumpeters Freddie Keppard and Manuel Perez, as well as black innovators such as trumpeters Buddy Bolden and Joe Oliver, trombonist Jim Robinson, and guitarist Bud Scott. Blessed with an uncanny memory for musical detail, Morton mimicked the keyboard style of all the self-taught, rough-hewn New Orleans virtuosos he had heard in the District, somehow bringing back to life the high-speed precision of Sammy Davis, the novelty piano of Albert Carroll, and the florid virtuosity of Tony Jackson.

And, of course, Morton talked about his own innovations, the facets of primordial jazz that he felt he had authored first.

"He played and played," recalled Singleton, "and after each number he'd turn around on that stool and tell us how he wrote each number and where it came from. It was a real lecture, just for the benefit of me and Lil and Louis."

In this impromptu session, and in countless others, the two most formidable forces in jazz—one a galvanic trumpeter and inspired improviser, the other a virtuoso pianist and innovative composer—met, like two wings of an art form that could not fully take flight without both. Each pointed the way for generations of musicians still unborn, but each was heading toward a very different fate.

If Armstrong was the latest sensation in jazz, in effect the public face of a still youthful art form, Morton was its master planner, the man who put to paper the complex arrangements that made urban America dance. The virtuosity that Armstrong poured through his horn Morton drew from his pen, each musician codifying an art form through distinct means but with more long-lasting effects than either may have imagined.

Unable to match Armstrong's draw in Chicago—to say nothing of the sheer decibel power of his trumpet—Morton could not claim the celebrity of Satchmo, who was emerging as a coast-to-coast icon unprecedented in American music. But Morton, in turn, was spared the popular and commercial strictures that Armstrong's success was starting to place upon him. Unencumbered by fans yearning to be thrilled by the popular tunes of the day or by the heaven-bound high notes that were making Armstrong America's first pop star, Morton could go about composing, orchestrating, and recording an ensemble music more intricate, subtle, and sophisticated than mass tastes might have dictated. It was a sound predicated not on the unrivaled prowess and virtuosity of a single spectacular soloist but on the complex interaction of several members of a jazz band, each dispensing a music more composed than improvised, more strictly controlled by its leader and conceptualizer, Jelly Roll Morton, than anything bandleaders such as the youthful Duke Ellington or the master Sidney Bechet were yet producing.

Now, as the summer of 1926 was coming to a close, Morton finally was about to have his chance to record the intertwining instrumental riffs and meticulously developed horn themes that had been resonating within him for more than two decades. His piano playing, after all, was a kind of distillation of the ensemble music he had heard in New Orleans, though updated with new harmonies and innovative contrapuntal voicings. Now he was preparing to record this music as he had written it for ensemble. For, to Morton, New Orleans music wasn't about one horn but about many, each entering and exiting the musical texture at his command, forming passing chords of his own making and blue-note dissonances richer than any soloist—even one as protean as Armstrong—could achieve alone. Morton's concept was not better than Armstrong's but different, more evocative of Morton's musical autobiography and of the way jazz had emerged in the city of his birth, New Orleans.

Finally given the chance to hire the best New Orleans musicians in Chicago, to gather them in the recording studio, and to pay them to render the notes precisely as written, Morton prepared to show the world an expansive vision of jazz. It was a music as fresh as the latest hit tunes but still rooted in the sounds of the social rituals—the funerals and parades—of his New Orleans childhood.

Morton had been developing this concept for years, testing it with ten fingers on a piano but longing to hear it played by cornets and reeds and drums and piano and bass. This would be New Orleans music in all its polyphonic glory, and if he could pull it off—if he could get the famously headstrong New Orleans musicians all pulling in the same direction at once, a big "if," to be sure—the world would hear modern jazz as Morton alone understood it.

This was to be an enormous undertaking, and not just artistically. A lone wolf if ever there were one, Morton until this point in life had put his faith almost entirely in himself, relying on his writing, his pianism, and his wits—as well as his occasional forays into card sharking, pool hustling, and pimping—to stay solvent. But to record the music as he conceived it, he needed to convene the greatest New Orleans men working in Chicago and persuade them to pursue a single vision—his. They had to understand and articulate his tremendously detailed music yet dispatch it as fluidly as if freely improvised.

Morton never had attempted anything so far-reaching, nor had anyone else. But Morton was about to take his shot.

The events of September 15, 1926, neatly summed up the nature of black life in Chicago and across America. On that day, the National Association of Colored Waiters and Cooks held its first convention, on the South Side of Chicago, proclaiming that "the day of the white waiter is passing." On that day, WGN Radio in Chicago joined in a nationwide forty-six-station hookup designed to prove that the medium had arrived as a national phenomenon, with Sam 'n' Henry—the precursors of Amos 'n' Andy—mugging buffoonishly in the WGN studios.

And on that day, at 9 A.M., Jelly Roll Morton walked into the Webster Hotel, a fifteen-story brick edifice facing Lake Michigan on the Near North Side of Chicago, carrying a bundle of music under his arm. He was going to oversee the greatest jazz ensemble recordings yet created, as sure an expression of the vitality and intellectual achievement of black culture as any yet documented. Morton had been rehearsing the New Orleans boys intensely in his South Side apartment and at the musicians' union nearby. Realizing how much was at stake, he did not go easy on his men. He was "exact with us," said New Orleans musician Omer Simeon, whose expansive tone and tightly expressive vibrato made him one of Morton's favorite clarinetists. "Very jolly, very full of life all the time but serious. We used to spend maybe three hours rehearsing four sides, and in that time he'd give us the effects he wanted, like the background behind a solo. He would run that over on the piano with one finger, and the guys would get together and harmonize it . . . the solos—they were ad lib."

Apart from the improvised solos, however, the musicians played scores painstakingly written and edited by Morton, who noted key signatures, time signatures, phrasings, and expression marks with care and precision. Only the most versatile instrumentalists could have held down a chair at these sessions, for each had to be able to read a Morton score at sight, improvise brief solos based on the themes of the composition at hand, and capture the blues-tinged flavor of New Orleans music as Morton perceived it. Even musicians with national repute had to prove their worth. Simeon, for instance, already was a noted New Orleans clarinetist who had come to Chicago in 1923 and was working in Charlie Elgar's Creole Orchestra in Milwaukee at the time. So he was surprised when he got the call to visit Morton in Chicago—for an audition. "We used to go to his home for rehearsals, and the first time I was there he handed me a piece called 'Mamanita,' which had a pretty hard clarinet part," recalled Simeon. "I guess he was testing me out, and I knew he was pleased when I read it off at first sight."

Simeon got the job, though he had no idea that the Morton sessions eventually would rank among the most revered dates in the history of recorded jazz. Even so, it was clear to him that something extraordinary was happening on that pivotal morning of September 15.

"Melrose spared no expense for a record date—anything Jelly Roll wanted he got," observed Simeon, who never had seen a white businessman rush around like this at the behest of a musician of color. "Melrose worshipped him like a king." Or at least he appeared to, hastening to obtain any novelty instrument or unusual sound effect that Morton requested. To Melrose, these sessions were crucial, too, for if New York–based Victor succeeded with these disks—all using

Melrose publications—the Chicago publisher would enjoy the kind of national exposure that small-time labels such as Autograph and Paramount and Gennett could not match. It was Melrose who had persuaded Victor to make these recordings, and he was going to do everything within his power to ensure that they succeeded.

This was the biggest opportunity to come Melrose's way since Morton had first appeared in his store more than three years earlier, for Victor stood at the forefront of the recording industry in America. Through costly research, the firm had upgraded the electrical recording process dramatically from the days when Morton and Oliver—two years earlier—had cut their first electrical disks, duetting on "King Porter" and "Tom Cat" in December 1924. The Victor engineers, whose paperwork listed the day's artists as "Jelly-Roll. Mortons Red Hot Peppers. (Colored)," brought state-of-the-art technology to the date, and Morton was ready to take full sonic advantage of it.

For starters, Morton had hired the top New Orleans musicians within a hundred miles for these sessions, including trombonist Kid Ory and banjoist/guitarist St. Cyr—both veterans of Armstrong's Hot Five recordings. They were joined by clarinetist Simeon, bassist John Lindsey, and drummer Andrew Hilaire. Only cornetist George Mitchell was not from Louisiana, but his roots in Louisville, Kentucky, evidently were close enough. With so many New Orleans originals at his command, Morton baptized this band his Red Hot Peppers, an apt choice judging by the emotional temperature of the music they produced. The records they made on this day rendered most other jazz disks outdated. Even Armstrong's Hot Five recordings, which had set a new standard for solo virtuosity in jazz, did not approach the complex compositional structure, the thick layering of themes, and the vivid orchestral colorations that defined every Morton tune that the bandleader and his Red Hot Peppers played. Moreover, the first three pieces Morton chose to record practically summed up the fundamental ingredients of New Orleans jazz, as he viewed it.

One scarcely can imagine how listeners in 1926 reacted to "Black Bottom Stomp," a glorious merger of robust New Orleans ensemble jazz, lively Chicago-style tempo, and two-beats-to-the-bar stomp rhythm. Named for a bawdy dance that was heating up the city's South Side clubs, Morton's "Black Bottom Stomp" captured the rowdy spirit of Roaring Twenties Chicago so concisely it could have served as an anthem for the period.

From its first notes, the piece bristled with crisp dialogues among the instruments, Simeon's clarinet riffing against Mitchell's cornet, while Morton and the rhythm section churned out fiercely syncopated backbeats. Between refrains, each of the players took a brief, improvised solo, Ory's whinnying trombone riffs, Mitchell's searing cornet lines, and Simeon's elaborate clarinet phrases dispatched at a breakneck clip. St. Cyr, meanwhile, played comparably aggressive solos on banjo, his hand strumming faster than the eye could see. Morton, for his part, turned in a leonine solo, his buoyant left hand and fast-flying right producing a nearly orchestral burst of sound. And toward the end of the piece, when the ensemble texture thickened and the bass drum started pounding on the offbeat, the tension became practically unbearable, sending the tune headlong to its climax.

In this remarkable miniature, lasting all of three minutes and eight seconds, the Red Hot Peppers set off a revolution, proving on record—for the first time—that a formally conceived piece of music could embrace several improvised solos yet retain the cohesiveness of an artfully composed piece of music. It was as if the energy and drive of big-city jazz, with its relentless rhythmic pulse and impossible-to-notate solos, finally had been harnessed, or at least captured on disk for the world outside Chicago to hear.

Morton could not have done this alone. He needed the New Orleans players, who knew how to drop in a two- or four-bar break with split-second precision, somehow merging their own musical vocabularies with the letter and the spirit of Morton's tunes.

"Jelly marked out the parts we liked, and he always had his manuscripts there and his pencils and he was always writing and changing little parts," recalled Simeon. "Jelly left the solos up to us, but the backgrounds, harmony and licks were all in his arrangements. He was easy to work for, and he always explained everything he wanted.

. . . He'd tell us where he wanted the solo or break, but the rest was up to us."

By allowing his players to create their own music within the context of his, Morton was establishing a new standard and method for recording ensemble jazz, in effect codifying the principles by which this music would be conceived for decades to come. Ultimately, he was establishing that a remarkably detailed music, complete with improvised passages, could work perfectly—so long as the piece was carefully composed and the players steeped in the traditions and performance practices of New Orleans music.

If Morton's "Black Bottom Stomp" addressed the rambunctious side of New Orleans–Chicago jazz, Charles Luke's "Smoke House Blues" (published earlier as "Creole Blues") spoke to the slow and smoldering southern blues that Morton had heard in New Orleans since the turn of the new century. Though the tune was Luke's, the treatment was indelibly Morton's, with its constantly changing combinations of instruments, its wide-open spaces for Ory's trombone laments and Simeon's clarinet arabesques, and its flirtations with poignant minor-key chords. The tour de force, though, came in Morton's solo, his right hand spinning a silken melody embellished with grace notes and turns, ravishing not only in the cushioned quality of his tone but in its unexpected pauses and silences, its unpredictable rhythms, and its arialike delivery. At the conclusion of this haunting piano soliloquy, a spoken voice on the recording proclaimed, "Ahhhhh, Mister Jelly!"—the voice belonging, of course, to Morton himself. Finally, his Red Hot Peppers let rip with "The Chant," by Melrose arranger Mel Stitzel, the aggressiveness of the tempo, relentlessness of the syncopations, crispness of the ensemble attacks, and red-hot quality of the cornet solos all affirming that Morton had created a virtuosic band capable of tossing off the most demanding jazz band scores yet written.

When these musicians played their last notes of the session, at 1:10 P.M., Morton went home knowing he had come closer than ever to making permanent the sounds that until this day had resided entirely in his inner ear.

Yet he had just started his work. Nearly a week later, on September 21, Morton and his Red Hot Peppers were back at the Webster Hotel, this time adding clarinetists Darnell Howard and Barney Bigard to the mix, as well as an unidentified cornetist and a sound effects man, whom Morton had engaged to expand, deepen, and vary the ensemble sound. Morton opened "Sidewalk Blues" with a whistle and car horns, a bit of novelty to catch the listener's attention, then followed it with some satirical dialogue, inspired by his days as a vaudevillian. "You're so dumb, you should be the president of the deaf and dumb society," said Morton, while the machines were recording. "I'm sorry, boss, but I've got the 'Sidewalk Blues,'" responded St. Cyr, and with this comic intro, the music making commenced. "Jelly was great for effects, as on 'Sidewalk Blues' and 'Steamboat Stomp' and later on like the opening on 'Kansas City Stomp,'" recalled Simeon of this session. "I had never heard anything played like that before. Jelly thought it up, and anything he needed for his effects, Melrose would go out and get it."

On the second date, Morton used reedists Howard and Bigard for certain trio passages and asked Melrose partner Marty Bloom to handle sound effects, such as the Claxton car horn that honked rudely on "Sidewalk Blues." The church bells that pealed on "Dead Man Blues" and the foghorn whistle that opened "Steamboat Stomp" gave a dramatic context to these recordings, as if each cut were as much a story as a piece of music. Indeed, after the tolling church bells that opened "Dead Man Blues," the musicians played a brief musical quotation from the famous New Orleans funeral march "Flee as a Bird to the Mountain," then proceeded with up-tempo themes. In so doing, Morton effectively captured on record a musical portrait of a classic Crescent City funeral, with a slow dirge leading to the graveyard and exuberant music for marching back to town.

Roughly the same cinematic principal applied in "Steamboat Stomp," its opening foghorn and background chatter followed by a banjo solo, as if the banjoist were sitting alongside the shore, playing jubilantly as the passengers boarded the boat. Some of the most amusing scenes, however, played out when the microphones were off.

"I remember on the second date, Melrose walked in with a bottle of scotch," noted Simeon. "We usually had a bottle around as the dates would be early in the morning, and we had to get our spirits up. Anyway, Jelly had two drinks, and we had to stop the session for awhile and open all the windows so he could get some air. He wasn't much of a drinking man. Melrose sure got a big kick out of that."

Finally, for the last session of the year, on December 16, Morton stretched out again, adding two violinists and a bass clarinet for "Someday, Sweetheart." And though the fiddles and bass clarinet robbed the music of some of its authentic New Orleans jazz flavor, they also showed Morton reaching for new colors, tones, and textures, essentially merging the spirit of a New Orleans jazz band with elements of classical orchestral music.

Practically everything Morton did in this session, in fact, smacked of innovation. On his "Grandpa's Spells," the bass riffs that John Lindsey played in dialogue with the band foreshadowed the bass-and-band dialogue that the great bassist Jimmy Blanton made famous fifteen years later with the Duke Ellington Orchestra in "Ko Ko." On "Doctor Jazz," Morton made his recorded debut as singer, his lazy phrasing and bluesy style saying a great deal about how jazz was sung in old New Orleans. And on "Cannon Ball Blues," he played a piano solo backed by the entire band (including a bowed bass), a detail of orchestration to be imitated by others for generations to come. The man could hardly cut a track without introducing a new idea to recorded jazz. On "Someday, Sweetheart," for instance, Morton wrote a part for Simeon to play on bass clarinet, an unusual choice for jazz bands of the day. "Jelly wanted it, and Melrose rented one somewhere," recalled Simeon.

Took a little time to get familiar with it, and I didn't like it too much. Jelly was always fond of effects and wanted to be different. He was always trying to find something different, and whatever he wanted, we would have to do. He was fussy on introductions and endings, and he always wanted the ensemble his way. . . . Some more of Jelly's effects cropped up on the third date. He had two violins on 'Someday Sweetheart.' . . . On 'Original Jelly Roll Blues,' Johnny St. Cyr played a guitar, and the drummer used castanets to give a Spanish style effect. Jelly was sure full of ideas, and he used them.

Within months, the *Chicago Defender* chronicled the impact Morton's recordings were making on the city. "Sidewalk Blues," the paper noted in 1927, was the "current sensation" in Chicago, while the innovative "Grandpa's Spells" was "played in a manner which would indicate that grandpa was a gay old bird with a foot as active as that of a twenty-year-old high stepper."

But the extraordinary confluence of Louisiana musicians who had made these recordings possible and had turned Thirty-fifth and Calumet into a crossroads of black culture and innovative jazz was starting to come undone. Black ministers decried the increasing noise and licentiousness of the neighborhood, and with a mayoral election looming, Big Bill Thompson—possibly the most corrupt Chicago mayor in a long line of them—decided that he had to appear to be taking action. On Christmas Day, 1926, Chief of Detectives William Schoemaker and Captain John Stege launched raids on both the Sunset and the Plantation, arresting nineteen customers for violating Prohibition laws. But just so the mobsters and bootleggers didn't think that Thompson was serious about shutting down Thirty-fifth and Calumet, Chief of Police Collins "denied the raids on two 'black and tan' cafes early yesterday morning were forerunners to a general cleanup," reported the *Chicago Tribune*. And even though "young boys and girls are frequent visitors at the two places, and the conduct of dancers and patrons is shameful," Collins continued, the police "will not interfere unless violations are openly made."

Party on, the Thompson administration was saying, drink your liquor and snort your dope and satisfy your lust, just don't be flagrant about it. The approach worked like a charm, with black ministers dutifully pledging their support to Thompson in the pages of the *Chicago Defender*, backing him for both the February primary and the March general election just around the corner in 1927. Meanwhile, the police kept going through the motions of picking up revelers nightly, packing them into paddy wagons, and hauling them off to the district station just long enough to catch their breath before returning to the party still fully under way.

Amid this bedlam, Morton noticed a petite singer-dancer wearing next to nothing every night of the week at the Plantation, her smile at least as bright as his, thanks to three diamonds that flashed in her teeth. Morton picked her out from more than a dozen pairs of legs, motioned her over to his table, and discovered something more than just a Creole beauty. As the two conversed, Morton learned that Mabel Bertrand had been born in New Orleans—in the French section, on Rampart Street—the daughter of a Creole physician father and a Shawnee Indian mother, her looks as exotic as any Morton had seen. By enchanting coincidence, she came from the same New Orleans Catholic parish as he and had been raised with the same liturgy. Better yet, Mabel Bertrand—like Morton—had learned to fend for herself from childhood, her father and mother having died when she was young. But because she had enough pluck for a woman twice her ninety pounds, Mabel at fifteen had fled the Catholic boarding school in which she had been placed and headed to Manhattan, where she had learned to sing and dance from a veteran trouper named Billy Arnat. He had taken her on the road to London, Paris, Hong Kong, and beyond. But Arnat had become too possessive, insisting that Mabel marry him, so she had bolted while they were in Oklahoma City, where she had found refuge with the local Shawnee chief. She had eventually made her way north to "a job in the best club in Chicago," she said, the Plantation.

Morton heard practically his own story in Mabel's, while Mabel was astonished that someone of Morton's wealth and stature would have any interest in actually talking to her. Most of the men who called her over had something else in mind. When it came time to order drinks, Morton pulled back his jacket to reveal his infamous pearl-handled revolver, then got out his roll of cash—three thousand to four thousand dollars, Mabel estimated. She was impressed, though she resisted Morton's proposals for an evening of companionship, or said she did. When Morton said he was leaving but would come back for her, she scoffed. "A man making fifteen or sixteen hundred dollars a day? That's out of the question for you to be interested in a little nightclub entertainer like myself."

Neither Morton nor Mabel realized that the scene of their flirtation—the music and laughter that swirled around them at the Plantation—was about to disappear. As the 1927 mayoral election neared, Big Bill Thompson, on February 1, ordered his cops to shut down the Plantation for good, citing liquor violations. The move immediately took some of the steam out of Thirty-fifth and Calumet and signaled the end—at least for a year or two—of high times in Bronzeville.

At first, Morton was unfazed, enjoying the commercial and critical success of his Victor sessions. These triumphs bolstered him, and on June 4, 1927, the composer headed back into the recording studio, but this time at a new location (the Victor suite on Oak Street, downtown) and with a largely new cast of his Red Hot Peppers, most notably clarinetist Johnny Dodds and drummer Warren "Baby" Dodds. Like Morton, the Dodds brothers ranked as early-generation jazz royalty, having played on the seminal recordings of King Oliver's Creole Jazz Band, while Johnny Dodds had been integral to Armstrong's Hot Five from the beginning, in 1925. Once again, Morton gathered around him the originators of the new music, the latest Red Hot Peppers lineup including New Orleans guitarist Arthur "Bud" Scott, alto saxophonist Paul Anderson "Stump" Evans (another King Oliver alum), and a return by cornetist Mitchell. For these musicians, recording with Morton and with each other was like attending a New Orleans family reunion, albeit a hardworking one.

Said trombonist Kid Ory, "Morton was a very tough man to work for. He knew what he wanted and would not permit any variation from the arrangements he had written. They were to tough to play—the tempos were difficult—lots of key changes." Morton kept taut control of his sessions, with the score—and his interpretation of it—paramount. Moreover, this new, larger version of his Red Hot Peppers sounded weightier, mightier, and more redolent of the earliest days of New Orleans jazz than the earlier incarnation (particularly with stand-up bass replaced by tuba, the instrument that always played the bass lines in the New Orleans marching bands). When this unit began to swing, as it did ferociously in "Billy Goat Stomp," its rhythmic momentum and drive were more formidable than on the earlier Red Hot Pepper recordings, if only because of the sheer size of the ensemble sound. Add to this the steeped-in-blue quality of Johnny Dodds's clarinet in a cut such as "Wild Man Blues," and the Red Hot Peppers clearly were taking on hues only hinted at during earlier recording dates.

But the most radical recording of this session was of Morton's "Jungle Blues," a piece in which Morton dared to hover on essentially one chord for its duration. This created not only unprecedented dissonance for a jazz recording but virtually dispensed with the very notion of chord progressions, which had been essential to jazz since its dawning at the turn of the century. By obsessing on this single chord, which musicians call the "tonic," Morton in effect was looking back to nineteenth-century blues—which often focused on a single pitch. But Morton was also glancing ahead to the nonchordal innovations of Miles Davis, which musicians termed "modal" jazz. It was decades after Morton's recording of "Jungle Blues" before musicologists understood the radical nature of this recording, which critic Martin Williams, among others, considered the first modal piece of jazz.

Six days later, Morton and the band returned to the Victor studio downtown, the composer unveiling for the first time in jazz the clarinet-piano-drums trio, a brand of chamber jazz that sounded equally convincing in the hard-charging tempo of "Wolverine Blues" and the lazy pace of "Mr. Jelly Lord." The drummer on the session, Baby Dodds, credited Morton with inventing the jazz trio genre, a breakthrough for the art form. Yet there was a slight technical problem in recording the trio, for Morton relentlessly stomped his foot on the ground to keep time. A technician complained that Morton's pounding heel sounded like a couple of bass drums and rigged a mattress about eight inches square to place under Morton's foot. The padding absorbed the thumping sound, and Morton was able to keep time the way the old-time New Orleans players always had.

This was Morton's last Chicago recording date and perhaps the pinnacle of his recording career. Richer, better dressed, and more deeply immersed in writing and recording music than at any other time in his life, Morton did not notice an almost imperceptibly subtle slip in his stature, in his fortunes, and in his relationship with Walter Melrose. On the contrary, Morton believed he had nowhere to go but up, yet the start of the decline had commenced, even if he didn't know it.

In July 1927, with Morton's landmark Victor Records sessions concluded and his fame at a higher pitch than ever, no less than the Music Corporation of America (also known as MCA), one of the top presenters of touring acts in the country, came courting. The firm, which had started out in Chicago and recently had expanded with offices in New York, belatedly realized that a musical revolution was brewing in its own backyard, on the South Side of Chicago, and that a national audience probably would react to the likes of Morton and Oliver and Armstrong as passionately as Chicagoans had.

The chance to be the first black jazz bandleader booked by MCA seemed historically significant to Morton, as it did to the *Chicago Defender*, which noted that Morton and his players represented "the first race organization that [the MCA] concern has on its books." And why shouldn't Morton have been first? He knew full well that his records were making him an international name, with ensembles from the Red Nichols–Miff Mole unit in New York to Gregoir Nakchounian and his Russian North Star Orchestra in Berlin among dozens recording Morton's tunes, rendering them the soundtrack of Jazz Age America.

But the MCA contract, arranged by Bill Stein (who ran the Chicago office, while his brother, Jules, operated out of New York), also represented the first hint that Walter Melrose was getting ready to cut Morton loose. Deciding that he didn't need black artists anymore, Melrose was preparing to switch over to musicians of the white variety, whose music soon became his stock-in-trade. So on a hot summer afternoon in 1927, while MCA's Bill Stein stood outside the Woods Theatre chatting with the song pluggers who worked in the beehive of offices stacked atop this Loop palace, Morton and Melrose manager Marty Bloom walked by.

"Apparently, Morton was becoming a little difficult and demanding with Melrose, and maybe Bloom saw a chance to unload his troubles on someone else," recalled Karl Kramer, a youngster in the MCA office at the time. "So he suggested that we sign up Jelly as an MCA band."

Neither Melrose nor Bloom let on exactly how Morton was becoming "difficult and demanding," though a couple of sore spots stood out. For starters, there was the payment due Morton for the Victor recording sessions. Though the disks had been immediate commercial hits, Melrose had paid Morton simply a flat fee for the sessions, with no artist royalties. The contract for Morton's great Red Hot Peppers dates, in fact, was between Melrose Brothers Music of Chicago and the Victor Talking Machine Company of New York, and it provided for all money to be paid to Melrose, none to Morton. This was a routine arrangement for black artists, who—unlike their white counterparts—did not make contracts directly with record companies and were not paid by them. It was the white impresarios who cut the deals with the white labels, so that operators like Melrose were in a position to deny black artists their royalties. Melrose relished this opportunity, bragging about it in a letter to RCA. "I am wondering if you would be interested in four sides of jam-up Dixieland," Melrose wrote, years later. "I could deliver these recordings exclusive of studio cost for five cents per, double-faced records free of all publisher and artist royalties. Some years ago I had a similar [arrangement] with your firm on Jelly Roll Morton." Melrose, in other words, set up his record deals to grab all the royalties himself, while the instrumentalists and composer collected none.

But Morton, who could see that his records were selling fast, couldn't understand why he shouldn't get a cut. Nor did he appreciate Melrose adding lyrics to his compositions, thereby making himself partner on Morton's songwriting royalties. Adding to the egregiousness of Melrose's methods, the man's lyrics were worse than amateur, as in the dreadful text he grafted onto Morton's "Sidewalk Blues": "My baby's gone and I got the blues/It sure is awful to be lonesome like me/Worried, weary, up in a tree."

Melrose was neither the first nor the last music publisher to hit on this way of slicing into composer royalties, nor was Morton his only victim. At roughly the same time, in fact, Melrose also added lyrics to music by Earl Hines ("Midnight in New Orleans" and "Lazy Mornin'"), Charlie Davis ("Copenhagen"), the New Orleans Rhythm Kings ("Tin Roof Blues," later reworked as the 1954 Jo Stafford hit "Make Love to Me"), and Louis Armstrong, Benny Goodman, and Frank Trumbauer ("High Society"). But once Morton got wind of Melrose's tactics, he balked. "Walter Melrose never wrote a hit in his life," Morton later wrote. "Melrose is my publisher, he [Melrose] inserted words to some of my hit tunes without my knowledge or permission & is receiving [royalties]."

But Morton was dealing with a man who had become one of the craftiest finaglers in the already corrupt world of music publishing, grabbing rights and royalties from other publishers as adroitly as he did from his songwriters. A year earlier, for instance, on January 12, 1926, the copyright on Scott Joplin's "Maple Leaf Rag" ran out, inspiring Melrose to file his own copyright on the tune before Stark & Sons of St. Louis had gotten around to renewing theirs. Because Stark & Sons, the original publisher of "Maple Leaf Rag," were famously casual about such details, Walter Melrose saw his opportunity and seized the biggest hit they had.

By now, in the summer of 1927, Melrose had so much money coming his way from so many illicit sources that he didn't need Morton anymore. But to the composer, the issue of money was becoming increasingly important, for Morton—like other black jazz musicians of the day—was finding that the Chicago scene was drying up in the wake of the South Side police raids. Even Morton, already the leading jazz composer-arranger of the day, was starting to settle for jobs decidedly less glamorous than when Thirty-fifth and Calumet was at its peak, and the distasteful nature of these gigs turned Morton's normally ebullient mood sour. "The few contacts I had with him . . . bring back to memory the most disobliging person I have ever met," remembered Dr. Edmond Souchon, a guitarist and physician whose high school dance Morton played. "Admittedly, we were adolescent pests, but we were hiring him. And at no time can I ever recall him obliging by playing a request. . . . To our requests, he would scarcely glance over his shoulder—disdainfully and scornfully—and grunt something about 'there are six requests ahead of yours.' We would slink off, while he proceeded to play exactly what pleased him."

But if Souchon had known anything about Morton, he would have realized that although Morton indeed smarted at working a high school dance, there was something more behind his unfriendly demeanor than just an abrupt decline in his fortunes. Equally important, Morton did not take requests. He was now a Victor recording artist, no longer a brothel piano player. The composer might have made ample compromises in life, certainly so far as his Catholic upbringing was concerned, but when he sat at the piano, he called the tunes or didn't play at all. This was not Creole pride but an unspoken philosophy on the nature of his art, and Morton clung to it until his last days, even though he would be desperate for cash.

For now, though, anyone could see that jazz in Bronzeville was slowing down, at least for the moment, with musicians such as Armstrong, Noone, Bechet, Condon, and others flocking to New York, Paris, and beyond. None had better reason than Morton, who was wearied and perplexed by Melrose's tricks. So Morton, always ready to return to the road when prospects were heading south, took MCA's offer for a national tour, setting out for a year and taking with him Mabel Bertrand, the dancer he had spotted at the Plantation Café. She accompanied Morton during a year's worth of one-nighters for MCA, a tour in which Morton occasionally shattered racial barriers that had been generations in the making. Though bookings were plentiful for Morton and the ordinary pickup band MCA misleadingly promoted as his Red Hot Peppers, their date in Herrin, Illinois, stood out. "At first, there was some resentment in that town about engaging a colored band; in fact, there was almost a small riot," noted Kramer. "But after they heard the orchestra the dancers went crazy over the stomp beat, and, as I remember it, the orchestra returned to Herrin several times in the next few months."

Morton still had that touch, the ability to seduce a potentially hostile audience with the sheer lyric beauty and irresistible dance beats of his music. If Chicago had fallen under his spell for fully four years, if a backwater town such as Herrin had been beguiled, surely he could ravish New York.

Or so he thought.

six

FREE FALL

*T*he girls positioned themselves strategically around the room, some sipping drinks, others dragging on cigarettes, all offering their services for ten cents a dance, if that's all you wanted. Anything more cost extra, but that could be negotiated on the dance floor, where lonely men rubbed up against female flesh while the band played the shortest possible versions of every tune in the book. The instant the music stopped, every girl whispered promisingly into the ear of her customer: Want to keep going? It's just a dime.

No, it wasn't the most glamorous spot in Harlem, but if you were out at night and alone, the flickering marquee on the corner of 125th Street and Seventh Avenue beckoned you inside. Then you lumbered up a flight of stairs to get to the dance floor, and as soon as you walked in you felt as if every girl in the place was staring at you, trying to grab your attention. They called this seedy room the Rose Danceland, a blatant steal from a genuinely fabled spot, the Roseland Ballroom, where the best swing dancers in New York City convened in midtown on Broadway. But could anyone, even the most gullible out-of-towner, confuse this hole with the plush and spacious Roseland? Did anyone truly believe that this was some new Harlem branch of the most celebrated palace in the kingdom of swing? Perhaps it didn't matter, since music and dance were not what the Rose Dance-land ultimately was selling, which was a pity, since the man fronting the band was Jelly Roll Morton.

When Morton arrived in New York after his MCA tour ended, in February 1928, this was the best job he could land, which should have warned him that Manhattan was not pining for his services. But if New York couldn't care less that a former king of New Orleans, Chicago, and points west had arrived in town, the young musicians in this seedy place immediately recognized the stature of the man who stood before them.

"Everybody looked at him and began talking," recalled Tommy Benford, the house drummer, of the day Morton first walked into the place. "The proprietor brought him up to my brother [bandleader Bill Benford] and introduced him. . . . Well, when he said 'Jelly Roll Morton,' everybody was enthused. We'd all heard of him but had never seen him. . . . Everybody was amazed because, you know, at that time there wasn't anybody around playing that particular style."

Yet with the exception of a couple of newspaper ads mentioning that Morton was leading the house band, New York barely noticed Morton's arrival. While the tuxedoed Duke Ellington was broadcast-ing nationally from the high-toned Cotton Club on Lenox Avenue, while Fletcher Henderson was packing them in at Club Alabam on West Forty-fourth, while McKinney's Cotton Pickers were whipping the lindy-hoppers into a frenzy down at the Roseland, the father of them all was working a house just this side of a brothel. It almost was as though Morton had come full circle, providing background music for the purchase of sex, as he used to do from the piano at Hilma Burt's place in the District, nearly a quarter century earlier. The only significant difference was that everything was cheaper here in Harlem—and Morton older and grayer.

"The Rose Danceland was a dime-a-dance joint—you know, you take an orchestration, you play the introduction, you play down one chorus, you repeat, play down to the second chorus, and you stop," recalled Manzie Johnson, who subbed occasionally as drummer for the band. "I didn't enjoy that too much. . . . Jelly didn't like the start-

and-stop business either, and he must have been down on his luck or he wouldn't have done that kind of work. But the place did pay you good money. It was just a stepping stone for Jelly. Maybe he wanted to acquaint himself more with the New York musicians. . . . I think that maybe he was on his way down—anyway, about leveling off. At one time he had a big name."

To Morton, the Rose Danceland didn't look so bad, if only because it filled his pocket with cash, which he displayed at the slightest provocation, just as in the old days. There was no reason to rush to a bigger and better gig, anyway, since his tunes—the pieces that he had begun creating in the District at the start of the century—now were working hard for him, spreading his name and his sound across the country and around the globe. Just a month after Morton arrived in New York, in fact, Fletcher Henderson rerecorded a rhythmically charged version of "King Porter Stomp" for Columbia in New York. At about the same time, McKinney's Cotton Pickers—a Detroit outfit soon to rank among the most celebrated swing machines in the country—went into the studio for the first time, recording Morton's "Milenberg Joys" in a radiant Don Redman arrangement for Victor. Even Benny Goodman, the kid who had watched and studied Morton's rehearsals in the Melrose music shop back in Chicago, was breaking into the business on the strength of Morton's art. Under the auspices of publisher Walter Melrose, Goodman put together a Chicago band drawn mostly from the ranks of Ben Pollack's orchestra, including trombonist Glenn Miller and cornetist Jimmy McPartland, igniting his recording career with Morton's "Wolverine Blues." A few months later, the soon-to-be "King of Swing" returned to the well, recording Morton's "Jungle Blues" for Brunswick in New York.

With Morton's tunes spinning on turntables across America, the man could bide his time, so he spent his days heroically trying to transform the sorry band at the Rose Danceland into something worthy of his name and his art. Before show time, he drilled the players in this music, relentlessly making them repeat his phrases the way they had been played back in New Orleans. First he worked the brass section, then the reeds, then the rhythm players, each facing a different set of technical and musical problems that seemed virtually impossible to solve to East Coast musicians unfamiliar with Morton's ways. When the rehearsals ended and the performances began, Morton presided as if he were some Toscanini of the Jazz Age. "A lot of times we'd play one of his own tunes—that means he'd start playing it, then he'd stand up and start directing the band, sometimes with the baton and sometimes he'd grab one of my drumsticks" to wave at the musicians, recalled Tommy Benford, astonished that anyone would take a job in a dump like this so seriously.

When the Rose Danceland engagement settled into something of a routine, Morton made his move, taking this third-rate band into the Victor studio in New York on June 11. But judging by the results, Morton was deluding himself if he believed that such an ensemble could make any impact in a city where Ellington, Henderson, Chick Webb, and the like were upping the tempos, volume, and ensemble precision of the modern big band. That Victor went along with this self-deception, anointing this band the Red Hot Peppers, practically amounted to an insult to everything that the original unit back in Chicago had achieved on record. With clarinetist Omer Simeon as the only New Orleans musician in the band (apart from Morton himself), the new Red Hot Peppers very nearly mauled several of Morton's most delicately crafted compositions. The messy ensemble playing, flat-footed rhythms, and jerky melodic lines instantly showed Morton, and anyone who listened closely to the recordings, how steeply the bandleader had fallen after just a few months in New York.

If Morton were to get anywhere with his music, he needed the New Orleans men who had swarmed into Chicago more than a decade earlier. But these black and Creole artists, who had taught Chicago how to swing, were not so easily found in Manhattan, and those who turned up there made minimal musical effect on the town. Jazz was taking utterly new directions in New York—faster, louder, more frenetic, more virtuosic, more driven—and any lukewarm attempt to revive last year's New Orleans sound was doomed. Surely Morton cringed when he heard the muffed notes of trombonist Geechie Fields, the heavy-handed drum work of Tommy Benford, and the leaden tuba playing of Bill Benford on Morton's New York recordings of "Kansas City Stomp," "Shoe Shiner's Drag," and "Boogaboo." Each of these records, and others, represented the antithesis of Morton's flowing, graceful pianism on these cuts. The new men simply didn't get it.

At one recording session, Morton played a fairly sophisticated extended chord, which threw off guitarist Lee Blair, who tried to match it but landed on a clinker. Morton instantly stopped the band and asked Blair what he was trying to pull. Those wrong notes "made me kind of sick," Morton snarled.

The musicians' often smudged, earthbound playing affirmed that Morton no longer was leading a band of the stature that his scores required, that he was utterly out of his element. Only on "Mournful Serenade," Morton's radical rethinking of King Oliver's "Chimes Blues"—recast at an exquisitely slow tempo—did Morton approach the aesthetic level of a few months earlier in Chicago. But the success of that tune was owed, in large part, to the sweet fact that most of the key passages were played by Morton and Simeon, the two New Orleans veterans in the band. Morton's beguiling keyboard touch, as well as his ability to keep a melody flowing even when it was rhythmically agitated, gave the piece its sense of serenity, while Simeon's fast and oft-throbbing vibrato referred more closely to Louisiana blues than to New York hustle. Even so, Tommy Benford's bludgeonlike drum work and Fields's oft-grinding tone marred the effect.

But for Morton, it wasn't just the record dates that were falling flat, for his public appearances were leaving New Yorkers strangely unmoved, at least compared with the responses he had been accustomed to receiving since playing behind a screen in Storyville's brothels, while his customers writhed and moaned before him. Up in Harlem, where stride piano genius James P. Johnson was proving that a left hand could bounce along the keys at breakneck speed and Fats Waller was making the ivories jump in tunes such as "Handful of Keys" and "Smashing Thirds," Morton's gently fluid lyricism sounded almost archaic. The Harlem piano players, from Eubie Blake to Willie "The Lion" Smith, simply were playing faster, harder, and more brilliantly than anyone who had come before. If Morton's goal was to evoke at the piano the full sonic breadth of a New Orleans jazz band, he was playing the wrong game, for his Harlem rivals were letting loose with all-out hot piano, pursuing digital virtuosity and keyboard pyrotechnics as thrilling ends in themselves. Yes, there still were distinct pleasures in listening to Morton re-create on the keyboard the many intricately interweaving lines of a New Orleans jazz band. But in New York, noise, fury, and phenomenal technical accuracy were deemed higher musical virtues.

"He had ideas, he was original, but I don't think the other guys in the band thought he was much of a piano player," recalled drummer Johnson. "He wasn't in a class with James P. and Fats Waller—my God, no. He could sell himself—he could *tell* you he was a great piano player. But the guys in New York just laughed at him."

For the first time in his life, Morton wasn't crushing the competition; he was being mocked by it. The warm touch, blues-steeped melodies, lazy southern tempos, and somewhat retro two-beat-to-the bar stomps had no chance against the sheer onslaught of sound that the New York piano men were unleashing. Nor did Morton's struggling band at the Rose Danceland approach the sumptuous orchestral colors that Ellington's organization was creating at the Cotton Club or the visceral swing energy that Henderson's state-of-the-art swing band was cranking out at Club Alabam and the Roseland Ballroom.

For Morton, everything was going awry in Manhattan, though not quite enough to make him step back and reassess. He was taking in enough money to maintain the old lifestyle, but now he was deemed second-rate or, worse, passé. Yet even if he had been able to gather around him the New Orleans musicians he had led and recorded so ingeniously in Chicago, he probably wouldn't have fared much better in Manhattan, for his music, his manner, his bravado— virtually everything about him—rubbed New York the wrong way.

"He had went to Chicago, and he had success in Chicago, and then he went to New York with the same beat, and it didn't catch on," said New Orleans jazz guitarist Danny Barker, who had befriended Morton in Manhattan.

> They didn't go for bluesy jazz in New York. And when he made his best music, it was a laidback tempo that they loved in the South: If you're dancing with a woman, you don't want to be rushing nowhere, you want to hold on, feel around, pull her close to you, move in and squeeze her and see if she'll allow you them liberties. New York wasn't from nothing laid back. The New Yorkers, they're grinding. The famous dance then is the Lindy Hop, so they don't want nothing laid back. . . . And anyway, America is always waiting for the new thing. That's the way America is. And Jelly wasn't no new thing.

So far as New York was concerned, Jelly Roll was decidedly the old thing—a New Orleans pimp who had made it big in Chicago—his very name a throwback to the days when jazz and sex were practically inseparable, the very rhythm of life in the District. With his bulky Chesterfield shirts and gold suspenders and diamond-encrusted tooth, Morton appeared to New Yorkers as if he still were selling women rather than music, while his long-winded soliloquies—a holdover from an era when New Orleans musicians served as their own press agents and publicists—grated on those who bothered to listen.

Morton's only saving grace, in fact, was that at least his name still held some allure in the hinterlands, so at the start of 1929 he picked up a job playing a chain of ballrooms in Pennsylvania and Ohio. At first, it seemed like a decent engagement, but it quickly showed that Morton's options were running out. "It was pretty rough, and we couldn't make any money," said New Orleans reedist Paul Barnes.

> In fact, at one time we went a couple of days without food. At the taxi [dance joint] we got paid every week; on the road, it depended on what we took in at each dance. . . . One day we got

into Washington, Pa., very late, with nothing to eat, and we were
so hungry that Jelly pawned his diamond ring so the band could
have some food. Coming back to New York from this trip we
had only $10 apiece. . . . I remember now that we wore tuxedo
suits on that tour, and how we acted "big time" in our tuxedos
and wouldn't let anybody know we were broke and hungry.

Appearances were everything to Morton and therefore to his
band. No matter how much your stomach growled, you were to look
as if you just had feasted on caviar. And if you were weary and aching
from hundreds of miles logged on the road, you pulled yourself together and strode grandly into a town as if your reputation preceded
you—which, in Morton's case, it generally had. When Morton and
the band rolled into some obscure country burg, word quickly spread
that one of Capone's gangster musicians had arrived, and before long,
someone inevitably hollered, "Pack your pistols 'cause Jelly Roll Morton's band is here—from Chicago!"

Though running out of cash, Morton indeed still had his name,
which is why a publisher on the make named Ralph Peer pursued him.
To Peer, a veteran record producer scouting for tunes for his Southern
Music Co., Morton was a godsend, a down-on-his-luck former hit
maker who suddenly had become eminently affordable. At first, Morton resisted Peer's seductions, insisting that he needed the blessing of
Walter Melrose back in Chicago, though, legally, Melrose had no hold
on Morton. But Morton was going to be as loyal to Melrose as he expected anyone to be to him.

"Mr. Peer asked me would I do some recording for him, I again
refused," Morton recalled. "'Would you record if I could get Permission from Melrose?' he stated.

"In reply, I stated that if that could be done, that would be okeh.
The next day or two we met, Mr. Peer produced a wire stating it was
okeh to record, signed by Walter Melrose."

That was all Morton needed to see. On December 6, 1928, the
composer returned to the studio, recording original tunes that he had

penned for the occasion, many spilling over with fresh concepts in jazz. In "Red Hot Pepper," Morton's big band churned out brilliant brass-section riffs and rapid-fire call-and-response dialogues between solo and ensemble. In "Deep Creek," he presided over a big-band blues as dark and mournful as any he ever had written. Yet for all the substance and originality of this music, the performances by his touring big band, now dubbed Jelly-Roll Morton and His Orchestra, proved technically inferior, rhythmically choppy, and badly lacking in reed and brass solos of distinction. Even Morton's own playing suffered from the company he now was keeping, his pianism overpedaled and thematically unclear in solo tunes he recorded on July 8, 1929, including "Pop" (a revisiting of "Seattle Hunch"), "Frances" (similar to "Mamanita"), and the aptly named "Freakish," with its daringly chromatic chord changes, unusual syncopations, and unorthodox stops and starts.

Nevertheless, as a composer Morton somehow was unfazed by the downward spiral of his career, his as-yet-unshaken self-confidence enabling him to unfurl brashly original works in the studio from July 8 through July 12, 1929. He ennobled the Charleston dance craze in "Burnin' the Iceberg," which transformed a hackneyed rhythm into a sublimely expressive riff; he subverted big-band tradition in "Tank Town Bump"—bringing his phalanx of hard-swinging horns to a screeching halt so that Morton himself could play a single, long-held note on the piano and linger on it. Here was a great jazz composer asserting his eminence, placing himself at the center of the orchestral music swirling around him. It was as if Morton were saying that he remained the lord of his world—Mister Jelly Lord, as he sometimes called himself—even if that world had shrunk significantly in less than a year. The ensemble performances sounded more than a little vulgar, considering the plodding rhythm section in "Courthouse Bump," the astonishingly inaccurate intonation on "Sweet Aneta Mine," and the woefully inelegant ensemble playing of "New Orleans Bump" (particularly compared to Morton's earlier recording). But Morton's pen would not stop yielding significant new work. Unfortunately for him,

the new tunes made virtually no impression on the record-buying
public, which had moved on to newer stars, Ellington, Lunceford,
Calloway, Henderson, and Armstrong chief among them. Worse,
Morton was about to be sabotaged by his former Chicago publisher
and friend, Walter Melrose. For no sooner had Morton gone into the
studio to begin recording for Peer than Melrose dug a knife deep into
Morton's back.

"[Walter] Melrose wrote me a letter and told me that I would get
no more royalty from him and that I could do whatever I wanted to
do about it, because I had doublecrossed him for Ralph Peer," Morton explained later. "I then figured there that that telegram [which
Peer had produced earlier] was a fake. I showed the letter to Peer and
he then stated that the wire from Melrose automatically turned my
contract over to the Victor Co.," a bizarre interpretation suggesting
that Peer was either confused or willfully misleading Morton.

Either way, Melrose had no legal right to cut off royalty payments
to Morton. The composer's royalties for the tunes Morton had
recorded with his Red Hot Peppers in Chicago and for versions
recorded by everyone from Benny Goodman to Fletcher Henderson
were legally Morton's for as long as he lived, and long after. If Melrose had a legitimate dispute—which he did not—it would have to be
settled by a judge.

Yet Melrose vowed that he no longer would send Morton his royalties, and he meant it. To Morton, this was the worst of all the blows
he had been dealt since coming to Manhattan, not only because of the
money he stood to lose but because it cut his last tangible link to the
glory days in Chicago and severed his relationship with a man whose
friendship he had prized. From this point forth, Morton was adrift in
New York, the Chicago years receding into the storied past, to be remembered fondly and longed for but never again matched. Though
Morton now realized that he and Melrose were finished, he couldn't
get the loss out of his mind.

"Chicago was the place he liked to remember best, so we talked
mostly of Chicago," remembered record collector Kenneth Hulsizer,
who befriended Morton in New York.

He seemed to like to talk about the old days in Chicago, the people he knew, the things they did and what had happened to them. He had been one of the best known colored musicians in Chicago about 1925 when he was playing piano in the Melrose Brothers Music shop. He had known almost everyone, and they had all known him. He remembered it as a pleasant period. About New York, where the money was, he was bitter. He hadn't been successful there. He had never fitted into the picture in New York. He had never "caught on."

But the bad news kept coming. In 1930, RCA bought Victor Records and immediately dropped Morton, while continuing to record younger men, such as Ellington, Armstrong, and Bennie Moten. With Morton's reputation fading and his bands running from mediocre to terrible, he was becoming the odd man out in New York, a relic deemed expendable to a growing concern such as the new RCA Victor. So after Morton walked out of Victor's studios in New York on October 9—having recorded a new piece, "Gambling Jack," and an old one, "Fickle Fay Creep" (known as "Soap Suds" on a 1926 record)—he disappeared from the record industry for nearly a decade.

The great raconteur and braggart, the man who had once had more women, suits, and rackets than anyone else in the music business, was being discarded and knew it. Reduced to playing hokey prom dances at local colleges, Morton was watching himself fade from public consciousness, to him an unimaginable and unfathomable fate. When he led a band at Princeton University in 1930, one of the students walked up to the stage and had the temerity to ask, "Who is Jelly Roll Morton?"

Morton was appalled. "I'm the great Jelly Roll Morton—you're looking at the great Jelly Roll Morton," he said.

The kid still didn't get the picture. "Are you the one who's playing the piano?"

Morton still couldn't believe the depth of ignorance he now was battling. "Well, who else would be playing piano?" he said.

Answered the kid, point blank, "I'd never heard anything about you yet."

"Son," replied Morton, "you've got a long ways to go. Just listen to this."

Between increasingly infrequent engagements, Morton began killing time in front of the Rhythm Club in Harlem, at 132nd Street and Seventh Avenue, a haven for musicians left underemployed by the Great Depression. Standing near the curb, Morton entertained younger players with stories of old New Orleans, his impromptu speechifying more popular than any of his stage shows. Opulently garbed in his Hart, Schaffner & Marx suits and impeccably pressed shirts and freshly shined Florsheim shoes, he expounded upon the magnificence of New Orleans musicians and the shortcomings of their New York counterparts. "You are your own worst enemy," Morton told the musicians, deriding them for not practicing enough, not showing up for rehearsals on time, not playing the music exactly as it was written.

But Morton missed the point. The New York men weren't ignoring all of their rehearsals and playing poorly on everyone's compositions—just his. "I tried to help Jelly organize a band," remembered guitarist Danny Barker. "I asked around, like [trumpeter] Dave Nelson and a couple of other New Orleans musicians, and they said, 'Jelly's hard to work with, well not exactly, but he wants you to play that old-time music, and the boys don't want to play that kind of music, you see in fact they *can't* play it.'"

A thousand miles and a couple years removed from Chicago, Morton was alone but for his relationship with Mabel—or May, as he called her. In the cramped room they rented up in Harlem, she cooked him hot gumbo filé, washed and pressed his clothes, and took his suits to the dry cleaner after a single wearing. But Morton was losing ground, and he poured his frustrations into his curbside rants, imploring youngsters such as guitarist Barker and trombonist Trummy Young to wise up while there was time and avoid the disasters that were befalling him.

"I want to tell you one thing, you cannot play around, just because you think you're so great," Morton railed. "I'm telling you those white boys are not playing corny any more. They're coming up right along. I hear them playing my tunes. They're getting the *idea* of how to play hot. Once they get it, they're going to use it. Then they're gonna sell you for five cents a dozen."

A few of the young players got the message. "He'd tell us to watch our business transactions, so we wouldn't be cheated or work for nothing," said Young. "He felt hurt, I wouldn't say bitter, he felt hurt that people had taken advantage of him in the past."

Morton was slip-sliding into oblivion. Though he had recorded thirty-four cuts for Peer's Southern Music between 1929 and 1932, Morton's career as a performer was unraveling. On July 16, 1933, he played John Young's Cabaret and Beer Garden Restaurant in Hartford, Connecticut, where the cover charge was twenty-five cents. On October 7, he opened a week's engagement at the University Grill in Albany, New York, making all of fifty dollars, from which he had to pay the band. While Morton was earning pennies playing in the middle of nowhere, Duke Ellington was bowing in his first Hollywood film, *Check and Doublecheck*, in 1930 and conquering Europe in 1933, while Cab Calloway was following close behind, starring in Hollywood's *The Big Broadcast* in 1932 and blazing across Europe in 1934. A new royalty was taking its place in the jazz pantheon, leaving no room for a fallen king.

Yet as Morton's descent gathered momentum, his music paradoxically seeped deeper into American culture. Fletcher Henderson scored a major hit in 1932 with Morton's "King Porter Stomp"—renamed "New King Porter Stomp"—while Bennie Moten's Kansas City Orchestra recorded "Milenberg Joys" for Victor in the same year. By 1934, the Casa Loma Orchestra, Wingy Manone, Claude Hopkins, and even the Dorsey Brothers' Orchestra were waxing Morton tunes, at a time when Morton himself couldn't get within shouting distance of a recording studio. Desperate to find some work—any work—Morton reasoned that if he couldn't make records, he'd settle for playing the piano and telling his stories on the radio. With cash-starved Depression-era America increasingly tuning in to the only form of musical entertainment that was free, Morton reasoned that there had to be a job on radio for a musician who could speak as glibly as he always had. So he dropped by the offices of the National Broadcasting Company, in the RCA Building on Rockefeller Plaza, in April 1934, looking for a spot on the airwaves, and filled out an application. The response came quickly.

"We . . . regret we cannot give you the audition you seek," read the rejection letter sent to him on April 25, 1934. Undaunted, Morton tried WINS Radio, where he succeeded in securing a show of his own—then quickly lost it. "Dear Mr. Martin," read the kiss-off letter from WINS, sent September 28 to his address at 323 West 137th Street, blowing the name of a once famous man.

> We regret to advise you that due to a rearrangement in our program schedule caused by the fact that beginning October 1 we lose two hours of our operating schedule, it is necessary for us to discontinue your programs over this station. Please be assured that we have the highest regard for your talents and will communicate with you at the earliest opportunity in regard to another series of programs.

None occurred.

With Morton's tunes becoming increasingly prevalent on radio, he knew that he ought to be receiving money from ASCAP, which was collecting flat percentages from every radio station in America and divvying the proceeds among its members. If the radio stations were playing Morton's music and ASCAP was taking in a portion of the proceeds, he clearly deserved a cut.

ASCAP disagreed.

"Dear Sir," opened the form rejection letter ASCAP sent to Morton on October 25, 1934. "We are returning to you herewith application which you forwarded to us. Please be advised that all applications must be proposed and seconded by members of this Society."

This was ASCAP's ingenious way of keeping membership limited and white. By excluding potential new members, ASCAP ensured that the composers who already belonged would collect a larger slice of the royalties pie. And by requiring that all applications be proposed and seconded by an ASCAP member, the organization effectively kept blacks out, since ASCAP's nearly two hundred charter members included only two men of color (the classical composers Harry T. Burleigh and James Weldon Johnson). Morton knew neither, so his chances of getting into ASCAP were slim to nonexistent. Even Louis Armstrong, by the mid-1920s and 1930s the biggest black musical star in the world, was not admitted until 1939.

So, as far as he could tell, Morton was finished in the music business. In a gesture of desperation, he took his last dollars and sank them into a fledgling New York cosmetics firm that quickly failed. Yet at the very moment that Morton seemed to be hitting bottom in 1935, all he had to do to hear his music was turn on the radio, where his old New Orleans tunes—reorchestrated for uncounted big bands—were swinging the nation. Benny Goodman, in fact, was savoring his first hit with Morton's "King Porter Stomp," a tune that transformed an obscure Chicago clarinetist into a king himself—the official white "King of Swing." Goodman's sensational, explosive arrangement had come to him from the pen of the black bandleader Fletcher Henderson, whose swing band had gone broke in 1934. It was "King Porter Stomp," Goodman believed, that saved him in 1935, when his first national tour was bombing coast to coast, until he reached Oakland, California. "I called for 'King Porter Stomp,' one of Fletcher's real killers," said Goodman. "That number started off with Bunny Berigan playing a trumpet solo, the saxophones and rhythm behind him. Before he played four bars, there was such a yelling and stomping and carrying on in the hall that I thought a riot had broken out. When I went into my solo, the noise was even louder. Finally, the truth got through to me. We were causing the riot." The Oakland triumph foreshadowed the even more spectacular success Goodman achieved in Los Angeles, at the Palomar Ballroom, playing "King Porter Stomp" and swing tunes inspired by it.

But because Walter Melrose wouldn't pay Morton royalties on "King Porter Stomp" and because ASCAP had rejected Morton's application for membership a year earlier, Morton wasn't earning a dime from one of the hottest tunes in the country. "King Porter Stomp" stayed on the charts for fully a month in 1935, benefiting just about everyone associated with it but the man who had conceived it three decades earlier in the District. With no work, no money, and no options, Morton had no choice but to flee Manhattan and forget about music, or at least that was the plan. He told Mabel to stay behind in New York to watch over the Melrose and ASCAP business, while he headed to Washington, D.C., to become a fight promoter and leave the whole rotten jazz business behind him.

You could smell the hamburgers burning on the grill even before you walked into the place, and it followed you right up the stairs to the second floor of the squat building at 1211 U Street, in Washington, D.C. As if this stench weren't bad enough, the fumes of a wood-burning stove permeated the Jungle Inn, a shoebox-shaped room impersonating a jazz club. With a dozen small tables scattered in a twenty-by-forty-foot room and an old spinet pushed up against a wall, it wasn't exactly elegant, but Jelly Roll Morton was long past worrying about appearances. At the moment, he was lucky to be working anywhere, for his fantasy of managing fighters in Washington in 1935 went nowhere—the fighters got drunk and wouldn't train, he said. What else was Morton to do, what else did he know how to do, but sit himself down at the piano and reel out tunes, just as he had since his youth when all else failed? That's how he had ended up in this dive, talking himself into a business partnership with one Cordelia Lyle, who owned the place. If she supplied the booze, he would provide the melodies, and he surely kept his end of the deal. As always, Morton had ideas. He was going to build a great band. He was going to invite movie stars and celebrities. He was going to host movie auditions.

Many scholars believe that Morton is seen at the piano in Hilma Burt's brothel in New Orlean's Storyville district.

Hogan Jazz Archive/Howard Tilton Memorial Library, Tulane University.

Tom Anderson's Annex Café and Chop House stood as the gateway to the plush brothels along Basin Street, fronting the railroad tracks.

William Russell Collection/Historic New Orleans Collection, 1968.

Roy Carew, Morton's late-in-life
friend and business partner, in
about 1937.

*William Russell Collection/Historic New
Orleans Collection, undated.*

Roy Carew in his later years, long after Morton's death.

William Russell Collection/Historic New Orleans Collection, undated.

Tony Jackson, the only New Orleans piano player Morton regarded as his superior.

William Russell Collection/ Historic New Orleans Collection.

Freddie Keppard, whose hot band of first-generation jazzmen was causing a sensation at the Tuxedo Dance Hall, in the District, in 1908.

William Russell Collection/Historic New Orleans Collection.

Laura Monette, Morton's grandmother, who disapproved of her grandson's life in the District and threw him out of the house.

William Russell Collection/ Historic New Orleans Collection.

Louise Monette, Morton's mother.

William Russell Collection/Historic New Orleans Collection.

Possibly the earliest known photo of Morton, undated.

William Russell Collection/ Historic New Orleans Collection.

Morton, in blackface, with Rosa Brown, about 1914.

William Russell Collection/ Historic New Orleans Collection.

Morton, before 1920.

William Russell Collection/ Historic New Orleans Collection.

TEENAN JONES PLACE.
3445 S. STATE. ST.
CHICAGO ILL.
Worthington STUDIO.

Morton is easy to pick out (second from right; see detail below) posing in front of Teenan Jones's Elite Café, around 1915. His impeccable attire reflected his rising status in Chicago entertainment, while the decorations on the building announced an Elks convention in Chicago.

Photo by the Worthington Studio, Chicago. William Russell Collection/ Historic New Orleans Collection.

Morton (third from left) as part of a revue at the Cadillac Café, in Los Angeles, c. 1917–18.

William RussellCollection/ Historic New Orleans Collection.

Morton with Anita Gonzalez in Los Angeles, 1918.

William Russell Collection/Historic New Orleans Collection.

Morton at his pinnacle as a recording artist, during a 1926 Victor photo session in Chicago.

Photo by Bloom. William Russell Collection/Historic New Orleans Collection.

Morton and His Red Hot Peppers in Chicago, 1926. From left: Omer Simeon, Andrew Hilaire, John Lindsay, Morton (seated), Johnny St. Cyr, Kid Ory and George Mitchell.

Morton during a 1926 Victor recording session, in Chicago. From left: Andrew Hilaire, Kid Ory, George Mitchell, John Lindsay, Morton, Johnny St. Cyr, Omer Simeon.

William Russell Collection/Historic New Orleans Collection.

Morton, in 1926, with inscription: "With best wishes to my friend Omer Simeon, 'Jelly Roll' Morton."

Photo by Bloom. William Russell Collection/Historic New Orleans Collection.

Jelly Roll Morton band in the Victor Studios in New York, July 1929.

William Russell Collection/Historic New Orleans Collection.

Site of the Jungle Inn, at 1211 U Street, Washington, D.C., where Morton spent three lonely years—from 1935 to '38—as piano player, bartender, barrel opener and bouncer.

William Russell Collection/Historic New Orleans Collection, 1968.

Morton at a Bluebird/RCA Victor session in New York, September 1939.

William Russell Collection/ Historic New Orleans Collection.

Morton portrait,
taken at the Bluebird/
RCA Victor session on
September 14, 1939.

*William Russell Collection/
Historic New Orleans
Collection.*

Morton's autograph.

"JELLY ROLL" MORTON
(ORIGINATOR OF JAZZ)

- STAFF WRITER -
TEMPO - MUSIC PUB. CO.
145 W. 45TH ST., NEW YORK, N. Y.

Morton's late-in-life
business card

Morton, promoter Harry Lim, and impresario Steve Smith at the second Bluebird/RCA Victor date in New York on September 28, 1939.

William Russell Collection/Historic New Orleans Collection.

Morton's last address in New York, 209 W. 131st St., where he lived from 1939 to '40.

William Russell Collection/Historic New Orleans Collection.

Morton at the 1939 Bluebird/RCA Victor session in New York, September 1939.

William Russell Collection/Historic New Orleans Collection.

Morton, at the piano, leading his Bluebird/RCA Victor session in New York on September 14, 1939.

William Russell Collection/Historic New Orleans Collection.

Morton in New York,
c. 1939.

*William Russell Collection/
Historic New Orleans Collection.*

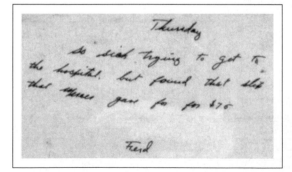

Morton's Last Will and Testament, June 28, 1941.

William Russell Collection/Historic New Orleans Collection.

Morton's death certificate.

William Russell Collection/ Historic New Orleans Collection.

Morton could barely write a straight line in June 1941, a month before he died: ". . . so sick trying to get to the hospital," he wrote, "but found that slip that Mercer [a record producer] gave for for $75."

William Russell Collection/Historic New Orleans Collection

It all flopped, for nothing could succeed in getting crowds to come to a drafty second-floor joint on a rough block in the black part of town. But even if Morton had landed in the most lavish den in Washington, the city was no more going to embrace him than New York had. It just wasn't that kind of town.

"The better night clubs in this town are stiff, expensive joints frequented by Uncle Sam's employees, who fear that someone will see them with their hair down," noted *Down Beat* at the time.

> Bands in these clubs, which bowed before Guy Lombardo's altar a few years ago, are now aping [Benny] Goodman, with about as much fire as a Salvation Army lass walloping a tambourine. Once a night some of the bands will play a blues in B-flat, but it sounds more like an Hawaiian love song. The Negro joints are a bit better, but on week nights they are dead, and on Saturday and Sunday nights they are overrun with queers.

Aside from the occasional group that wandered in looking for a few drinks late at night, the Jungle Inn was about as desolate as Washington clubs got. Morton hardly could believe it had come to this. At a time when Armstrong was becoming an international star and Fats Waller and W. C. Handy and Ethel Waters were ascendant, Morton in 1936 was trying to hustle radio jobs, briefly landing one on WOL in Washington, then getting canned shortly thereafter. So he was back at the Jungle Inn, serving drinks and running out to restock bottles of beer when customers had guzzled their way through Cordelia Lyle's tiny stock. In the midst of this ignominy, he tried to console Mabel, who yearned for him to return to New York.

"I don't want you to worry," he wrote to her. "Things are tough everywhere, and we are not the only ones that's catching Hell. There are plenty worse than us. I know things will turn out all right. . . . Enclosed you will find $17. See if you can pay up the interest on the things that's nearest to be lost. I will send you something Monday. I thank God I am able to send you something. Yours. Ferd."

In a quixotic series of moves, Morton and his partner at the Jungle Inn changed the name of the saloon, to Blue Moon Café and to the Music Box, as if that would help. Visitors proved so scarce that Morton practically leaped off the piano bench whenever a passer-by stumbled in. "After being welcomed at the door by Jelly Roll Morton himself, we grabbed a ringside table just in time for the floor show," noted a rare review in the *Washington Daily News*, euphemistically describing the scattershot solo entertainment. "Of course, the high spot of the entertainment was Jelly Roll Morton's ivory tickling, which we think is tops."

Yet the squib in the *Washington Daily News* was enough to get the word out to the jazz cognescenti that a genuine legend was in town, and in short order *Down Beat*—the nation's preeminent chronicler of jazz and swing—noted the disparity between the venue and its legendary showman. "I found the legendary Jelly Roll Morton playing in a low down dive called the Jungle Inn, at 1211 U St., smack in the center of the town's jig district," wrote James Higgins in *Down Beat*.

> And is not only playing but owning half interest in the place, acting as an out-of-sight bartender and barrel opener and, in between these duties, serving as M.C. and bouncer. There have been few kicks more terrific than the sound and sight of Jelly playing the blues, his thumping heel beating out the slow rhythm, his eyes closed and his head thrown back and the sad notes sprinkling from the keyboard into the low-ceiling, smoky den. Frankly, there are not many that listen.

Worse, the uninitiated complained about the tunes on the jukebox—Morton classics such as "Wolverine Blues" and "The Pearls." "They don't know nothing about jazz," Morton growled. "No one wants that stuff any more. . . . I don't know what I'd do if a few friends didn't drop in. People don't know the old jazz any more."

Yet at least one man in Washington did, for he had heard the old jazz when it still was new and he was standing outside Hilma Burt's sporting house in 1904, on an evening when the young Ferd Morton was at the keys. Roy Carew hadn't met Morton in person on that night, but thirty-four years later he was about to find him at the Jungle Inn and try mightily to return him to a place of honor in a jazz world that now scorned him.

Roy Carew stopped short. While casually leafing through the newspaper at the kitchen table of his white-frame house, he looked twice at the headline streaming across three columns of page 6 of the *Washington Daily News*. Even before Carew fully understood its meaning, the story and accompanying photo of an aging Creole piano player instantly took him back more than three decades, when Carew had shown up for his first day of work at the Hibernia Bank Building in New Orleans. The passing parade had introduced Carew to the raucous musical life of turn-of-the-century New Orleans, and before long he had heard practically everyone in town worth hearing, from Buddy Bolden and Tony Jackson to the most notorious piano player of them all, Ferd Morton.

More than three decades later, the same piano player was staring up at Carew from the pages of the March 18 edition of the *Daily News*, underneath a headline proclaiming: "Jelly Roll Charts Jazz . . . Years Encroach but His Fingers Know the Ivories as of Yore." As Carew pored over the story, everything about the District—the music, the brothels, the drugs, the stench, and the violence—came back to him, almost as vividly as if he were again investigating the streets of Storyville for the first time. Though Carew had left New Orleans about the same time Morton had, peddling Remington typewriters across the South, he had practically lost touch with the jazz life. Instead, he had become the upstanding, white collar worker his family expected him to be, attending college, getting married, and now toiling in anonymity as an auditor for the Internal Revenue Service, where his wife also worked. It was a dull but reliable occupation that certainly beat hawking typewriters, since it rescued Carew from the rigors of the road.

Now Carew, who had buried his memories of New Orleans, unexpectedly was basking in them again, thanks to a newspaper article that was about to change his life and Morton's. "Jelly Roll Morton is getting along in years but age hasn't diminished one jot the flexibility of his fingers," said the article in the *Daily News*. "In his Blue Moon night club at 1211 U-St NW yesterday, he spun thru a fragment of his best repertoire and his version of 'Tiger Rag' is something to shout about from the housetops." With these words, Carew nearly could hear the thunder of Morton's left forearm as it pressed against the keyboard, imitating the cry of a tiger, just as Morton used to do back in New Orleans. But if this description told Carew he ought to visit the Blue Moon soon, the passage that came next underscored the urgency of the visit. For Morton in this article rhapsodized on the great New Orleans pianist that Carew had befriended decades earlier—Tony Jackson. Morton called him "the world's greatest single-handed entertainer," and Carew couldn't have agreed more. So he resolved to visit Morton as soon as possible, for here was a man who not only had been in New Orleans at the dawning of jazz, when Carew was young, but understood the genius of Jackson, Carew's long-lost friend. "I simply had to look up Jelly Roll Morton and find out what had become of Tony," Carew later explained, though the task proved more difficult than he had imagined. For starters, the article referred to Morton's venue as the Blue Moon Night Club while the sign out front said Music Box. Worse, the Music Box sign was posted up on the second floor, with no marking on the building itself at street level. But after phoning twice and deciphering the signs, Carew gingerly walked up the wooden stairs to the place where Morton was said to work.

"The day I first got to see Morton was a cold, raw day in late March, and for heat in that large club room all they had was a good sized oil stove; it certainly seemed totally inadequate," remembered Carew.

I don't doubt that, financially speaking, the Washington night club venture was unfortunate both for Jelly Roll and the woman who went into the business with him. . . . On that March day I mention, she and I sat by the oil stove and talked about current events until Jelly Roll arrived. As he entered the room and walked slowly over to where we were sitting, he gave me the impression of a tired man. He evidently felt the raw cold, for his overcoat collar was turned up and he seemed to have pulled his shoulders up to bring the collar closer about his throat. He really was a sick man then, but no one knew it.

As Morton approached Carew—his gray hair making him look every bit of his fifty-four years—Carew stood up and introduced himself as an old friend of Tony Jackson's from New Orleans and Chicago. The mere mention of these places lowered Morton's guard, and the pianist invited Carew to sit down near him by the stove.

Finally, two men whose lives had barely intersected a lifetime ago, in New Orleans, were establishing contact three-and-a-half decades later. The admiration that Carew lavished upon Morton warmed the composer in that icy room more than the creaking oil stove ever did. For Carew, the most haunting moment came when Morton sat down at the piano and "played a long stretch of music that was clear cut and very smooth, of a characteristic Spanish type that sounded almost the same—if I can trust my memory—as what I stood and listened to at that time in front of Hilma Burt's."

Alone in Washington without Mabel and dismayed by the turn his life had taken, Morton told Carew the whole incredible story—the disasters in New York, the triumphs in Chicago, the turbulent romance with Anita in California, the freewheeling years rambling along the Gulf Coast, the battle to survive in Storyville, the disgrace of being tossed out of his family's home in New Orleans. Each time Carew returned to the club thereafter, Morton picked up the saga, fleshing out details, tracing the arc of his life, arguing that he had been first to capture jazz on paper, first to publish it, first to record it in all its New Orleans glory, first to explain to anyone who would listen the precise manner in which it had come into being. For this, the music industry had repaid Morton with a pungent mixture of derision, contempt, and neglect. "Now you know how it is," Morton said, concluding his lament.

Carew was overwhelmed by the amount of information Morton summoned and amazed that the great man shared it with him. Easily persuaded that Morton had been wronged, that the music world owed this man something more than a bleak existence in a cold and empty Washington club, Carew decided to take action, to help Morton—if he could think of some way to do it. As it happened, the first opportunity presented itself just days after the two men had begun to forge their friendship, when Robert Ripley's nationally broadcast radio show referred to W. C. Handy as the creator of jazz and blues. After everything Carew had heard from Morton, Carew smarted at this assertion. How could Handy—who had been born in Alabama, had led a generic marching band in Memphis, and now worked as a publisher in New York—possibly have earned such a title? The man had never even set foot in New Orleans.

With Morton's facts and stories and musical descriptions resonating in his ear, the soft-spoken Carew primed himself for battle. "In your broadcast of March 26, 1938, you introduced W. C. Handy as the originator of *jazz, stomps* and *blues*," Carew wrote on his typewriter, in a five-page, single-spaced letter that Morton signed on March 31. "By this announcement you have done me a great injustice and also have misled many of your fans," continued Carew, assuming Morton's voice and paraphrasing the words that Morton had told him.

It is evidently known beyond contradiction that New Orleans is the cradle of *jazz*, and I myself happened to be the creator, in the year of 1902, many years before the Dixieland Band organized. *Jazz* music is a style, not compositions, any kind of music may be played in *jazz*, if one has the knowledge. The first stomp was written in 1906, namely *King Porter Stomp*. *Georgia Swing* was the first to be named swing, in 1907. . . . Paul Whiteman claimed the name of King of Jazz for years with no actual knowledge of it. Duke Ellington claimed title of jungle music, which is no more than a flutter tongue on a wind instrument, mostly trumpets or trombones to any denomination of chord, which was done by Keppard, King Oliver, Buddie Petit, and many other brass instruments.

Trying to capture Morton's pride in New Orleans's great black and Creole musicians, and to give them the credit they deserved, Carew wrote, "These untruthful statements Mr. Handy had made or caused you to make will no doubt cause him to be branded that most dastardly imposter in the history of music."

Carew and Morton sought to prove that Morton and his black and Creole New Orleans brethren had been crafting real jazz in the first decade of the century, years before Handy had begun publishing the simplistic blues tunes that used the same structure and chord changes as thousands of others before them. How could a man such as Handy possibly have invented a music that emerged in New Orleans at the turn of the century before Morton's eyes and ears? How could Handy's blues tunes even be mentioned in the same breath as Morton's New Orleans ensemble pieces and Keppard's exultant high notes and King Oliver's deep blues sighs?

In this letter, Morton's rage met up with Carew's righteous indignation. Though all the world soon assumed that Morton had written this letter, the mangled dates, spellings, and musicological errors affirm that the letter was Carew's handiwork (at several points, Carew inadvertently referred to Morton in the third person). But Carew, to his eternal credit, was using his well-worn typewriter to give the largely forgotten piano player a voice, a way to be heard outside the tawdry club to which he had been confined. Moreover, Carew shrewdly sent the letter not only to Ripley but to the *Baltimore Afro-American* and to *Down Beat*.

The spirit of this letter—and the battle it was sure to provoke—inspired Morton. No longer would he bide his time, sulking in Washington. On the contrary, he would begin laying plans to retake his place at the pinnacle of a jazz world he had helped create. "All the Art Tatums and Teddy Wilsons don't even phase me," he proclaimed in a letter to the British journalist Earle Cornwall, sounding like a

wounded lion reasserting his preeminence. "They have the greatest respect for me. They don't come for fear of being shown up. I am the
one that educated Chicago, Detroit, N.Y., N.O., L.A. and they all
know it. . . . I shall take back my former position of first place."

By night, Morton toiled at the Music Box. By day, he drove his
Packard sedan to the Library of Congress, where folklorist Alan Lomax recorded Morton's recollections of life in New Orleans. Though
Morton wanted to talk music, Lomax grilled Morton about sex, mayhem, and murders in New Orleans, the sensational tales that Morton
gave him reluctantly. To keep the bawdiest anecdotes flowing, Lomax
repeatedly filled Morton's glass with whiskey, and as he did, the stories became more colorful, raunchy, and exaggerated. The composer
didn't realize that by giving Lomax the dirt he wanted, he was helping
to soil his own reputation for generations to come.

But when speaking unfettered and unfiltered by anyone else's pre-
conceptions—particularly in his letters—Morton railed about his
plight. Determined to tell the story that Carew had reawakened
within him and to demand what was rightly his, Morton composed a
letter to no less than the Chief Justice of the United States Supreme
Court, Charles Evans Hughes, hand-written on May 13, 1938. "As a
last resort I thought I would inquire of you to be directed in the right
channels of protection, which I don't seem to be able to find," he
wrote in his own hand.

> I have written musical compositions under my name, published
> by Melrose Music Co., Chicago, in the neighborhood of 30 num-
> bers. Several were considered very big hits. My name appears on
> compositions, contracts on royalty basis. I have been unable to
> collect royalties on any of these tunes since 1929. . . . I wrote Mr.
> Melrose some time ago. His respond [sic] was not satisfactory
> with an understanding that I would not get no money. These
> tunes may be traced through the copyright dept. Library of Con-
> gress. . . . I am here financially unable to go to the scene to try &
> protect my interest which would mean much to my dependants
> and myself. I would like to know what would become of my

rightful property. That is why it take the courage to write to you, realizing this is not in your department & not able to find any laws that able to protect me. Due to financial conditions, which have been tremendously embarrassing, if action isn't taken imedi- ately [*sic*], I fear it will be of no use.

Three days later, Chief Justice Hughes's secretary posted a re- sponse: "Your letter of May 13ᵗʰ addressed to Chief Justice Hughes has been received. He is not at liberty to advise you, as he can deal only with cases which are brought before the Supreme Court in accor- dance with the statutes and rules." The letter was addressed to Mr. Fred Morton.

Nevertheless, fired up by the injustices his own words recalled, Morton went on a tear, writing to the White House, in care of James Roosevelt—FDR's son and secretary to the president—about his downfall and suggested a WPA-style plan to put bands and bandlead- ers to work across Depression-era America. Evidently impressed by Morton's words, James Roosevelt personally wrote right back to Morton, thanking him for the letter and referring Morton's suggestion to the Secretary of Labor. "No doubt you will hear from her in the near future," wrote Roosevelt.

Morton seemed to be making headway, or at least getting the at- tention of important people, so he pressed on, next taking a swing at Walter Melrose himself: "I am writing to you to notify you that my royalties is far over due," Morton concisely said in a letter Carew typed on May 14, but Melrose did not answer. This was galling, for Morton knew that Melrose had received the letter, since he had sent it registered mail, the receipt showing that Melrose had signed for the letter on May 18.

While Morton waged his letter-writing campaign, the dispatch that Carew had sent to *Down Beat* and the *Baltimore Afro-American* jolted the world of jazz, reminding everyone that Jelly Roll Morton— once rich, famous, and revered—had not been silenced. On the front of its August 1938 issue, *Down Beat* blared an extraordinary cover line: "W. C. Handy Is a Liar! Says Jelly Roll." Inside, the headline

riffed on the theme: "I Created Jazz in 1902, Not W. C. Handy, De-
clares Jelly Roll Morton—Whiteman Claimed to be King of Jazz with
no Knowledge of it." The letter, typewritten by Carew in Morton's
voice, seethed with the composer's claims and accusations, proclaimed
Morton's hard-won innovations, and reminded readers across the
country that it was Morton who had cracked the code that made it
possible for him (and thereafter everyone else) to write jazz chords,
rhythms, and melodies on paper. How could anyone compare
Handy's work with his?

"Mr. Handy cannot prove anything is music that he has created,"
Carew wrote, fusing his words with Morton's to produce a text almost as hot as the music that had once made Morton famous. To underscore Morton's importance, the letter pointed out that there would
be no Walter Melrose without Jelly Roll Morton, for it was Morton
who had advised Melrose to put out band versions of Handy tunes
such as "St. Louis Blues" and "Beale Street Blues." "I was the brains
of the business," wrote Carew-Morton. "All this was new to Melrose.
He was told to talk to me. I selected the *St. Louis Blues* and *Beale St.
Blues*, but the only way he [Melrose] accepted them was that my
arrangement would be used."

Down Beat excerpted this letter (and rewrote parts of it) in not
one but two issues, the sensational treatment drawing an equally incendiary response from Handy, whose own letter, published in *Down
Beat* in September, fueled the contretemps, making Jelly Roll Morton
the talk of the jazz world once more. "'I Would Not Play Jazz if I
Could,' Writes Father of The Blues," *Down Beat* screamed in its headline, adding: "W. C. Handy Says Jelly Roll's Attack is the 'Act of a
Crazy Man.'" "Jelly Roll Morton says I cannot play 'Jazz,'" wrote
Handy.

> I am 65 years old and would not play it if I could, but I . . . had
> vision enough to copyright and publish all the music I wrote so I
> don't have to go around saying I made up this piece and that
> piece in such and such a year like Jelly Roll and then say some-
> body swiped it. . . . If I didn't know him I would think he is crazy

and it is the act of a crazy man to attack such fine men who have done outstanding work like Paul Whiteman, Duke Ellington.

Handy articulated in print what everyone else in the music business had been saying behind Morton's back, that he was crazy, jealous, and lying about his achievements. Though Morton classics such as "King Porter Stomp" and "New Orleans Blues" had been famous long before anyone had heard of Handy, Morton had become a joke in the music business, so Handy glibly defended his reputation by mocking Morton's. Certainly Handy dared not question the truthfulness of Morton's claims. Instead, he simply made sport of Morton, the biggest, easiest, most tragicomic sitting target in all of jazz.

Yet years later, Handy practically conceded the central point that Carew and Morton had been making. Though Handy's "Memphis Blues" in 1912 became the first published blues, the essence of this simple piece and hundreds like it was in the air and in the ancient roots of black culture. Handy conceded in his memoirs, years after Morton's death:

> The twelve-bar, three-line form of the first and last strains, with its three-chord basic harmonic structure (tonic, subdominant, dominant seventh) was already used by Negro roustabouts, honky-tonk piano players, wanderers and others of their underprivileged but undaunted class from Missouri to the Gulf, and had become a common medium through which any such individual might express his personal feelings in a sort of musical soliloquy. My part in their history was to introduce this, the "blues" form to the general public, as the medium for my own feelings and my own musical ideas.

Handy, formally educated and unacquainted with the insides of the brothels and saloons and honky-tonks where Morton had learned his art, in effect acknowledged that he essentially had popularized a blues genre "already used by Negro roustabouts," writing down its three basic chords and copyrighting them. And though Handy didn't say so, the "Negro roustabouts" for whom he held such obvious contempt included whorehouse piano players like Morton himself. Morton did not have a fraction of Handy's formal training in music, yet Morton took the larger leap, proving that entire jazz compositions—with their themes and counterthemes and solo breaks and ensemble riffs and clear thematic development—could be notated on paper in copious detail, so that others could re-create the music precisely as the composer had envisioned it. While Handy was copyrighting his three blues chords, Morton was inventing a universe of harmony, melody, rhythm, and ornament.

The verbal brawl over the authorship of jazz and blues, however, was intensifying, for Walter Melrose—the same publisher who hadn't paid Morton royalties for nine years and had ignored his most recent plea for payments past due—now weighed in, on Handy's behalf! In a follow-up letter published in *Down Beat,* Melrose wrote:

Dear Mr. Handy,
Replying to your letter of recent date relative to an article published by the [*Baltimore*] *Afro-American* in which Jelly Roll Morton was credited with making certain claims in connection with your composition St. Louis Blues, I wish to say that I was indeed surprised at facts thereto. In the first place Morton had nothing to do with my firm taking over your compositions for orchestra and band. They were accepted by me strictly on their merits and reputation. . . . It is hard for me to understand why he has made such a claim.
Sincerely yours,
Walter Melrose.

This marked the first time that Morton had heard from Walter Melrose in nearly a decade, yet the man who had withheld Morton's royalties and had refused to communicate with him now was asserting that Morton had had no hand in picking tunes Melrose did not publish until after Morton's arrival in Chicago. Perhaps Melrose had forgotten that in 1923 he had bragged in the *Phonograph and Talking Machine Weekly* that the great Jelly Roll Morton "Joins Writing Staff of Melrose Bros." Perhaps Melrose no longer remembered that the Melrose operation had been in the red until Morton showed up, that Morton had given the firm its first run of hits and its lustrous arrangements, that Morton had written orchestrations for others to copy, that Morton had led rehearsals in the shop, helped composers finish their tunes, and attracted to the store everyone from the rising Louis Armstrong to the teenage Benny Goodman.

Apparently, in the years when Melrose had cut off Morton's money and refused to answer his letters, the publisher had decided that he had done it all himself, a notion that also came upon his then-estranged brother Lester, who later declared, "Old Jelly was a good orchestra man, but he couldn't write music; we had to have an arranger take down his stuff."

Now at least it was clear exactly where everyone stood. Walter Melrose—whose business had been built on Morton's genius—was dismissing the composer's role in the publishing firm's success, wiping away Morton's history as Melrose's first great artist. Carew and Morton, meanwhile, were launching a battle to give the first jazz composer his due. And *Down Beat* was selling copies by stirring up passions in the feud among these figures and others.

As the contretemps brewed, Morton kept a rigorous pace for himself, working virtually around the clock and earning almost nothing for it. Carew said:

> During the spring and summer of 1938 Jelly was often at the Library of Congress, patiently recording many historic examples of ragtime and early jazz, and giving historical comment on the changes and progress of popular music in New Orleans, sacrificing a considerable amount of time during the day which normally he would have spent in rest. Also, he often stayed at the Music Box after hours to entertain a group of friends and acquaintances who had a fondness for his unique playing and singing—a bit of

old New Orleans brought across the years, into the nation's capital. This also took time from his rest, which he could ill afford to
lose, although he was doubtless pleased to do it.

Still determined to reclaim his name, Morton persuaded a two-bit
local label, Jazz Man, to record his piano solos on "Winin' Boy"
(with vocal), "Creepy Feeling," "Honky Tonk Music," and his newest
tour de force, "Finger Breaker" (mistakenly called "Finger Buster" on
the recording), a piece so fast and furious it could give up-and-comers
such as Teddy Wilson and Art Tatum something to sweat over. Or at
least that was the plan. With "Finger Breaker," Morton created a solo
piano piece that nobody could say was as old as Storyville itself, its
fast-flying notes in the right hand and perpetually bouncing left dazzling the few friends who visited him at the Jungle Inn.

"I made a good recording today, it's a great number, do you want
to hear it?" Morton asked Carew, who was startled that Morton still
could attain such virtuosity, despite his travails.

"He went into it and really made the instrument talk," said
Carew. But "Finger Breaker" and the other Jazz Man records went
nowhere, while a clarinet-piano duo Morton planned never got
started because the clarinetist didn't show up. So Morton persuaded
a few young musicians to join him in some ensemble recordings,
only to discover that the only tune they could play was "Dinah," of
all things. "Why shouldn't they play that all right?" Morton rhetori-
cally asked Carew. "They've been playing it ever since they were
babies."

Meanwhile, rejection notices were pouring in from a long list of
presenters, to whom Morton had written looking for work. "Dear
Mr. Martan," began a form letter from the Vic Schroeder Agency in
Omaha, Nebraska, of all places, which noted that it already represented a great band—the Lawrence Welk Orchestra. The Turnpike
Casino in Lincoln, Nebraska, told Morton to forget it, while Freder-
ick Bros. Music Corp of Cleveland wrote, "We are not intent on
adding any bands to our organization." Even Gennett, the minuscule
label in Richmond, Indiana, that was one of the first to record Mor-

ton, in 1923, when he was still on his way up, wasted few words: "We doubt, therefore, if your plan would be of interest to us."

The relentlessness of the rebuffs and the day-and-night schedule were wearing Morton down, and Carew could see it in the composer's gait and in his eyes. "Had Jelly been younger, these activities might have built him good will for the future," Carew recalled, "but at 53 they took a toll from his health, and he gained little."

Carew, however, had another idea: If Morton were to create updated jazz arrangements of Scott Joplin's classic rags, tunes such as "The Entertainer" and "Maple Leaf Rag" might conquer new audiences while bringing Morton some quick cash. Testing his theory, Carew brought a few of Joplin's scores to the Music Box, where Morton quickly read through them, agreeing that the pieces could be modernized. But then Morton began noodling something else on the piano, a plaintive theme that Carew found unusually effective.

"That's a good tune," Carew told Morton. "What is it?"

The composer explained that he had written it for the clarinet player who had never shown up at the recording studio; Morton had decided to call it "Why." Though it had no lyrics, its title succinctly summed up the question that haunted Morton at this low point of his life. When Carew suggested that Morton add lyrics, the composer nominated Carew for the job.

Though Carew's lyrics proved little better than those Walter Melrose had grafted onto Morton's music more than two decades earlier, at least Carew did his work out in the open, for Morton to see and hear. The two fast friends cobbled together four songs, each marked by a poignant melody and a lumbering lyric and each signed by Jelly Roll Morton and Ed Werac—the latter being Carew's name spelled backward (possibly because Carew did not believe his bosses at the IRS would approve of such a side venture). Together, they prepared to publish "Why," "If You Knew," "Sweet Substitute," and "My Home Is in a Southern Town," all (with the exception of the blues "Sweet Substitute") conceived roughly in the popular manner of the day, with a fairly simple, easily remembered melody taking the place of the sophisticated ensemble pieces that were Morton's forte. These may not have been the finest pieces Morton ever wrote, but he hoped they might be memorable enough to readmit him to a music world that apparently no longer had much interest in the intricacies of vintage New Orleans–Chicago jazz.

With four finished tunes to their credit, the two men sat in this gloomy, nearly empty nightclub and in a burst of optimism and self-delusion decided to create their own publishing house, christening it Tempo-Music Publishing Company, anointing Morton composer, Carew office manager and would-be lyricist. They ran the meager operation out of the decrepit club and Carew's home, Tempo's modest means epitomized by the crude pencil drawings that Carew created for the sheet music covers, which might have been amusing if Morton's situation were not so grim. Yet Tempo-Music at least gave Morton something to hang his hopes on. Encouraged by the new possibilities, he briefly went to New York in September to price the printing of sheet music and to arrange with his old friend Clarence Williams, who now had a publishing business at 145 West Forty-fifth Street, to use Williams's office as a New York mail drop for Tempo-Music. Friendship only went so far, however, with Williams agreeing to the arrangement only if he received 25 percent of Tempo's New York profits, a steep price but one that Morton and Carew had to accept.

"I don't believe I ever had more good opportunities than I have now," Morton told Carew, "or less money to spend on them."

Mabel, alone and worried in Harlem, no longer could bear to have her husband languishing in Washington, his increasingly desperate letters persuading her that she needed to travel to the Music Box to save him. He would die in this place if he didn't get out, she said, and she almost was right. On a bloody evening at the club in the fall of 1938, Morton chided a loudmouthed customer who had had a few too many. The men exchanged words; Morton slapped the customer, sat down at the piano to cool off, and a few moments later felt a sharp blade slice into his back. As blood oozed out of him, he rose up and took the punk down.

"I was back of the bar mixing a Pink Lady when I heard the scuffle," recalled Mabel.

> When I come out from behind the bar I couldn't hardly tell which was which, they were so covered with blood. The blood was just gushing out of Ferd like out of a stuck beef. I took a heavy glass ashtray and I struck this young man just as hard as I could in the head. Then we pulled Ferd away—Ferd was on top by then—and Ferd grabbed an iron pipe and was going to kill him, but Cordelia grabbed Ferd and the fellow got away.

The cops took Morton to the hospital, where he got patched up, but by the time he was ready to return to work, Cordelia said business was so bad there was no point in his returning. Anyway, with Mabel back in the picture, Cordelia gave up hopes of keeping Morton for herself. So the composer found a gig playing at Thirteenth and H Streets in a second-floor bar owned by Nattie Brown, a retired boxer. This was a cruel irony, since Morton had come to Washington three years earlier presuming that it was the boxers who would work for him. Regardless, no one showed up to see Jelly Roll Morton at Nattie Brown's place, so Brown fired Morton after a week.

Finally, he had reached the end in Washington. Mabel still pleaded with him to come home with her to New York, and at last he agreed that there was nothing else to do. So he met with Carew to finalize their business plans: Morton would start up a band in New York to play the new pieces he was writing, while Carew would represent Tempo-Music in Washington by filing and guarding copyrights. It wasn't much to go on, but with a smart IRS man like Carew working on his behalf, Morton might have a chance. Certainly he believed he did.

Shortly before he and Mabel packed up, on Christmas Day, 1938, a young jazz record collector named William Russell visited him at the club and asked Morton his plans.

"Tell them to move over," said Morton. "The king is coming back."

seven

LAUGHINGSTOCK

*T*emperatures hovered around freezing on Christmas Day, 1938, when Jelly Roll Morton and Mabel climbed into their car, a new Cadillac sedan. Even if Morton's rusting Packard could have withstood the drive north, which he doubted, there was no way he was going to reenter Manhattan steering anything less than the best, which was why he had picked up the Caddy at Eichberg-Auction-Sales, trading in the Packard as a down payment.

On Christmas morning, he slid behind the wheel, Mabel slipped into the roomy passenger seat, and they headed to New York, skidding along an icy and deserted two-lane road. The slow and treacherous journey ended before nightfall, and though he was bone tired as he rolled into Manhattan, Morton stopped into the first Western Union office he saw and, at 4:09 P.M., sent a cable to the last man who believed in his worth as a musician, Roy Carew, back in D.C.

"ARRIVED SAFE TOUGH DRIVE ON ICE GOOD POSSIBILITIES MERRY XMAS—JELLY ROLL MORTON," read the dispatch. Within hours, temperatures in New York dipped below freezing and icy winds began blowing in from the northwest. Still weak from the nightclub stabbing he had suffered a few weeks earlier, Morton felt these chill gusts cut through an overcoat he considered too thin for New York, but it would have to do.

When Carew received the telegram, sometime after 5 P.M. on Christmas Day, he was surprised to detect a streak of optimism in Morton's words, so he celebrated the holidays with a bit of hope. Maybe Morton was right, maybe he did have a shot at New York City this time. Buoyed by these thoughts, on December 28 Carew sat down at his typewriter—the same one on which he had pecked the Ripley letter that briefly had catapulted Morton back into the spotlight—and cheered him on:

> I received your telegram and was pleased to learn that you arrived in New York all right. I was pretty sure that there might be ice and difficult driving, and am glad that you got through all right. From the newspaper accounts there has been some real winter weather up that way. I hope that those "Good Possibilities" you mentioned pan out all right, and I know that if anyone can make them pan out you are the one. I have no doubts along that line. Let me know what turns up.

So Morton set to work, renting a tiny office on the fourth floor of 145 West Forty-fifth Street (the same address Tempo-Music had been using as a mail drop), in the heart of the Broadway theater district. As 1939 dawned, he began prowling the frozen streets of Manhattan, visiting publishers, booking agencies, managers, union headquarters—anyplace he could think of to jump-start a career that had been mired in a Washington dive for more than three years, an eternity in the music business. He had to let New York know that he was back and decided that the best way was to round up a crack band and let it rip with the music he knew he still had in him. If he were leading a plush swing ensemble playing his best new tunes, he could take on the likes of Benny Goodman and Artie Shaw, who were becoming crossover movie stars playing a music that Morton first had taught the world how to put on paper.

But it wasn't easy persuading musicians to rehearse for nothing—no money, no jobs, no prospects—simply because Jelly Roll Morton wanted them to. A few, such as the tenor saxophonist Happy Caldwell, whom Morton knew from back in Chicago, were willing to go along with him, up to a point. But as soon as a paying job came along, they vanished, most never to return.

"Things were really tough about that time," said New Orleans guitarist-pianist Frank Amacker, who, like Morton, had studied piano back home with Professor Nickerson.

> He was having a hard time—a great man like that—trying to get a break. . . . Half the time the guys didn't come to rehearsal, oh, maybe one or two, and we couldn't do much with one or two. But he would try to run over the manuscripts he had. . . . There were some beautiful numbers. "Sweet Substitute" was one we rehearsed at that time. And we really had a good time when he rehearsed with the full band. It wasn't a *big* band, but a jazz band like he had in Chicago, that type of sound—one trumpet, one clarinet, one trombone. He was sure he could get a job and keep the guys together, but they'd drift off.

When Morton wasn't rehearsing this shell of a band, he was working his way through the office towers of Manhattan's entertainment industry, yet he now lacked the energy, the physical strength, and even the wind that he had once had in abundance. He could not climb a flight of stairs without losing his breath, and occasionally he felt as if a knife were digging into his chest, doubling him over in pain for a few seconds or more.

As if this misery weren't bad enough, now Ralph Peer's Southern Music Co., which had lured Morton away from Melrose almost a decade ago, wasn't responding to his requests for royalty payments either. The only money trickling in arrived in the form of cashier's checks from Carew—ten dollars here, twelve dollars there—which kept food on the table and paid the two dollars for renting a rehearsal room for Morton's would-be band. When the first payment on the Caddy came due, late in January, Morton had no choice but to ask Carew to pick it up. He did.

Amid this gloom, however, Morton somehow saw hope where anyone less messianic would have found despair. Though utterly lacking in funds, a band, or possibilities, he wrote to Carew on January 18, "I am sure that we will have a better band than Basie," perhaps even believing it. Yet there still was no money from Melrose, whom Morton had been hounding to return his old scores, and to provide an accounting of sales of records and licensing of his tunes—and to cough up the cash due. "I wrote Melrose Co & asked them for my statement with the music [scores]," he wrote to Carew. "I got the music but not statement. Maybe he will send it soon."

That he did, though not precisely as Morton intended, for in February the check that Melrose had been denying Morton for fully a decade finally arrived. When Morton saw the envelope—which Carew had received in Washington and forwarded to New York—he almost wept. Though he could not fathom why Melrose had waited so long to make good on his debt, he was not going to question his good fortune.

So he tore open the envelope from Melrose Brothers Music Co., pulled out the check, stared at its numbers in near disbelief, and felt as if the wind had been knocked out of him once more. For Walter Melrose was squaring his debt to Jelly Roll Morton for precisely $86.94, a sum that supposedly covered the composer's cut of some of the biggest and most enduring hits of the Jazz Age.

This was more than even Morton, an unflagging optimist, could bear.

"I received the check from Melrose," he wrote to Carew on February 7. "The check was [not] near what it should have been. . . . He had the nerve to send me a check in D.C., the one you seen, for $87 for nearly 10 years & lot of those numbers were good sellers, when I wasn't getting a penny on them. King Porter, Wolverine & a few others have never stopped going over."

Carew was beside himself, the soft-spoken tax man seething over this latest injustice.

"The statement covered 5 years and 3 months (Feb. 1, 1933 to April 30, 1938) and amounted to $86.94 on 20 numbers—an average of less than 83c per tune per year," he later wrote to a friend. "Think that over. . . . That subject makes my blood boil."

Morton didn't know it yet, but the only reason Melrose even bothered sending Morton this pittance was because the publisher was cashing out of the business, selling his firm to Edwin H. Morris & Company, Inc., of New York, and therefore closing out the books once and for all. The Depression had made the sheet music business decidedly less appealing than it had been in the Roaring Twenties, when a hit tune could sell a million copies or more. Now, the action was in radio and recordings, but the big labels in New York—such as RCA Victor and Columbia—weren't letting pipsqueaks like Walter Melrose dictate the contracts anymore. So Melrose, who had developed a distaste for black music and musicians and had switched to publishing four-square college songs such as "Sweetheart of Sigma Chi" and "Ramblin' Wreck from Georgia Tech," was getting out of the business altogether, kissing off Morton for a lousy $86.94.

"So the money wasn't very hot," Morton wrote to Carew, with remarkable restraint. "Of course, it all helps until I can go to work. Rehearsing there are lots of incidentals. I had to get a pair of shoes, my feet was simply on the ground. Paid rent, got my tuxedo out of pawn."

Morton's world was closing in on him. Most days, he felt as if he were choking, his body aching, his stomach churning, a heavy weight pressing on his chest. When MCA promised him an audition, he briefly believed things might be looking up, if only because MCA—now one of the biggest booking agencies in the country—was sure to recognize his stature. This was the same firm, after all, that had promoted Morton and his Red Hot Peppers as its first black jazz band in the 1920s. But this time, MCA was trifling with him. On March 16, MCA boss Bill Stein blew Morton off in a terse telegram—"LEAVING TOWN REGRET UNABLE TAKE CARE

OF AUDITION FOR ABOUT TEN DAYS"—never to contact his former star again.

Each setback took its toll, but as Morton's body gave out, medical attention proved a luxury well beyond his means. "I did not have a doctor & really could not afford one, & I was unable to get about on my own power, so therefore I did not get to a hospital," he wrote to Carew, on March 23. Yet as Morton's health declined, *Down Beat* magazine—one of Morton's last and only allies in the music business—was beating the drum for him, proclaiming in its March issue, "Jelly Roll Morton has left for New York, where he plans to form a new band and crash the big time again." If the editors at *Down Beat*, back in Chicago, understood how far from the big-time Morton had fallen, they might not have published such a statement.

With nowhere else to turn, Morton imagined that perhaps he could get a cut of the money ASCAP was taking in on his tunes, so he began filling out forms and sending in scores proving that he was a bona fide songwriter, a prerequisite for joining the organization. The application process took weeks to complete, and the waiting period dragged on for months. Meanwhile, there was at least some comfort in knowing that John Hammond—the self-styled talent scout who was pushing Benny Goodman at the moment—had agreed to audition Morton's fragment of a band. But when the big date arrived, it was all the ailing composer could do to drag himself to the theater. "I got out of the sick bed to make the audition," he explained to Carew on April 9, "& had to go right back to bed [afterward]."

The lack of cash, the feverish auditions, the avalanche of paperwork to ASCAP all amounted to more than a sick man could bear. Morton's heart pounded so hard and fast against his chest that in mid-April Mabel finally rushed him to Presbyterian Hospital at 622 West 168th Street, then begged Carew to help them pay the hospital bill. Mabel wrote to Carew on April 20:

Jelly has been very sick for two weeks but he wouldn't give up. The day Mr. Hammond heard the band he was having heart attack. . . . So the landlord said to take him to medical center at once[.] He gave me his address so I could get Jelly in hospital[.] They don't take you in medical center if you lived in Harlem[.] So gave my address 4520 Broadway [and] 190 St. Washington Heights—if Jelly would have stay five minutes longer he would have died. I thank God and this Gentelman. . . . When your not a payer or anything you have to do the best you can. . . .

    Sincerely, Mrs. Mabel Morton.

Carew was shocked by Morton's precipitous decline and soon boarded a train to New York. If Carew's visit palpably lifted Morton's spirits, the doctors' methods did nothing significant to restore Morton's health. After tormenting the composer with a painful spinal tap, the physicians recommended the one remedy Morton least could afford: rest. So when the hospital released Morton, at 1 P.M. on May 7, the composer felt little better than when he had arrived. Leaning on Mabel, Morton slowly ascended the two flights of stairs to the room they shared, Number 3-A, on the right side of the stairwell, at 207 West 131st Street, then passed out when he got inside. By the next day, he realized he no longer had the strength to climb the sixty-seven steps to his fourth-floor office on West Forty-fifth Street and gave it up, his chest pains and pervasive exhaustion later being diagnosed as congestive heart failure. From now on, he holed up in the Harlem walk-up, in a building owned by Mamie Wright, an old New Orleans pol from the District, who now was letting rooms in Harlem for ten a week. From here, Morton heroically waged a one-man campaign to get back his money, his credit, his career, and his name.

Since Carew no longer was within earshot, he poured out his troubles to musicians who lived in the same building, such as trombonist Wilber de Paris. "Practically every night we'd sit out on that stoop and talk," recalled De Paris. "Sometimes he'd mention some of the bad breaks that he got, and of course he'd blame a lot of them on musicians that didn't show up or couldn't play when they did show up."

The desperation of Morton's situation was not lost on him, particularly when he thought of all the men who were getting rich off his art.

"One of the things I would of like to had you do before you left N.Y. was to visit some of those music publishers, so you could of seen what gorgeous palaces some of them have," he wrote to Carew on May 9, "& many has been in business a very short while." Morton, on the other hand, had been working every facet of the trade since the dawn of jazz itself and didn't have a spare dime to spend on his failing health.

"I find myself very weak in my lower extremities," he wrote Carew on May 10. "I tried to walk a little bit, I walked a couple of short blocks & was tired. Of course I have to climb two flights of stairs. I find that my worst task. I surely need a rest as the Doctors stated & to take it easy. Well, one must make the best of things. I made an endeavor to the park but could not make it to-day."

When Morton regained a bit of his old strength in the middle of May, he commenced writing a swing number he dubbed "Good Old New York," though he acknowledged to Carew that his band, which he had hoped would play it, "is just about broken up." Worse, after a follow-up visit to the hospital, the doctors gave Morton a depressing diagnosis.

"I was examined again & finally was told what my main troubles were," Morton wrote on May 30. "I have hardening of the arteries of the heart & was told that it was incurable, but if I did not exert myself, I would be able to do alright. I was very sad over the report at first but after a second thought, I had a different decision. I was not expecting to live when I went there, & I am at least living yet." That was about the best that Morton could say about his status, that at least he still was breathing, though not much more.

Desolate at his friend's plight, Carew practically had run out of words of encouragement and knew too little about the music business to propose a practical solution for Morton's dilemma in New York. Yet Carew realized that he had to come up with something for Morton to hang onto, some goal or scheme, however improbable, that might at least keep the composer from giving up entirely. And the best that Carew could do, knowing it wasn't much, was to remind Morton that the World's Fair was going to be held in New York City in the summer, and that the Negro Elks were going to convene in Harlem by the thousands for their fortieth-anniversary national convention. Organized decades earlier as a counterpart to the larger Elks organization, the Negro Elks—formally known as the Improved Benevolent Protective Order of Elks—had been familiar to Carew since that hot day in 1904 when he had seen them march in the black Labor Day parade. If Morton could orchestrate a march that he once had played for Carew and rename it for the Elks, perhaps Tempo-Music could print up some copies and peddle bales of them.

Like a drowning man groping for something to grasp, Morton seized the idea. Though he knew full well that the sheet music business was over, that the only real money being made these days in music was in records and on radio, he had absolutely nothing else with which to delude himself.

"That idea is great," he wrote to Carew on May 30, even as his situation worsened. Just a few days later, in fact, he lamented to Carew, "I had clothes in pawn that was past due. Some was sold & I managed to save some." Nevertheless, the prospect of trying to reclaim a touch of triumph with a big-band version of "We Are Elks" mysteriously restored some of the old vigor to Morton's step. Somehow convincing himself that deliverance was at hand, he immediately set about printing up new stationery and emblazoning it with the words by which he defined himself. "JELLY ROLL MORTON'S ORCHESTRA" streamed across the top of the page, and in smaller type Morton proclaimed himself "Originator of JAZZ—STOMP—SWING" and "VICTOR ARTIST," though Victor hadn't given Morton a second thought for nearly a decade. Then, in case anyone still hadn't gotten the message, Morton completed the engraved letterhead with one more proclamation: "World's Greatest Hot Tune Writer."

Bolstered by a pile of his fancy stationery, a half-baked plan to score a sheet music hit, and several good new tunes still playing in his head, Morton willed himself into decent health, or at least into a passable approximation of it. He started going out to the clubs again, hoping to get one of the better bands to give the completed "Good Old New York" a run-through. But even the fledgling trumpeter-bandleader Harry James, who recently had left Benny Goodman's big band to start his own, wouldn't give Morton the time of day, so the composer had to settle for Hot Lips Page, whose seven-piece outfit could not do justice to the large-scale orchestration. As soon as Page and friends began sight-reading the score, Morton realized it was beyond them. "The men must be of the very best calibre to be successful" playing his music, Morton wrote Carew on July 10. "But it is so hard to get men that's qualified to play."

Even so, Morton drew solace from knowing that he had completed his orchestration of "We Are Elks," which he now regarded as his ticket back into the music business and an opportunity not to be wasted. "We haven't much time to lose, the time is flying," he wrote to Carew on July 10. "I almost feel sure they will be playing it in the Elks parade. The idea is to sell it at the convention. I think it will pay for itself immediately. I intend to be active as possible to make the number go. The idea is to sell to anyone that want[s] to buy to it [to] re-sell. . . . My idea of the cover is the Elks colors and big Elk head (prominent)."

With these words, Morton threw himself wholly into making "We Are Elks" a hit, obtaining price quotes from various printers, putting the finishing touches on the music ("I think the piano score on 'Elk' is perfect," he wrote Carew), and dreaming of the money that would start flooding in once the Negro Elks convention began in mid-August. He pawned more clothes to pay for printing the music, investing in a staggering thirty-two hundred copies of a tune no one had heard of. At the same time, he checked his mailbox daily, eager to learn the fate of his application to ASCAP, though no information was forthcoming. "I don't understand ASCAP," he wrote Carew on July 27. "All the summer without having a meeting to enroll new members, after waiting nearly 6 months for their approval," added Morton, suspecting something must be afoul. "The government should look in to this matter with a sharp eye."

Disgusted by the long wait, Morton dropped in on the ASCAP offices, only to be told there was nothing more he could do now. "I guess they intend to make slaves out of the people in the music world," he bristled to Carew on August 1. "It's strictly peonage. The government will get a hold of those babies soon, & they will change the whole situation. . . . I cannot get money on my own tunes that are earning money for the publishers and I understand they can keep anyone out that isn't in already if they want, according to their by-laws. They are outright crooked."

The injustice of the ASCAP stranglehold ate at Morton, who could not let go of the subject. "ASCAP tightens everything so that no one can move without seeing them first," he reiterated to Carew on August 4. "They have an outright monopoly and the government does nothing about it. . . . They are all on the collecting end and none on the protecting end."

But at least he had his ace in the hole, "We Are Elks." By the middle of August, as the convention was preparing to invade the city, Morton persuaded a representative of the Elks to give him a concessions booth at the convention headquarters—inside the 369th Regiment Armory, at Fifth Avenue and 143rd Street—so that he could sell his music. Unfortunately, the old chest pains and weakness in his legs were returning:

> I had a check up at the hospital last Monday [Aug.] 14th & another one to-day Aug. 21st. The doctor advised me to take it easy as possible & advised a rest & told me it would be about a year before I would be good and strong, by doing as he advised. I asked him for a diet. He said it was not necessary[,] just guide myself along. . . . Well, it is rather hard to get around on account of me getting so very weak, but I must do the best I can, to try to get the number started, & you cannot place any dependance in anyone around this entire eastern portion of the country, they seem to be all out to do you [in] if they can.

At last, on August 21, the Negro Elks, as they informally called themselves, began arriving in Harlem, and Morton was ready for them. He proudly stationed himself at his concessions booth at Elks headquarters and positioned Mabel just outside, so that they couldn't miss the throngs. But with the temperature hitting ninety-one degrees that scorching afternoon, hardly anyone seemed interested in getting near the headquarters.

"I am hoping & trying to do something in this convention with 'Elks,' and I do trust something good will come out of it," he told Carew. "This is their first day to-day, they don't seem to be a lot of money spent anywhere. I have taken good observation of things, but to-morrow is the parade & things may be different. There wasn't anyone at their headquarters today[,] it was blistering may be the reason. Things dont seem to have gotten underway as yet."

The next day, August 22, roughly 20,000 Negro Elks swarmed into the streets of Harlem, more than half participating in a massive parade. A crowd estimated at 250,000 to 400,000, "packed six deep along the streets and perched on rooftops and in windows . . . cheered the beturbaned Elks as they strutted, resplendent in white flannel, purple and yellow uniforms," reported the *New York Times*. The seventy-five bands and drum and bugle corps commenced the festivities at Bradhurst Avenue and 145th Street, wending their way east to Lenox Avenue, south to 116th Street, east to Fifth Avenue, south to 110th Street, west to Seventh Avenue, north to 142nd Street, and east to Fifth Avenue again, making a great noise every step of the way. Despite all this activity—or perhaps because of it—no one came by Morton's concession stand to buy a copy of "We Are Elks." Once the last group of costumed Elks had strutted past the crowd, everyone fled the oppressive heat and humidity that had been trapped amid the skyscrapers of New York. "It was so hot you could not pull anyone on in there," Morton told Carew. "Every one was interested in the parade & was only buying ice cream, & some soda, & some sandwiches."

But Morton was not yet ready to give up on "We Are Elks." He found a group of Negro Elks cloistered at the Imperial Lodge, played the tune for them at the piano, and soon had everyone in the room singing and marching behind him in a pitiful re-creation of the second-line parades he had witnessed in his youth on the streets of New Orleans. Everyone loved the tune, loved Morton, loved the spectacle of it all. They applauded and called him back half a dozen times to take a bow and play another.

Yet they did not buy one copy of "We Are Elks."

The debacle forced Morton to pawn his watch and one of his few remaining suits to pay off the printer, and by Wednesday, the day after the parade, he knew that his latest scheme for economic survival had imploded.

"The streets seemed clear. The streets are never clear on 'ordinary days' here," he wrote Carew, dumbfounded to see Harlem all but empty in the very week he needed its boulevards teeming with prospective buyers. "They seemed [to] have vanished like thin air. That was all of the Elks one day, the day of the grand parade." Afterward, the Negro Elks flocked to the World's Fair and danced to the music of bands led by Harry James and Benny Goodman, who played tunes by Morton, as well as songs based on his ideas.

At the women's headquarters, Morton unloaded a dozen copies, leaving him with 3,188 unsold.

"I feel terrible about this disappointment[,]" wrote Morton, "but I guess no one can control fate."

New York had picked its king, and it wasn't Jelly Roll Morton. But back in Chicago, in the halcyon 1920s, Morton never would have guessed that the throne would go to the kid in short pants who had watched him rehearse in the Melrose shop, Benny Goodman.

Yet there was no point in denying it: Goodman had been crowned the King of Swing, his 1938 concert in Carnegie Hall already enshrined in legend, for it had brought the hot music of New Orleans and Chicago to white listeners, many presuming that Goodman had authored it. Most did not know that the arrangements came from the hand of the black bandleader Fletcher Henderson, nor that some of Henderson's biggest hits had originally sprung from Morton's imagination, reflecting the composer's hard early years in New Orleans and on the Gulf Coast during the first decade of the century. The music of

Morton's youth now belonged to someone else, and if he were going to have a chance to get his newer tunes heard, he had to hope that Goodman remembered who he was and might be willing to take a chance on an old jazz man from Chicago days. So early in September, Morton prepared for Goodman new, radiant arrangements of three pieces: "We Are Elks," "Good Old New York," and "Mr. Joe," the latter a sleek, remarkably modern reorchestration of a tune Morton had penned years earlier in homage to Joe "King" Oliver. If Goodman chose to record any or all of these, Morton might be able to let the world know that he hadn't disappeared into the New Orleans brothels from which he had come, that he still knew how to make musicians swing and audiences move.

Goodman wouldn't see Morton, so the composer left the scores with Goodman's manager, John Hammond, and hoped for the best. While awaiting a verdict from the King of Swing, Morton pressed on, recalling a tip he had received in Washington about a man who was opening a traditional jazz record shop and might be able to put together a recording session or two for Morton. Determined to get back in front of the microphones, Morton put on one of the best of his remaining suits and made his way to Stephen W. Smith's new HRS Record Store, on Seventh Avenue at Fifty-third Street.

"He was dressed well and was flashing a tasteful amount of expensive jewelry," remembered Smith. "He was rather thin but not tired looking. . . . I assumed his thinness was due to age rather than sickness. He was interested in making a recording session, as I was, so the wheeling and dealing started."

Surprised that the venerable Jelly Roll Morton had appeared in his obscure little shop, Smith welcomed the man like royalty, not only promising the recording sessions that Morton desired but delivering on them: Smith pitched Bluebird—a boutique division of RCA Victor—on the idea of an old-time New Orleans recording led by the grand old man himself. With Morton's name recently back in the news, thanks to the coverage in *Down Beat*, Bluebird gave Smith the OK.

Though Morton was ailing and broke, he wasn't going to let this opportunity slip through his fingers, so he told Smith to convene the best New Orleans men in New York, and Smith did his best, engaging Sidney Bechet and Albert Nicholas on reeds, Wellman Braud on bass, Zutty Singleton on drums, and Morton himself at the piano. With five of nine musicians from back home in Louisiana, the band just barely deserved the name Bluebird gave it, Jelly Roll Morton's New Orleans Jazzmen.

At about 1:30 P.M. on September 14, the musicians started to arrive at Victor Studio No. 3, at 155 East Twenty-fourth Street, between Lexington and Third Avenues, and no one could miss the deep lines that now marked Morton's face, nor the silver that was showing plainly at his temples. But they greeted him and each other warmly, meanwhile waiting anxiously to see if Bechet—alongside Morton the foremost soloist in the group—would make it in time from a gig he had been playing a couple hundred miles away.

Bechet appeared moments before the band was ready to start, yet there was one more delicate matter to resolve: Many in the studio believed that Bechet, the first great soprano saxophonist in jazz and an improviser on a par with Armstrong, didn't know how to read music and might have trouble finessing arrangements he hadn't yet heard. Producer Smith stood by petrified, not knowing whether to broach the subject with Bechet and risk humiliating him or to say nothing and allow a musical train wreck to ensue. But Morton himself resolved the situation, stepping up and placing his arm around Bechet, one of the few players in jazz Morton rightly considered his equal.

"Before Sidney could give more than a cursory glance at the parts on his stand," recalled Smith, "Jelly casually and gently walked him to the piano where with the remark, 'You remember this one, Sid,' he ran the numbers off on the keyboard under a steady stream of jive concerning everything except music." Morton, in other words, finessed the problem, discreetly showing Bechet the tunes on the piano without letting on that he was. Only a man who had endured his own share of humiliation would have concocted this ruse to spare the dignity of another old New Orleans musician.

With Bechet prepped for the day's recordings, Morton sat down at the piano and led the band in a run-through of "High Society," a vintage up-tempo New Orleans tune that enabled everyone to shake away any anxieties before the recording mikes were turned on. If it was old-time New Orleans that Bluebird wanted, that's what Morton was going to give them, even if he yearned to unveil some of the new pieces and sleek big-band arrangements he had been penning for Tempo-Music but still had not heard played by a fully staffed big band.

Smith and the suits from Victor—Artists-and-Repertory man Leonard Joy, John Reid, and his staff of engineers—fell into a hush as Morton began to work. The composer opened the recording session with "Didn't He Ramble," a timeless New Orleans funeral song that had saluted more spirits in the graveyard than any other. Morton himself had played this music as a kid, at the turn of the century, before he knew how to read a note, blowing the somber refrain of "Flee as a Bird to the Mountain" into a trombone as the procession wended its way to the cemetery. After the weeping and moaning was done, the New Orleans musicians always switched to the up-tempo strains of "Didn't He Ramble," leading the bereaved and the second-liners back to town for free food and drink, when Morton enjoyed some of the most copious meals of his misspent youth.

Now, standing in front of his men several decades later, Morton waved his arms, signaling the start of "Flee as a Bird to the Mountain," after which trumpeter Claude Jones stepped in front of the microphone and lamented, "Ashes to ashes, and dust to dust. If the women don't get you, the whiskey must." Then, with Morton egging the musicians on, everyone let loose with great cries of anguish and mourning, as if a funeral truly were taking place. When the chorus died down, Morton leaned in to the mike and cried, "Such a good man," his voice dripping with piety. In so doing, Morton recalled "those mean old hypocrites down in New Orleans, the low down folks who used to tag after a man's funeral and say nice things about him when they done all manner of slandering when he was alive."

Morton's re-creation of a New Orleans funeral on "Didn't He Ramble" proved so true to the spirit of a Crescent City funeral that the New Orleans men in the room marveled at what had just transpired.

After the microphones were turned off, Braud said, "1895—That's the way they used to play," realizing that for a few moments, a handful of musicians had transported themselves right back to the very origins of jazz, which they had witnessed. By evoking this pungent, blues-drenched musical language and pouring so much world-weary feeling into it, they had conjured up a sound that was rapidly disappearing in New York, as jazz ineluctably evolved into something newer, leaving behind its past—and those who still represented it.

After this extraordinary start, the band prepared to launch into "High Society," another well-worn item from an earlier age. "It wasn't a dance in New Orleans until they played 'High Society,'" Braud recalled. But Morton didn't like the first run-through, insisting that the musicians "get in on time with the last strain. Anybody can make a bad record," he reminded them. "But anybody can't make a good one. I don't want to make no bad record."

When it came time for Morton to sing and play "I Thought I Heard Buddy Bolden Say," he ran through several raunchy off-color verses to get warmed up, the bawdy lines drawing smiles from the New Orleans men, who recalled how salty the old songs used to be. As if to add color to a tune that already overflowed with it, Morton opened with a chord that carried more dissonance than Victor's representatives at the session were equipped to comprehend. "It's a discord, but it's *supposed* to be a discord," Morton explained to the execs, whose puzzled facial expressions said a lot. "That's an E-flat diminished seventh."

Then Morton slipped into the blues on "Winin' Boy," evoking his days as a young man exploring the Gulf Coast, when he had bragged about the "windin'" pelvic thrusts that had made his reputation long before his music had. This time around, though, Morton had to clean up the lyrics a bit, singing:

I'm the winin' boy,
Don't deny my name,
I'm the winin' boy,
I don't deny my name.

The voice was deeper and craggier than in Morton's youth, the tempo slow and mournful, the message poignant as Morton sang, "Don't deny my name."

When the session ended, the musicians put down their instruments and began talking among themselves, but Morton stayed at the piano, playing the new works he had been writing, hoping some of the boys from Victor might be interested in hearing music that wasn't thirty years old and perhaps might even consider recording it.

"Jelly played piano almost incessantly throughout the session, during breaks and between takes of the recorded numbers," recalled writer Fred Ramsey, who observed the proceedings. "He played long solos; some were the same pieces the band recorded, like 'Windin' Boy.' It may be that he was only trying to entertain everyone, but possibly the idea was partly to try to interest the Victor people, hoping that some of the executives would hear some of the solos and want to record them."

But there were no takers, the studio quickly emptying out, with Morton left alone at keyboard. By the time he got home, to Harlem, Morton was so exhausted that he had to spend several days in bed recovering. After nearly a week's pause, he gathered up the strength to write Carew about the desperate state of his finances and the injustices of the music racket. "ASCAP sure is giving me the run-around & keep[s] collecting money from my tunes, & I am unable to collect 1c," he wrote on September 19. "I think that is terrible. It almost make[s] one lose their head, when one knows much lesser important people are drawing money from their tunes. I don't know just what to do about it. I guess I will have to think [of] some way out."

It took two weeks for Morton to be well enough to complete the Bluebird sessions, but this time he lacked the strength he had had the first time around. Worse, the proceedings were turning ugly. A week after the first session, Victor had tried to strong-arm Morton into signing over the publisher's copyrights to the label, but Morton was hell-bent on preserving them for Tempo-Music, and he paid dearly for insisting.

"Just to-day the Victor sent me a paper to sign that would give them the rights to the tunes," Morton wrote to Carew on September 21.

> I would not sign it & in turn I gave them your address in Washington & told them the copyright was owned by Tempo. I was imediately demoted, & the drummer [Zutty Singleton] was made the contractor for the next engagement which is Thursday 28th next week. Of course I will have to do all the work & he will get the leadership fee & credit, but I am getting Ala[bama] Bound in, & the title must be changed to—Don't you leave me Here. So I guess its worth the demotion.

Yet RCA's brutal move soured Morton for the session of September 28, which started falling apart even before it began, since Bechet called to say he couldn't get into town on time. As a result, the balance of the band shifted, with the New Orleans players no longer dominating, and a rebellion ensued. After the band ran through "Climax Rag," de Paris said, "I just can't play that old stuff. I can't get into it at all. I really can't." And when "Don't You Leave Me Here" came around, with Morton savoring its bluesy lyric and tempo, one of the boys in the band moaned, "The tune's too slow." De Paris chimed in again: "Ain't no life in the tune." So the musicians kicked up the tempo, making a mockery of the piece and of Morton, who inevitably got swept up by the stampede and sang the tune at a clip that defied his every instinct.

Morton no more could understand the musicians' insurrection than they could understand the music he wanted them to play and the world from which it came. "The trumpet tried his best to ruin this batch," Morton later recalled, referring to de Paris. "He was just as hateful as could be. I still can't figure what was wrong with him."

Thanks to such antics, "the session seemed to be falling apart," observed Ramsey. "The men were simply running through the routine of one try after another without giving their best, and Jelly himself was not in his best form. Tired and ill as he was, he did not have the drive he displayed at the first session. Something wrong had happened," continued Ramsey, who did not know of Morton's battle with Victor over publishing copyrights, "and later there were recriminations, accusations. Perhaps it was the absence of Bechet or the lack of sufficient rehearsal before the date. Perhaps it was because the men simply couldn't relate to Jelly Roll. At times it almost seemed as if the men were trying to destroy Morton, simply by failing him."

Dispirited by the events of the afternoon, Morton simply returned to the piano, gathered clarinetist Nicholas and drummer Singleton around him, gave them some additional scores, and began playing precisely the relaxed, blues-tinged music he had hoped to produce at this session from the start. With the three men from New Orleans speaking a vanishing musical language they still shared, a new mood came over the room, which started filling up with listeners from elsewhere in the building. They had come to hear where that sublime music was coming from, and who was making it.

Harry Lim, a jazz promoter, wandered in, photographers began taking pictures, listeners began whispering to one another—something remarkable seemed to be happening. Realizing he finally had captured something worth preserving, Morton asked the Victor executives if they would like to record his trio music. They said no and left, and Morton and friends simply played on, this music lost for all time.

"You never really had the feeling that he was giving up," recalled Ramsey. "And I felt this in his playing that day at the Victor session. He started playing these long solos, and knowing that they were never going to be recorded, and well, it was sad, sad and tragic, and I had the feeling that this guy is going to be gone soon, and all that stuff we're going to lose."

In the days after the Victor sessions, Morton tried to rest and rebuild his strength, but the chilly, damp weather left him feeling cold all the time, unless he was under the covers of his bed. Still, there was work to be done, starting with the increasingly difficult task of getting Hammond and Benny Goodman to return the scores he had left with them for their perusal. If they weren't going to record his new music, the least they could do was return it, for Morton needed these scores if he was going to persuade anyone else to play them.

"Goodman is here, & I have been running my head off to catch him & also Hammond, & both seem to be very hard to catch," Morton wrote to Carew on October 10. "I have never been able to see Goodman at all. I do try every day—writing wont do. Hammond don't seem to answer my letters."

Worse, Morton's Cadillac was locked up in a garage across the street from the Rhythm Club, and he didn't have the forty-two dollars he needed to pay the storage fee and take it out. If he had the money, at least he could move around Manhattan without getting soaked every time it rained. "That is why I have made such a desperate attempt to get that car, so it would help preserve my health," Morton wrote Carew.

But when Morton finally got hold of the auto, he was dismayed to find that two of its tires were ruined. All he could do to replace them was to put a two-dollar deposit on three used tires at the Firestone shop at 187 West 101st Street, "to be called for not later than 15 days from the above date," according to the receipt. If he could get ten dollars by that time, the tires would be Morton's, free and clear. But the fact remained that the man who had once bragged to the boys outside the Rhythm Club that his car was so long "I have to go into Central Park to turn it around" in truth couldn't afford to purchase tires for it. Once he got the used Firestones, Morton hit on the idea of renting out the Caddy for funerals, a source of income more reliable than anything he was doing in music.

Too weak to work and too sick to go out in the rain, Morton was tumbling toward a dead end. If Melrose or Southern or ASCAP would pay him some of the money that his music was making for everyone else, he might be able to get going again, but nobody came through.

And all he could do about it was stand in front of the Rhythm Club and rail to anyone who would listen about how the music business had boxed him in.

"All you young studs, and you old ones, too, better learn these three rules," Morton said, as musicians gathered around to see what the old man was squawking about. "Write your music out. Send it to Washington to be copyrighted. And then hire a lawyer to see that you get a fair deal. I'm Jelly Roll Morton, and it's me telling you that none of those music publishers are worth the [gun]powder to blow them to hell," he said, waving his arms, pointing at one ignorant young musician or another.

> They make you promises—then they steal your stuff. You wind up begging them for a handout while they lollygag around in their big cars and yachts. Ya better wake up, ya stupid knuckle-heads. A Negro has to be 10 times as smart to get an even break in this business. Watch and see if some of those *peolas* [whites] don't come up with some so-called new kind of music. That's to get in the act. . . . I see more and more "Patties" hanging around Harlem. They bring their horns; line up at the bars with you, buy you a sandwich—and as soon as they get to know you, they say, "Let's go jam!" Go right ahead, you dumb SOBs. Go ahead and teach them your music so they can set up their phonograph machines, and then your children can someday read how you used to create and play music.

Most of the men just laughed, amused that a relic from New Orleans still had some fire, though precious little room to burn, at least so far as music was concerned. They taunted Morton, saying just the things that would goad him on, which they knew from having heard his grumblings a hundred times before.

"Those fellows around the corner would razz and kid him, and it would burn him up until he got red as a beet," said guitarist George Guesnon. "They called him old Mr. Has-been and such things."

Or they needled him about all the great piano players who now ruled Harlem, from the hypervirtuoso James P. Johnson to the fantastically entertaining Fats Waller to the ferociously hard-driving Willie "The Lion" Smith, who took part in the merriment. Eager to see if he could lure Morton to the piano, Smith on one afternoon arrived outside the Rhythm Club and proclaimed, "Gee whiz, my fingers are itchin,' just lead me to the piano. Lead me to a piano, my fingers are itchin,' I'm rearin' to go, I'm the Lion.'"

The other musicians on the corner told Morton he had just been disrespected. "Jelly, you hear this cat crackin' to you all about who he is, about leadin' him to a piano?"

But Morton wasn't going for the bait.

"Man, let the kid go and practice," Morton said. "Let him go and practice, man, he don't know what he's doin'."

The Lion headed into the Rhythm Club and walked downstairs, where they kept the piano and the pool table. In a few moments, it sounded as if all hell had erupted, the Lion roaring at the keyboard for all he was worth. Predictably, the street corner where Morton had been soliloquizing quickly emptied, as everyone rushed inside to hear the Lion in all his splendor.

Then one of the boys, in on the prank, ran outside and said, "The Lion is gone today, he's playin' all around the piano," which was about all that Morton could take. Unable to listen to so much adulation heaped upon the Lion—nothing but a cub when Morton first conquered Harlem in 1910—Morton finally, begrudgingly, walked down the stairs himself and watched the spectacle, waiting for his moment.

As the Lion played, his left hand vaulted quickly from bass notes to mid-register chords and back, while his right hand never stopped flying. All the while, he provided a running narration. "I'm in F," the Lion said, indicating that he was working in a simple key, with but one flat. "Now I'm in F-sharp," he announced, having modulated up just half a step, now working a key with six sharps, one of the most difficult. "Now I'm in C. I'm in A Minor." The listeners were impressed.

"These weren't pop tunes," recalled Nicholas, who witnessed the showdown. "This was fast fingering called stride piano—the left hand."

But as the Lion kept up his display, Morton edged closer to him, sizing him up, studying what the Lion could do and what he could not. When he had the Lion figured, he struck.

"Get up from there, you don't know what you're doin'," Morton scolded, and everyone burst out laughing, knowing that they had reeled him in, exactly as they had intended from the start.

Sure enough, Morton commandeered the piano, but he proceeded to put on a show such as none of these young busters had ever seen. He played fast—as fast as The Lion, and then some—and he started out in B, one of the most remote keys, with five sharps. His hands were a blur, but while he played, he, too, shouted out the names of the keys he was devouring. The young men could not believe it.

"That was the first time we heard Jelly striding, because he always played with an easy tempo—moderato," recalled Nicholas. "This went on for about 10 minutes, and Jelly was really goin', and everybody'd say, 'I didn't know Jelly could stride.'"

Morton, who reveled in their disbelief, simply kept playing. "Man, I invented all this kind of piano," he said. "Man, I invented jazz."

But Morton wasn't through with them yet. He stopped playing, asked them to turn on the radio, and in no time, "King Porter Stomp" turned up, this time in Tommy Dorsey's version.

"There, do you see what I'm talking about?" Morton crowed. "That's my tune. You see, I'm going to get some more money from that," he said, bragging about royalties he was finding impossible to obtain. "You see, you can't play nothin' without me."

With that line, recalled Nicholas, "The house came down. I mean, it was timed perfectly."

Almost everything that turned up for Morton in the fall of that year, 1939, had the quality of a mirage—alluring from a distance but im-

possible to grab up close. When the *We the People* radio program invited Morton to appear live, he relished the prospect of reaching New
York on one of the biggest radio shows in the town. "The program
presented people, more or less prominent, who had accomplished
worthwhile things, people with special talents, people who had interesting experiences," Carew later recalled, and Morton certainly filled
those prerequisites. But when the producers said they had no interest
in hearing Morton's new work, preferring him to play the old
warhorse "Tiger Rag," Morton had no choice but to comply, figuring
that some exposure—no matter how antiquated the music—was better than none. Unfortunately for Morton, a deluge came down on
Manhattan on the day of the program.

"When I appeared on 'We the People,' it just poured down & was
terribly cold," Morton wrote Carew afterward. "Of course I had to
be there at any rate, my word was at stake, although it did not even
mean car fare." The experience sent Morton back to his sickbed, but
even here there was no peace, for as Morton lay in bed he heard on
the radio the sides he had recorded for RCA in his last sessions, reminded once again that ASCAP was collecting the profits on broadcasts of these tunes, not he. Worse, when *Down Beat* raved about the
new Morton disks, calling them "a spectacular comeback with a
group of excellent and judiciously chosen musicians," the praise cut
two ways. For though the review gushed that Morton's return represented "the biggest surprise of the month," it also pointed out that
"Didn't He Ramble" and "Winin' Boy Blues" were "two ancient
tunes," as if Morton couldn't play or record anything new if he
wanted to. Meanwhile, Benny Goodman's manager, John Hammond,
still wouldn't return Morton's precious new scores.

The tension did not help the tightness around Morton's chest,
which was making breathing increasingly difficult. But to treat his
heart condition, Morton could afford only worthless over-the-counter
bromides.

"I got the Kepler's malt as you suggested[,] an 18 ounce size & am
taking it," Morton wrote to Carew on November 16, hoping that a
cheap over-the-counter cure for indigestion might relieve the pressure

engulfing his dying heart. "I believe it will help me. The druggist said it was very good to build resistance." Nevertheless, Morton had to admit that he no longer could work for an entire week straight, his energy shot after a couple of days. When he was strong enough to sit at the table and read or write, he barely could see the words the newspaper in front of him. "I had to get glasses[,] my eyes was so bad," he continued. "Bifocals, they are hard to get used to."

Finally, on December 4, as 1939 was drawing to a close, the letter Morton had been waiting for arrived: ASCAP, the organization that had flatly rejected him in 1934 and had ignored him ever since, congratulated him on being accepted. Though this was a belated development from an institution that had been profiting from his music for more than a decade, Morton was beside himself over this turn of events.

"I did not want to write you until I had something of real interest to tell you," he wrote to Carew on December 7. "We missed [a planned] recording date [due to illness] but something bigger has happened. . . . I have been accepted in ASCAP. I havent received my contract yet but I feel sure it is alright."

It wasn't. Two weeks later, ASCAP—which doled out payments not according to the frequency with which a composer's tunes were performed and broadcast but according to a subjective classification system—informed Morton that he had been placed in the lowest category ASCAP had. A pay scale that gave approximately $16,000 a year to white composers such as Irving Berlin and Richard Rodgers, who were placed in the top rank, paid $120 to nonwhites such as Morton, who were ranked at the bottom. Their music was deemed to have less intrinsic "value" than anything conceived for the Great White Way by Berlin, Rodgers, and other legit composers, who held the top offices in the organization.

This enraged Morton as much as the injustices that Melrose had dealt him for a decade. But ASCAP's scam was worse, because Walter Melrose was just another greedy publisher, while ASCAP purported to serve songwriters but, in fact, exploited them. Morton, already accustomed to tilting at powerful institutions, vowed to fight ASCAP, its slap at him unleashing a deep-seated anger born of a lifetime of be-trayals. Thanks to ASCAP, Morton was becoming radicalized, and he promised that he would bring down the entire organization.

"The situation is very disheartening sometime, but I will go on trying & trying again, as long as I can have a spark of energy left in me," Morton wrote to Carew on December 23, two days before the first anniversary of his doomed attempt to conquer New York.

"The ASCAP, to [my] way of thinking, has hurled a terrible insult at me. I guess it was a forced proposition to save themselves. So they made me a member to save trouble but I intend to re-send this insult real soon."

eight

A BATTLE ROYAL

*J*elly Roll Morton did not expect that the records he cut in New York in the chill of December 1939, and January 1940, would be his last. Though ailing, cold to the bone, and broke, he had too much to say in music, too many new tunes to play, to imagine that this would be his final chance to get them all down.

As he stepped into Reeves's Sound Studios on East Forty-fourth Street, on the afternoons of December 14 and 16, he came ready to play, a lifetime of melodies and riffs at his fingertips. Once again, the label—General Records—wanted Morton to play the old ones, and he was going to oblige in full, creating some of the most lush and ornate versions of his music that he yet had committed to record. Setting aside his pains and miseries for a few hours, he summoned a degree of energy and keyboard virtuosity that defied the present conditions of his life. With no band to worry about, no unruly musicians to cajole, and no musical scores to prepare, he played the piano as if liberated, his performances more daring in tempo and intricate in texture than anything he had recorded before. Somehow, Morton recaptured the fire of his earliest days, when he first was learning to compete in the piano dens of the District. But he also drew upon a musical sophistication and improvisational finesse that he could not have conceived of back then. The musical ideas and finger techniques and unorthodox chord progressions that he unleashed on these two afternoons had been earned, painstakingly, through nearly four decades in the music business. The boys outside the Rhythm Club might have considered him Mr. Has-Been, but nobody could play a piano quite like this, transforming the old New Orleans spirit into something fresh, spontaneous, virtuosic, and original. It was a sound so huge and symphonic, yet so detailed and complex, that—in its own way—it held its own against the wizardry of Art Tatum and the sleek melodicism of Teddy Wilson and any of the keyboard tricks of the piano men who now ruled in jazz.

Never before had Morton dispatched "The Naked Dance" so frenetically in a recording studio, his left hand flying—stride style—at a nearly manic clip, his tempo gaining momentum with every refrain, his chords more dissonant than ever, his keyboard attacks nothing less than ferocious. This wasn't turn-of-the-century New Orleans ragtime anymore; it was up-to-the-minute jazz improvisation, complete with weirdly chromatic key changes and a startling, repeated D-flat bass note where the ear longed to hear an E-flat. And yet the tempo perpetually increased, the piece spinning inexorably into some kind of frenzy.

When it came to "Mr. Joe," it hardly sounded as if Morton were playing a piano at all. The trumpetlike melody lines, the swelling midregister chords, and the perpetual rhythmic tension between the hands suggested instead the sinewy big-band orchestrations that Morton had been writing since he had hooked up with Carew, for some stillunplanned future release by Tempo-Music.

And then, inevitably, came "King Porter Stomp," the piece that not only had heralded the ascent of swing music in America through uncounted big-band recordings but also dated back to Morton's first awakening as a jazz musician in New Orleans. Morton had toiled over this piece for fully three years leading up to 1905, but the "King Porter Stomp" he now was recording belonged to a new era, and Morton knew it. You could hear it in the relentless swing dance rhythm that drove this performance, in the crashingly dissonant chords with which he made it modern, and in the buoyant left-hand octaves he used to slyly subvert its central pulse.

The man was summing it all up, bringing to the keyboard every crafty piano trick, sly rhythmic device, and daring harmonic innovation he had in him. And he wasn't done yet. On some numbers, he began to sing, his vocal tone and phrasing overflowing with the spirit of the blues. Into these pieces—the slow and sultry "Winin' Boy Blues," the mournful "Buddy Bolden's Blues," the somber "Don't You Leave Me Here"—Morton poured a decade's worth of sorrows and humiliations.

"At Jelly's request I sat in the studio with him as he recorded, and I thought at the time I was going through at least as many crises as he was," recalled writer Charles Edward Smith, who had organized the sessions for Gordon Mercer of General Records. "On 'Winin' Boy Blues,' for example, he closed his eyes on the humming passage. The clock was climbing up towards the three-minute mark. Gordon and the engineers motioned me frantically to nudge Jelly. I didn't. It was too good. Besides, I didn't dare. Jelly opened his eyes slowly and murmured, 'Oh, Mamie,' as the number came to its close," that last exhortation almost a sob.

Morton was reaching deep within for this music, creating sounds that were every bit as personal and as autobiographical as jazz audiences now demanded of their artists. The strength of these performances—and the sterling recordings he knew they would make—sustained him through a harrowing Christmas, during which he seethed over the blow from ASCAP. The very notion that ASCAP could send him a letter, in mid-December, informing him that performance and broadcast payments from his compositions were worth a pitiful $120 a year demeaned and injured him. So did the attitude of Benny Goodman's manager, John Hammond, who just before New Year's Eve finally returned the scores that Morton had lent him months earlier. But Hammond made clear that he was annoyed at Morton for pestering him about such a trivial matter. From Hammond's tone, Morton realized he had made another enemy.

So the dawning of 1940 came as a relief, if only because Morton could get back to work, picking up where he had left off in December with the General Records sessions. Again, he tried to gather as many New Orleans musicians as possible, filling the rest of the chairs with New York men. When he spotted several of them at the Rhythm Club the day before the recording date, Morton urged the musicians to show up a bit early, so that perhaps they could run through scores they never had seen before. "We're recording tomorrow," Morton told them. "We got to be there in the studio for 2 o'clock, so let's try to get there around 1:30."

As the players trickled in on the afternoon of January 4, they saw Morton intently editing and polishing the instrumental parts, and they began goading him. "Well, Jelly, we know you haven't been doing much lately, but we're going to put you on the map today," New Orleans trumpeter Henry "Red" Allen joked. "You got a good bunch with you, and we're going to make you famous. . . . What are we going to play?"

"Well, just wait a minute, you'll get your part. Just wait a minute," Morton replied, fixated on the scores and hardly hearing the jibes. Soon enough, Morton handed the parts to each of the players— trumpeter Allen, clarinetist Albert Nicholas, bassist Wellman Braud, and drummer Zutty Singleton, all from New Orleans, plus trombonist Joe Britton and alto saxophonist Eddie Williams. After the musicians quickly read through the scores, the tapes started rolling.

"We hit the thing and went on through it, one take—perfect," remembered Nicholas of the slow drag "Sweet Substitute." The tune, rich in southern blues sensibility and unhurried New Orleans rhythm, brought out the best in these players, and in Morton as well, for he caressed the tune, his softly sung lines and seductive moans and sighs providing a poignant counterpoint to Allen's piercing blues trumpet solos.

But then the battles began, as even the New Orleans men showed no patience with Morton's deliberate way of making a record. "Now look, Jelly, some of us have business to attend to after this session is through," said Braud, irked by Morton's habit of telling stories and jokes between cuts. "Let's cut out the time wasting."

In his youth, Morton would not have dared to speak to a bandleader in that way, much less a musician as famous as Jelly Roll Morton had once been.

"Gee, I'm sorry, Wellman, I didn't realize that you were such a busy man," said Morton, with irony. "OK, fellas, let's go. We'll start with that bass introduction that I've written out for you, Wellman."

Wellman blanched. "Ain't no written introduction here, Jelly," said Wellman, taking the bait.

"Oh, no—I must have left it at home," Morton answered. "Well, well, I'll just have to write it out again."

Morton picked up pen and paper, took his sweet time, and eventually came up with a bass solo that would have taxed better men than Braud. "OK, here it is, Wellman, here we go. . . . One . . . two –"

"Hell, hold on, Jelly," Braud protested. "Let me have a good look at this, give me a few minutes."

"I just don't understand you, Wellman," said Morton, going for the kill. "First you're in a great big hurry. Now you want to hang about and do your practicing, keeping all these poor fellows waiting."

Morton won the battle but was losing the war. The acrimony of the occasion was starting to show in the music making, with the underrehearsed "Panama" sounding ragged and a bit frenetic. "Good Old New York" went by at tempo too fast by half ("I'm sorry I had to speed up 'N.Y.,'" Morton later wrote to Carew, "but that was orders."). And the miking on "Big Lip Blues" proved so inadequate that some of the players sounded as if they were recording in a different room.

It was difficult to hold out much hope for these results.

"I had to make the recordings under difficult conditions," Morton wrote Carew two days later. "The men would not rehearse. The union demands pay for rehearsal, & the company was not willing to pay for it, so there will be bad spots. But there are much worse recordings."

Too ill to make the next scheduled date, Morton didn't reconvene the musicians until two weeks later, on January 23, when the band made a train wreck of "Why." But at least Morton was recording the tunes he and Carew had copyrighted for Tempo-Music, including "If You Knew," "My Home Is in a Southern Town," and "Swinging the Elks," a jaunty attempt at salvaging the "We Are Elks" fiasco by turning a peppy march into a loose-limbed swing romp.

And that was it, the end of Jelly Roll Morton's recording career, the last time anyone invited him into a studio to preserve what he had to offer. It was a dispiriting finish to an inspired recording career. After the last sessions, Morton and a young New Orleans musician he had invited to watch, banjoist George Guesnon, walked out together into the freezing night. They made it back to the 131st Street rooming house where they both lived, then later went out again to get some air and figure out exactly what had happened back in the recording studio.

As they walked, Guesnon read disgust on Morton's face, the loathing he had developed toward this city and its musicians and its cannibalistic ways of doing business.

"It must have been about dusk, night was just about to fall, and it was snowing," recalled Guesnon. "Him and I came out of the house and turned the corner into Seventh Avenue. I saw a poor woman scuffling and scuffling in that snow, and I saw her drop something small and black. I ran ahead and picked it up and saw it was a pocketbook. I didn't take time to notice what was in it. . . . I ran behind her and gave the pocketbook back to her."

As Morton watched this spectacle, he burst out laughing and hardly could stop, his hysterical guffaws quickly turning into a hacking, wheezing coughing fit. When he finally caught his breath, Morton let Guesnon in on the grim joke.

"All the time you told me you were from New Orleans I just took it for granted that you were, but now I truly *know* you are from New Orleans," said Morton. "There ain't nobody but a damn fool from New Orleans would have done what you did. If any of these cats from New York would have found her pocketbook, you can bet all the tea in China she never would have seen it no more."

The report came as a shock, even to Morton, who thought he already had heard about all the bad news that might be doled out to him for awhile. But he hadn't counted on how desolate he felt when he received news, a couple weeks after the last recording sessions, that his godmother Eulalie Hecaut was approaching death in Los Angeles. The great voodoo woman not only had seen to it that he studied music as a child but, at least as important, had taken him in when his family had thrown him out. Without Lalie, as he had called her as a child, there would be no Jelly Roll Morton, no life wandering the Gulf Coast and learning to survive through music and cards and pool and other forms of hustling, no triumphant records nor great jazz tunes heard around the world. Now she was dying, and he had to do something, particularly since her husband and sole support, the now blind Paul Hecaut, was in no better shape.

"My last near relative is suppose to be on a death bed in Los Angeles," Morton wrote to Carew on February 6, 1940.

> There are only two, & the other is stone blind & has been blind quite a few years now. These two was responsible for my little musical education, & is just the same as my mother & father. Of course there have been sickness in my family & death in the last five years enough to drive one crazy. I've got to go to try and protect a piece of property or more (if they still have more) but I know there's at least one fairly nice piece. It seems that I cannot get things to roll as I have in past years. This is God's work & no one can do anything about it. . . . If I am able to go to L.A. I will be able to record out there. They do a lot out there.

That's when the idea began to crystallize—Morton could go out west, attend to his godparents' affairs, and, perhaps, start anew once more, the thousandth fresh beginning for a man who inexplicably did not surrender each time he was beaten back to the starting line. The subsequent news that Eulalie had died only deepened Morton's resolve to head to California. The question was when, and what do about the ASCAP situation—whether to accept the pittance ASCAP had allotted him or fight for something better. Then there was the matter of the Melrose firm, which in early February sent Morton another check, for sixty dollars. He did not understand the purpose or significance of this payment, but he wanted to find out. More important, he wanted Melrose, who had insulted him in the pages of *Down Beat*, to make good on the money he had stolen from him, no matter how much or how little it was.

While Morton agonized over his next move, he wrote music, hoping his new big-band arrangements might turn Tempo-Music into a real publishing house with hits of its own. Granted, there was no money in it now, but there might be in the future. "No one would make orchestration[s] without pay, & play without pay & have all the other expense that goes with it with a chance not to make even carfare out of it but some struggling publisher like us," he wrote to Carew in February.

Yet Morton wrote prolifically, penning arrangements for a larger, more sumptuous orchestral sound than he ever had scored or heard before, meanwhile stripping his music of the baroque instrumental counterpoint that once had been his trademark. Now, he was writing the sleek, tuneful music that the dancers demanded, yet with a lazy New Orleans beat and blues-drenched chords that marked this music as unmistakably his. This was a new kind of New Orleans swing, a glorious merger of modern dance-band writing and at least the flavor of vintage Louisiana, scored for four saxophones and five brass, all moving together to create enormous blocks of sound and plush and luxuriant chords. As Morton wrote these scores, he practically could hear the shimmering horns, genteel rhythms, and burnished colors of "Mr. Joe" and the radiant reed choirs, easy swing backbeats, and colorful, snarling dissonances on "Oh, Baby." If Glenn Miller had proven that the dance-hall crowds wanted to swoon, Morton was going to give them something to sway to, but with more harmonic savvy and down-home blues than they knew existed. To make the youngsters feel at home, though, he tucked a lovely trombone solo into the middle of "Oh, Baby," evoking the music of Miller and Tommy Dorsey that the kids seemed to adore.

All told, this amounted to nothing less than a metamorphosis of Morton's art, from the brilliant wailing of so many horns that used to distinguish his music to the smooth and streamlined sound of the day. Yet nothing that Miller or Dorsey or Harry James or any of the rest had written approached the azure tonal quality or searing blues expression that defined Morton's new orchestral music. The melancholy phrases and complex extended chords and unmistakable southern sensibility distinguished Morton's new music from the rest of the big-band scores that Americans were accustomed to hearing.

When Mamie Wright, who owned the rooming house where the Mortons lived, hinted in April that the composer was making a ruckus on her piano, he simply continued to write and refine these scores away from the instrument, penning his orchestrations without a keyboard, imagining that the best players in the business were sitting before him. This music was too important and too valuable to stop writing now, for these were the arrangements that Morton planned to ride to triumph, once he had a big band to play them.

In the meantime, though, the jazz world was swinging happily without him, New York's Fifty-second Street aglow with the marquees of the Onyx, the Three Deuces, the Famous Door, the Hickory House, Jimmy Ryan's, Kelly's Stable, and the Yacht Club, among others. They called it Swing Street, and Morton had no place on it, though he wondered what it sounded like, what made the audiences flock there, how good the latest New York players really were—and whether he still could hold his own against them.

So he met up with New Orleans clarinetist Nicholas one night and checked out the strip. They started at the White Rose, at Fifty-second Street and Sixth Avenue, a joint where the musicians convened during intermission. Morton said his hellos, ordered a soda, took a few sips, then gave Nicholas the word: "Now I'm gonna go and see what these cats are layin' down, what they're talking about—'The Street' and all this humbug. Maybe we'll see what they're playin'.'"

At each stop, Morton sat at the bar, ordered a soda pop, listened, and analyzed every phrase and chord that was played. After a few minutes at any joint, he whispered to himself, "Uh huh, uh huh," as if he had unlocked exactly what the musicians were doing and thus was ready to move on to the next saloon. When he arrived at the Famous Door, he heard bassist John Kirby's uncommonly tight sextet, its playing so disciplined and its scores so meticulously engineered that Morton realized he finally was hearing something worth talking about. "Uh huh, uh huh," came the usual half-whispered remark, then, "Uh huh, I see, uh huh, they got something."

These words of praise inspired the boss at the Famous Door to ask Morton if he wanted a drink. "I'll take a Coke," came the usual response. At intermission, the boys came off the bandstand and headed directly to the bar, where they saw the old man himself and shook his hand. Trumpeter Charlie Shavers, pianist Billy Kyle, clarinetist Russell Procope (who had recorded with Morton in New York in 1928)—all were surprised to see one of the old pioneers checking out the new sounds. The "moldy figs," as players of Morton's generation derisively were being called, didn't usually come by, so this was something of an occasion.

"I know you're gonna play one with us," Procope said to Morton, and sure enough, when the band reassembled on the stage, Morton took Kyle's place at the keys. But once the musicians started playing, the band sounded radically different, as if Morton's keyboard work alone were turning an already excellent ensemble into something distinctive.

"With all due respect to Billy Kyle, it was a different sound," recalled Nicholas, who was startled by what he heard. "Without any practice Jelly played all their scores, and the people said, 'Who is that?'"

"Jelly Roll Morton," someone answered.

"That's him?" came the reply, as if astonished that the man still was alive, let alone playing a music unfamiliar to him with such insight. The crowd applauded fervently, acknowledging that something extraordinary had transpired, and the boss at the Famous Door made his move.

"Jelly, I've got an idea," he said. "Maybe we could get together and alternate with the band and you."

Nicholas couldn't believe it. Though he knew Morton still could play anyone off the bandstand, he never thought that anybody on Swing Street would be smart enough to offer Morton a job. But if that came as a surprise, Morton's response left him dumbstruck.

"Man, I don't play no intermission," Morton said, drawing laughter from everyone except Nicholas, who knew how much Morton needed the money, the visibility, and, above all else, the acceptance of a new public that had never heard of Hilma Burt's house or Tom Anderson's saloon or the piano players who once worked there.

"But I'm gonna pay you well," said the boss.

"There ain't that much money—I don't play no intermission," reiterated Morton, half-offended by the offer. Though financially desperate, Morton deemed that he did not need the engagement. Either he was going to lead his own big band in his own new scores or he wasn't going to play at all. On artistic matters, there was no room for compromise.

The boss persisted, and Morton laughed him off. "Man, I play for pleasure; I don't care what I make, I'm Jelly Roll Morton. There ain't that much money, man. How much I owe you for that Coke?"

Nicholas couldn't believe it. "That was Jelly: 'How much do I owe you?' Proud."

Yet, at other times—if the setting was right and the audience responsive—Morton played for hours without pause, and for a pittance. In April 1940, for instance, the jazz promoter Harry Lim invited Morton to lead a couple of the Sunday sessions at Nick's, a Dixieland joint in Greenwich Village at West Tenth Street and Seventh Avenue. Not surprisingly, Morton engaged the best New Orleans musicians in New York, with Sidney Bechet playing soprano saxophone, Nicholas on clarinet, Henry "Red" Allen on trumpet, and Braud on bass, plus the transplanted New Yorkers J. C. Higginbotham on trombone and Big Sid Catlett on drums.

"Jelly completely took charge," recalled Lim, who paid Morton fourteen dollars for a long afternoon's work. "He gave us an outline of history, as he usually does, and all those tunes he'd written. It was very entertaining, really. And there were cards on the table so people could write down a question and send it up. At intermission time, Jelly would sit at the piano and answer the questions."

When he wasn't orating on the evolution of jazz, Morton was playing the original classics that told his life's story, tunes such as "Winin' Boy Blues" and "Naked Dance," as well as old standards such as "Royal Garden Blues," "Basin Street Blues," and "Mamie Desdunes Blues." Once he felt he had the audience on his side, Morton even dared to sing the ribald lyrics he had heard back in New Orleans at the start of the century ("Mama, mama, look at sis, up on the levee doin' the double twist").

"It was a fantastic session, an extraordinary jazz experience, with all those New Orleans musicians present," said Frederic Ramsey, Jr., who with Charles Edward Smith had coauthored the landmark book "Jazzmen" in 1942, leaving Morton out.

> Jelly Roll was in superb form. He talked and sang, hardly ever leaving the keyboard, and he played non-stop during intermissions. It seemed that having finally received some exposure in New York City, he was out to show everybody that the great Jelly Roll was really back in town and ready to knock them all cold. He had the intensity. I know he must have been ill then, but you never would have suspected it. He did the whole "Tiger Rag," running through his demonstration of quadrille to rag.

So Morton still knew how to beguile an audience, which might yet have made him a hit in New York—at least as an intermission piano player. But that wasn't what Morton wanted. Neither money nor an audience's acclaim was his top priority, though he would have accepted either, on his own terms. He wanted a big band, and he wanted to play his music at his own tempos and with his own New Orleans musicians, period.

"If he really couldn't have things just the way he wanted them, he didn't want it at all," said guitarist Lawrence Lucie, who lived near

Morton's 131st address and informally studied music theory with him. "That's the kind of personality he was; he wanted to do things a certain way. Sometimes you have to bend a little bit, but he wasn't the personality to bend. . . . Sometimes you have to go along with the program. Jelly wasn't one to go along with just any program."

That much was clear from everything Morton did during these perilous days in New York. Though he needed the money and the visibility, he said no when invited to take part in a *New Orleans Jazz Album* that Stephen W. Smith was putting together for Decca. Morton would not participate if Smith was naming Louis Armstrong leader for the May 27 date and Red Allen and Zutty Singleton coleaders for the May 28 session (fronting a band that included Johnny Dodds and Jimmie Noone). As far as Morton was concerned, there was no reason that Jelly Roll Morton should get second billing to these men—or to anyone else, save perhaps the great Tony Jackson, who had been dead for twenty years anyway. Armstrong's fame was beside the point, because Morton had been famous when Satchmo still was in short pants.

So Morton told Smith he would not work as a sideman, which irked the producer, who was left "looking for another piano player but wishing Jelly had been more reasonable." Morton, however, believed he had spent too many years trying to appease record men like Smith, managers like John Hammond, and cheats like Walter Melrose and ASCAP—and now he was broke and they were not. He had paid dearly for acquiescing to the wishes of these men—all white, all in power—and he wasn't going to anymore. He wasn't going to act like Joe Oliver or W. C. Handy or the other black musicians who survived by keeping quiet. "Joe was more the old Southern-type nigger," Walter Melrose once said. "Like Handy. Didn't want any trouble with anybody."

Having written jazz standards before Handy or Oliver or Armstrong or Melrose or Hammond or Smith had arrived on the scene, Morton wasn't going to be the "old Southern'-type nigger" that Melrose preferred. Now he was going to make some trouble—as much as he possibly could.

"[They] try to tighten the noose around my neck," Morton wrote Carew. "I am sure I will be able to break it & it wont be very long either."

On April 17, 1940, Morton retained New York attorney Dorsey Spencer—of Newell & Spencer & Stafford, 420 Lexington Avenue—to sue Melrose, Southern, and ASCAP, the three entities Morton knew had been taking money that rightly belonged to him. He had tried to get his share by writing letters to Melrose, Southern, and ASCAP for years. None had provided Morton with the documentation he demanded: exact figures showing how much money they had made on his tunes and what percentage his cut was supposed to be. Southern had ignored him, Melrose had ignored then insulted him, and ASCAP had humiliated him, placing him at the bottom of the composers' pay scale. So Morton was going to strike back, hard. He was going to get every dime they had stolen from him, and he was going to make enough noise so that all the world would know. The document that the lawyer drew up sounded impressive, its language legalistic and precise:

> I, the undersigned, do hereby retain you as my attorney to take all steps, proceedings and actions necessary, or that you may deem proper, to collect for me any and all damages, claims and judgments that may be obtained by me or on my behalf, by reason of the publication, recording or other use made of my compositions by the Southern Music Corp. of New York City, the Melrose Music Corp. of New York City, the American Society of Composers, Authors and Publishers of New York City, and any and all other publishers, recorders or users who may have been or are indebted to me for such use.

With this sentence, Morton launched a full frontal attack on every aspect of the music industry he could think of, singling out not only those he knew had used his music without paying him but also anyone who had done so without his knowledge. This was Morton's declaration of war, and he intended to see it through. If engaging in this battle meant that the lawyer got fifty cents for every dollar Morton received, so be it. Better that it go to the attorney than to the thieves who were running the music industry in America as if it were their own private treasury.

"The lawyer would not handle my case but one way, & and that's 50/50," Morton told Carew, in April. "But so many other lawyers have double-crossed me when I tried to pay outright, so I thought I may get some fairness that way. He told me Thursday that he was preparing to open the case soon[,] 2 or 3 weeks. He was recommended through the hospital. He is not authorized to make a settlement without my approval."

While Morton awaited developments in his three-pronged assault on the music racket, he turned for solace to a place he hadn't visited since his childhood at home in New Orleans—the Catholic church. Though born Catholic, Morton had fallen away from religion since the day his family threw him out, thereafter leading a life that the church would not have approved. In his youth, he had been enthralled by the licentiousness of his new world, a place where drugs and money and sex and killings were the currency of everyday life. But even when he had stopped hustling women and cards to focus on music, in Chicago in the mid-1920s, he never had returned to the church, and the guilt he had felt through the intervening years now was surfacing. The only way he could confront it was in church, so he joined St. Aloysius, 219 West 132nd Street. The church gave him a Holy Name Society card, punched each time he attended mass. He went with Mabel virtually every morning, trying to rid himself of his sins and to interrupt his free fall.

"I am a staunch Catholic & all my people before me, & honor are one of their great teachings," he wrote to Carew on May 5. As if to underscore the point, he shared with Carew his guilt at missing mass when his body ached too much for him to attend.

"I haven't felt any too good this past week," he wrote on May 27. "The weather has been very bad this [week,] plenty of rain & very little sunshine & somewhat changeable temperature[.] The weather was so bad that I missed mass almost all the week. (I am a Catholic & usually go to church every morning.)"

When he wasn't attending mass or writing music, he was collecting articles on Catholics and Catholicism, including a two-page broadsheet newspaper spread on "The Cures at Lourdes as Vital Subject for Modern Medical Society," perhaps hoping that in faith there might be some cure for him as well.

The case against Melrose, Southern, and ASCAP was proceeding, his lawyer having drafted some of the initial paperwork. "The Lawyer sent a letter to me to come & sign the complaint," Morton informed Carew on May 30. "I started trying to read the data. Its really to[o] legal for me to understand thoroughly, so I decided to sign. At least some of it seemed right to me. . . . The atty seems very happy about the case & says we will go to the limit. Well I guess we might have some real money soon, maybe."

Momentum seemed to be gathering, for on June 6 Morton's attorneys served papers to the Melrose Music Corp., charging the publishing firm with taking proceeds that rightfully belonged to the composer. He celebrated this news, writing to Carew about it and, on another front, adding the sweet fact that on June 17 he finally would get his chance to appear before the board of ASCAP to argue his case.

At last, it looked as if the world was beginning to listen. "ASCAP promised to look into the case," Morton wrote Carew on June 20. "I don't know exactly what that mean[s], although it looks favorable, to me." Meanwhile, Morton's attorney, Dorsey Spencer, passed the case along to an associate, Saul A. Finkel, of 22 East Fortieth Street, New York. He served papers on George Simon, president of Melrose Music Co., and informed Morton that a hearing would be held July 9. "I am wondering," Morton wrote to Carew, "will I be present at the hearing? Which he don't state. There is so many crooked things [that] happen here." Insecure after so many defeats and disappointments, Morton worried that his case was proceeding without him, and, indeed, when July 9 arrived, his lawyer did not allow him to attend the hearing.

"So far no news yet, as to what happened about the case," he wrote on July 10. "I guess I will hear something soon, although it seems strange to me that I was not permitted to the hearing of my own case. The atty said he didn't need me. So I did not want to antagonize him, so I just had to trust, to the best of the outcome." He had no choice and, anyway, his attorney had assured him that "everything would result in my favor."

Another week passed, and still no word. "I havent heard from the atty in the case," Morton wrote to Carew on July 16, "so I went to the first one [Dorsey Spencer], & had him to call, but I wasn't able to get any satisfaction out of it, only that the other side claims we was suing for contracts not accounting. I am trying to get in touch with him to-day to find out what I can. I understand it will come up soon, but I don't know how soon."

No one was giving Morton answers, and he couldn't find out if or when a hearing had been held. The whole case seemed to be proceeding without him. Shut out of the biggest fight of his life, Morton tried to figure how he could get back in control when his attorney, Saul A. Finkel, delivered the final blow: Finkel was dropping Morton's case. According to the lawyer, Melrose's attorney was "a man of good caliber," and Morton had no real case. Moreover, the Melrose records for the past two years looked fine to Finkel.

Morton reeled at this development. How could Finkel have been satisfied that the Melrose records looked good for the past couple of years when Morton hadn't been paid by the Melrose company for nearly a decade, from 1929 to 1938, when the check for $86.94 had arrived? Furious at this latest outrage, Morton stormed into the office of attorney Dorsey Spencer, whom he originally had retained, demanding an explanation.

"The other atty [Dorsey] told me it was no need to go on because all the evidence was against me," Morton told Carew on August 12.

I wonder who is it that have power to protect copyrights & the rights of music. I haven't been able to find out. . . . I still haven't been able to get copies of my contracts & I did not get an ac-

counting [of royalties earned on tunes] either. I havent been able
to find out what judge this was. . . . I have had no voice one way
or other in the case. I don't know what judge[,] what room, what
transpired, or anything, & when I insisted on being present this
Finkel said (in half angry tones), Let me get gray over those
things, not you. . . . I just don't know where to turn for justice &
don't [know] what step to take next.

Despondent, Morton bolted from Spencer's office and headed to
see the biggest, most powerful lawyer he could think of—the district
attorney of New York, Thomas Dewey. The famous DA had a reputation for taking on crooks of all varieties, and maybe he would pick up
the cause. But Morton couldn't get past the secretary at Dewey's office. She explained that the DA prosecutes criminal matters and has
nothing to do with civil cases.

So it was over. Morton's crusade to collect the fortune Melrose
owed him had nowhere left to go. The royalties from the biggest hits
of Morton's life never were going to be his.

What Morton didn't realize—and had no way of learning—was
that even if Morton's lawyers had aggressively pursued the case
against Melrose Music Co., it was doomed, for Walter Melrose could
not be touched by these proceedings. By the time Morton had persuaded the attorneys to take his case, in 1940, the original Melrose
Brothers Music Co. did not exist, and its former owner, Walter Melrose, was basking in the sun on his new Arizona horse ranch, living
off the spoils of tunes by Morton and other songwriters he had swindled. Records show that Walter Melrose never really sold the company—he merely sold 217 copyright titles (26 of them by Jelly Roll
Morton) and the Melrose Music Co. name. The buyer, Edwin H.
Morris Co., of New York, therefore did not acquire Melrose's liabili-
ties. Instead, Edwin H. Morris Co. operated a new firm called Melrose Music and inherited none of Walter Melrose's debt to Morton or
anyone else.

Once the sale was completed, the new Melrose Music began
paying royalties on a timely basis (which Walter Melrose had not

done), which is why Morton had received that inexplicable check for sixty dollars from Melrose Music. The amount was tiny because the sheet music and record business had shriveled during the Depression.

Morton, in other words, had been entirely outmaneuvered by Walter Melrose, while Morton's own lawyers had denied him his day in court.

Carew was appalled.

"I think you are right about your conclusions in regard to the #2 lawyer, Saul Finkel," wrote Carew, concurring with Morton that Finkel had sold him out. "There seems little doubt that he figured there was more for him on the other side of the fence." But there was nothing Carew could do to help.

"It's too bad I'm getting old," wrote Carew, "and am handicapped by being down here [in Washington]."

The composer, who feared that he was coming undone, replied that he felt "very nervous [on] account of the dirty trick those lawyers did. I would love to get a settlement so I could end this whole thing. I am just about at the end of my rope now."

If the lawyers weren't going to pursue Morton's case against ASCAP, Melrose, Southern, and the rest of the corrupt music industry, Morton resolved to do it himself, lawyers be damned. Bruised anew by the latest series of blows, Morton in this dark summer of 1940 poured his rage into a letter-writing campaign to Thurman Arnold, assistant attorney general in the U.S. Justice Department's antitrust division. In this correspondence, Morton showed precisely how the music business had stolen his fortune and still was doing so.

After all these years and so much distress, Morton found a receptive ear in Arnold's Justice Department office and wrote:

I have been referred to you to unravel my situation, [which is] filled with many evils and diabolical [figures] . . . My letter [to Senator O'Mahoney] of Oct. 10th 1939 contained some of the

abuses [that] have been accorded me by the American Society of
Composers Authors & Publishers (ASCAP).

 . . . My grievances are that ASCAP have made collections on
many of my tunes from Radio, Hotels, Dance-Halls, Pavilions,
Theatres, Café's, Restaurants, Cabarets, & etc. all over the
world, since the year of 1915 [the year of his first published composition—and the first jazz work ever put on paper, "Jelly Roll
Blues].

 It was my style or creation of Jazz-Stomp-Swing that caused
such great expansion in the Jazz field, that's today considered one
of America's great industries. . . . I ask you, as one of the nations
great officials. Can outsiders take my personal earnings & deny
me a right to have a say? . . . I believe this sort of thing would be
against the constitution of the U.S.A. . . . My contributions are
many & have proved to be valuable in many instances. I am not
asking protection for something don't belong to me. I will be satisfied with my own earnings. . . . I believe a general investigation
would be the best thing ever happened if it comes from the right
source. I will be very glad to testify to any of the facts I know.

Morton signed the letter twice—as Ferdinand Joseph Morton and
as Jelly Roll Morton, perhaps acknowledging the distinction between
the man he was and the character he had invented for public consumption.

 Now Morton wasn't simply demanding justice. He was calling for
an investigation of the entire, iniquitous music-publishing industry,
offering himself as Exhibit A. He did not realize that precisely such an
investigation already was under way, with Assistant Attorney General
Arnold in the midst of collecting testimony from mostly black composers, songwriters, and bandleaders who had been denied their rights
and their cash by music publishers and by ASCAP. Eight days after the
Justice Department received Morton's letter, Thurgood Marshall, an
assistant attorney general, shot back a response that gave Morton the
first—and only—glimmer of hope he ever saw in his war against the
music business.

"The Department is conducting an investigation in the field of copyrighted music in order to ascertain possible violations of the antitrust law," Arnold's office informed Morton, who in this single sentence found a kind of vindication. "In connection with this investigation, it will be appreciated if you will furnish the Department the following information."

Now Morton realized the Justice Department was asking the right questions: Did Morton know the names and dates of publication of all his tunes? Had he ever been denied membership in ASCAP? Did he still have any of the rejection letters in his possession, and would he send them along? Did he know of any other composers who had had similar problems?

Morton had all the answers—song lists, publishers' names, and years of rejection by ASCAP (1928 and 1934), as well as information that the Justice Department hadn't thought to ask.

"Some members can get information that others cannot get," Morton wrote, referring to high-ranking board members such as Irving Berlin and Jerome Kern. "I was told by one of my publisher friends that I must have lost at least $75,000 by not being a member of ASCAP. I said I tried to get in for years, & evasive methods was used to keep me out. His reply was, 'they sure can keep you out if they want too.' I am wondering how can they take what belongs to me & do what they want with it."

Morton recited his litany of complaints to the Justice Department in several letters over a period of months, detailing his treatment at the hands of ASCAP and Walter Melrose. When a questionnaire arrived, peppering Morton with additional queries about his travails in the music business, Morton crisply laid out his case.

"Were you allowed any discretion in determining the terms of your contract with the music publishers?" the Justice Department asked. "No," Morton wrote, adding, "As a result you will have to except their terms."

"Were you allowed any discretion in determining the terms of your membership agreement [with ASCAP]?" the Justice Department asked. "Positively not," Morton answered.

"Have you made complaint to the Society [ASCAP] with reference to your classification and the terms of your membership agreement?" they asked. "Yes, made quite a few," Morton affirmed.

Meanwhile, the noise Morton had made at ASCAP headquarters during his meeting there on June 17 and thereafter persuaded the organization to promote him to a higher category—from "3" to "2." This meant that instead of getting $120 he would get $185, the highest amount ASCAP ever paid him in his lifetime. Morton knew full well that the category "2" designation was not the second highest ranking, as one might assume. Several higher categories—such as A, AA, and AAA—outranked the numerical ratings.

The ludicrousness of the $185 payment astonished Morton, who shared some figures with the Justice Department in his last letter to Arnold, on August 15. In this final dispatch, Morton produced numbers he had received from George Simon, president of the new Melrose Music Co., showing that from 1934 to 1937 alone the Melrose firm had collected thousands of dollars in payments from ASCAP for publishing Morton's tunes and for "writing them" (since Walter Melrose had secretly added lyrics to tunes by Morton and others), while Morton had received nothing. "I think this is out & out theft," wrote Morton. "I have not been able to get any part of this from Melrose. This have been going on for years."

Morton expounded on the subject of thievery in the music business to anyone who would listen. "ASCAP is a hard nut to crack," he wrote Carew on September 25. "I don't know if I will get anymore out of them, & they finally told me at the board that there is no way for me to measure my activities," meaning the frequency of performances of Morton's music. "They wont give statements & it is up to them to give you what they want too & as they see fit. I don't see how an organization of that kind can exist. You cannot get any information from those gangsters one way or other."

Morton understood precisely the stranglehold that ASCAP had on black musicians. There was no way for Morton—or any musician—to measure the "activities," or frequency of usage, of his music. This, in fact, was one of the reasons that ASCAP had been founded: Since musicians did not have the wherewithal to track performances of their works and bill the radio stations, nightclubs, and theaters accordingly, ASCAP would do it for them. In reality, ASCAP simply was collecting flat fees from broadcasters, theater owners, and the like, then divvying the spoils among a select group of mostly white composers.

Yet at the very moment ASCAP was turning its back on generations of black jazz and blues artists, it was expounding upon its beneficence, claiming in the pages of *Harper's Magazine* that before ASCAP, songwriters had suffered in ways that ASCAP now prevented. "The most tragic case in point, says ASCAP, was the life of Stephen Foster, whose music is among the best-loved in America," noted the *Harper's* article.

> He died in a hospital charity ward with thirty-eight cents in his purse because he had no financial reward for the popularity of his songs. Such a situation could not arise to-day, says ASCAP, because it assures ample payment to composers for frequently played music. Moreover, should once-successful writers fall into straitened circumstances ASCAP has made this pledge: "No member of ASCAP who writes successful music, or anyone else dependent upon him, shall ever want."

Despite the latest round of setbacks, Morton started over in the fall of 1940, somehow persuading a group of musicians to rehearse with him the big-band scores he had been writing since his return to New York nearly two years earlier. If his case against Melrose and ASCAP had yielded nothing more than paperwork and despair, if his lawyer didn't care to get him his day in court, at least he could write music, even if no one cared to hear it.

"I have been rehearsing a band in the past week[,] 15 [men] and a girl," he wrote to Carew. "If I am able to continue & believe[,] I will have a great band, one to compete with any of that type. But it is expensive to pay for rehearsal halls, & now and then the men want a dollar or two."

Nevertheless, Morton persuaded a few of the old men from New Orleans to rehearse with him at the Calumet Club, at 209 West 131st Street, next door to the rooming house where he lived with Mabel. Yet he could not forget about the music industry swindle that had left him all but begging musicians to play his scores, and he railed about it to a *Down Beat* reporter. "'Robbed of Three Million Dollars,' Says Jelly Roll," the headline proclaimed, and in this article Morton let out his last, great, anguished lament on how he had been wronged. Here was his final chance to explain the true story to anyone who cared to understand, perhaps as he would have told it to a judge had he been granted the opportunity.

"I've been robbed of three million dollars all told," Morton told *Down Beat*. "Everyone today is playing my stuff and I don't even get credit. . . . I am a busy man now, and I have to spend most of my time dealing with attorneys, but I am not too busy to get around and hear jazz that I myself introduced 25 years ago. . . . If I had been paid rightfully for my work I would now have 3 million dollars more than I have now."

Carew cringed when he saw the *Down Beat* piece, believing that Morton had erred by escalating his one-man war on the music industry. Even Carew, it turned out, had grown tired of Morton's complaints. "I believe I told you before that I don't think that kind of publicity does you any good," Carew wrote to Morton, on October 6. "Those boys [at *Down Beat*] play those things up and it puts you in a bad light with producers and others who could use your material[,] as well as yourself. No one knows better than I do that you have been robbed of material, but the outsiders believe that you are just beefing when you make big claims."

But denied a fair shake by the legal system and unable to liberate a penny from Walter Melrose or a decent slice of his royalties from ASCAP, Morton had nothing left in his arsenal except the truth, and his willingness to tell it. Now, having made his case in the pages of *Down Beat* and having written to every federal governmental office he could think of, Morton realized that the time had come to leave New York, for good.

So he contacted Ed Garland, an old friend from New Orleans who was playing bass at the time with Kid Ory's band in Los Angeles, and said that he was coming to California to handle Eulalie Hecaut's estate and to start over once more. Morton asked Garland to begin putting together a large New Orleans band that would be ready to rehearse once Morton arrived, his newly minted big-band scores in tow. Garland enthusiastically agreed to start recruiting top-notch New Orleans musicians who were willing to rehearse for nothing, and Morton made final preparations to leave Manhattan. He pawned a few more items of clothes and made a down payment on a new Lincoln; he got himself a chain and hitched his 1938 Cadillac to the back of the new sedan. Then he threw a few possessions into the Caddy and put the rest—mostly music scores—into two trunks he sent to Los Angeles by rail.

Mabel was disconsolate, fearing that Morton wasn't strong enough to make the journey.

"I asked him to let me go along," said Mabel, "but he said, 'No, I know my condition. I know if something was to go wrong, you'd have hysterics and it would make my heart attack worse.'"

Before leaving, Morton asked for a blessing from the priest at St. Aloysius, another nod to the Catholicism he was trying to reclaim. The priest pointed out that a cross-country trip in November could be hazardous. But Morton would not listen. "Father, I have just lost my godmother and my old godfather is out in California, blind and helpless," he said. "He needs my care. Besides, I've got to find someplace that is better for my health. This place is killing me by degrees."

There was no stopping this man when his mind was made up, so the priest blessed the Lincoln and the Cadillac and sent Morton on his way.

Said Mabel, "That was the last I saw of my husband."

nine

FLEE AS A BIRD TO THE MOUNTAIN

With a few suits and all his old Victor records packed safely into the new Lincoln, and the 1938 Caddy hitched behind it, Jelly Roll Morton pulled out of New York. He knew the journey west could be brutal in mid-October, particularly for a man with a weakening heart driving a two-car caravan across two-lane roads soon to be covered with snow and ice. But he had no other options, and the road, as always, was his last and only hope.

So Morton, with exactly forty dollars in his pocket, drove from Harlem down to New Jersey, then on to Pennsylvania, where he picked up U.S. Highway 30 west, driving through towns he had played when he still was on the way up. He stopped in several of them, hoping to pick up some work or a loan from someone who remembered him from back when. But there were no takers in Cincinnati, where Morton once had been a big draw; no recording dates in Richmond, Indiana, where he had launched his recording career in 1923; no gigs in Downstate Illinois, where he used to be the hottest touring act out of Chicago; no high times in St. Louis, Missouri, where he famously carved the competition, merely for sport. In this cross-country journey, Morton retraced a life lived on the road, at each stop remembering a sensational performance, a legendary recording date, a seemingly inextinguishable love affair, or a close brush with near disaster.

Now Morton was a stranger in these towns, his friends having long since moved away, his name no longer inspiring throngs to see the hot jazz musician from Chicago who carried an outsized roll of cash and a pearl-handled pistol and knew how to use both. No one wanted any part of him, not even Amide Colas, the elder of his two half sisters, whom he phoned in Lubbock, Texas. She told him not to bother driving south because she would throw him out if he dared show up at her door—their grandmother had told her all about him and the life he had led in the District, and she wanted no part of his seedy ways.

The only sanctuary Morton found was in the cheap roadside motels he slept in and in the Catholic churches that dotted the landscape. He stopped in some of them to pray for deliverance from his dire situation and for forgiveness for the way he had spent his life—or at least the sinful early parts of it. But apart from whatever consolation he may have received from on high, Morton found little solace on this journey, at least not until he reached the other end of the continent. Even there, in the Pacific Northwest, he thought his life had come to an end when both of his cars slid off the road in a snowstorm in Wyoming, soon forcing him to ditch the Cadillac in Montpelier, Idaho. Now his new Lincoln was almost as bent up as the old Caddy, but at least it took him to Roseburg, Oregon, where he looked up the woman who had loved and tormented him in the early days on the West Coast, Anita Gonzalez. Morton had not laid eyes on her in seventeen years and saw in her, at last, a friendly face. But she declined to mention to him that she now was married to a lumberjack named John F. Ford, who in turn did not know she was a Creole from New Orleans. Ford believed his wife was Cuban, because that's what she had told him.

Morton confessed to Anita that he was ill, though he needn't have, for Anita could see it in the sunken hollows of his cheeks and in the palpable effort with which he breathed and walked. He told her he was heading to Los Angeles to straighten out his godmother Eulalie's affairs and to start over in a warmer climate, and that if he was lucky, the royalties might start rolling in from ASCAP or Tempo or Melrose. He insisted, as always, that he had been robbed of $3 million and wasn't going to rest until he got it.

That was all Anita needed to hear. With 3 million reasons to leave her husband, she decided to liberate herself from pitiful Roseburg and return to the big-city life to see what might transpire. While Anita was gathering up the things she needed, Morton proceeded with his journey, stopping long enough in Rock Springs, Wyoming, to jot a few lines to Carew, who had no idea what had happened to his business partner: "Just a line to let you hear from [me] & let you know that I will never forsake you, until the business becomes a paying proposition. I left N.Y. because everything seems against us."

A few days later, Morton wrote to Mabel, detailing the hellish weather and horrific driving conditions that had battered his cars and nearly killed him. He attributed his survival behind the wheel neither to his wits nor to chance but to a greater power in whom he now was placing all his faith—in part because there was nowhere else left to place it. "Yes, the blessed mother really taken care of me in a-many ways in all the storms and danger I had to confront me," Morton wrote to Mabel from Yreka, California on November 9. "I did not get a chance to make many novenas on the road on account of driving all the time, but I said lots of prayers just the same."

But as Morton arrived in Los Angeles, around November 13, his worst fears were realized. Thieves indeed had run off with most of Eulalie's possessions during the last days of her life, taking the rest of them after she died. "Every thing was stolen," Morton wrote to Carew on November 21. "All the household goods, clothes, all was stolen from both. Diamonds & everything they had. It was simply a shame. . . . The old man is in fair health[,] at least about 80 years of age. Even stole every shirt but the [one] he had on his back."

At this point, Morton lacked the $42.29 he needed to claim the two trunks that he had sent a few weeks earlier from New York. They

contained his precious manuscripts—the last works he ever wrote—
and had arrived in Los Angeles on November 20. If he could get the
money together to claim them and if he could get a big band to begin
rehearsing the scores he had penned in his final days in New York, he
still might get his chance to show the world that he wasn't through
yet.

Indeed, with these scores—which no one, including the composer,
had yet heard played in full—he thought he might yet prevail in a music world that ultimately had no place for him.

Jelly Roll Morton's men met practically every day at Elks' Hall, 4016
South Central Avenue, and from the start of these rehearsals the composer knew that this was the best band he had ever had, playing the
most sublime music he had ever written. He could see that he had
chosen well in asking bassist Ed "Montudie" Garland to find these
musicians, for only someone like Garland—who had heard Morton
playing piano decades earlier at Mamie Christine's sporting house on
Basin Street and after hours at the Big 25 saloon—could have picked
the right players for this job. There was Bud Scott, the New Orleans
guitarist whose hot playing back at the turn of the century had persuaded Morton to give up the instrument entirely and switch to piano.
There was Kid Ory, the great New Orleans trombonist who had
caroused with Morton at Lulu White's in the District and had played
brilliantly on Morton's Red Hot Peppers recording dates in Chicago.
There was New Orleans trumpeter Mutt Carey, who had worked with
Ory in New Orleans in 1914 and a few years later with King Oliver in
Chicago at the Dreamland, at Thirty-fifth and Calumet. And there
was drummer Minor (Ram) Hall, who had brought his New Orleans
street beats to Kid Ory's band in 1916, to Oliver's California outfit in
1921–1922, and to New Orleans clarinetist Jimmie Noone's Chicago
outfit thereafter.

That was as many New Orleans men as Garland could round up,
but they were enough to set the tone and flavor for a mighty unit,
with Carey and Pee Wee Brice on trumpets; Ory and Jug Everly on

trombones; Theodore Bonner, Robert Garner, and Alfonso George on saxophones; Atwell Rose on violin; Scott on guitar; and Garland on bass. Better yet, Garland shrewdly had lined up Buster Wilson to play piano, so that Morton would be free to conduct the band and edit the scores. Even this lineup, however, was a bit short of what Morton had in mind, for he had scored these new arrangements for fully four trumpets and five saxophones—the modern big band in all its orchestral glory. But Morton quickly adapted his manuscripts to suit the instrumental forces at his disposal, thankful that at least a few great New Orleans musicians were willing to rehearse for free for a shot at playing Jelly Roll Morton's newest music.

When they began to read through these scores, the players were stunned not only by the originality of the music but by how far it had evolved from the great old Morton hits of the 1920s. For these were neither the fiery old stomps with which Morton had jolted Chicago's South Side in the mid-1920s nor the lazy blues reveries with which he had brought a distinctly southern sensibility north. This was something radically different, a plush, sumptuous ensemble music, with reeds and brass forming gleaming instrumental choirs, the band's phrases neither fast nor slow but gently pressing forward, above an undertow of deep swing rhythm.

Furthermore, the harmonies Morton now was writing were more dissonant and the chord progressions more radical than anything these players—or anyone else in jazz—had yet heard. "Those arrangements were very interesting," recalled Garland, who acknowledged that even some of the old New Orleans musicians had had some trouble with these scores, because they didn't proceed exactly as one might expect them to. "If someone didn't play their part right, Jelly'd run over it on the piano to show them," said Garland, marveling that a man who appeared so frail when he entered the rehearsal hall became so energized once the music making began.

On hearing this music played by New Orleans men, Morton realized that he not only had succeeded in grasping the sleek big-band style of the day but had radicalized it, stylistically pushing it miles ahead of the music that was making Ellington and Lunceford and Calloway rich and famous. This was his ticket back, a top-flight big band playing scores that offered something new in big-band music, a library of works that could reestablish Morton as the foremost jazz composer of them all. Among these scores, none was more outlandish than a piece he cryptically titled "Ganjam." It unfolded like the first movement of a symphony—complete with primary and secondary themes, a development section, and a recapitulation—and in it Morton introduced astringent chords, bizarre key changes, and exotic scales of a sort that would not be heard in jazz until at least the early 1950s. With "Ganjam," Morton took an enormous artistic leap, from the 1920s music that had made him famous (albeit typecasting him as a New Orleans–Chicago relic) to a genuinely avant-garde sound that presaged the direction in which jazz would evolve. This was a remarkable breakthrough, considering that Morton dated from the first generation of New Orleans jazz inventors and already had catapulted the art form forward once before—by proving that it could be written down. Now he was doing so again, offering a piece of art music so sophisticated and original that it could open up new possibilities for others, just as his groundbreaking publication of "Jelly Roll Blues" had in 1915.

Yet this crowning achievement had been authored by a musician who now was a laughingstock, a nearly broken man who had come of age in a long-forgotten, already mythic New Orleans. To the more famous young stars of jazz, Morton was a has-been at best, a sorry self-caricature at worst. But if these emerging jazz men had heard this music, they would have been forced to admit that Morton was the leader of them all, the most forward-thinking and accomplished composer in jazz.

Though the rehearsal band playing "Ganjam" wasn't staffed by as many horns as Morton had planned, at least it was letting this music sing out. As Morton conducted the players, setting tempos and cueing instrumental entrances with a wave of his baton or an extended forefinger of his right hand, he achieved a new pinnacle in his art, even as he was tumbling toward a new nadir of poverty and misery in his life. While his music played, however, only his art mattered. "Ganjam" and the other showpieces proved that Morton was back, once again the most prodigious jazz musician in the world, though no one but his band knew it.

Most of the jazz world dismissed Morton, presuming that he didn't know how to move past the stylistic clichés of the Roaring Twenties, yet in truth he was raring to conquer the music world again. For him, the challenge was to find an opportunity to perform and record this music, and to get paid for it, at least enough so that he could keep the men working.

"I have started organizing a band," he wrote to Carew on November 23, from a squalid room he had rented at 4052 Central Avenue, just down the street from the Elks' building where he was rehearsing. "I don't have to pay for the rehearsal hall so far, & it seems like I will be able to do something."

Morton was on his way, or at least tried to believe he was, contacting movie studios to let them know he was ready for work and joining forces with Benjamin "Reb" Spikes to start a new music publishing company in Los Angeles. The new partnership tantalized Morton not only because he and Spikes might make money publishing black music but also because the venture afforded Morton a chance to strike back at ASCAP. For the Spikes-Morton house would place all its tunes under the protection of a new organization called Broadcast Music, Inc., or BMI, a start-up competitor to ASCAP. Though Morton already was contracted to ASCAP as a composer, there was nothing stopping him from publishing tunes by Spikes and anyone but himself with BMI. In so doing, Morton hoped to help crack ASCAP's stranglehold on the music-licensing business.

"Broadcast Music, Inc., has signed to take the entire output of a new publishing company formed here by Jelly Roll Morton, famous old-time blues pianist and singer, and Benjamin ('Reb') Spikes, songwriter ('Someday Sweetheart') and one-time bandleader," reported *Down Beat*'s Hollywood office on January 1, 1941. "Harry Engel, [West] Coast chief of operations for BMI, said Spikes would be the composer in the new firm and that Morton would watch for and select songs by other Negro composers. . . . Engel said, 'We know there is a wealth of great talent among Negro song writers which has never been developed,'" a barely veiled reference to ASCAP's unstated but remarkably effective policy of keeping black composers out.

So Morton was back in business, his West Coast publishing venture about to get on its feet, his big band honing renditions of new Morton works that might catapult Morton back to the top. Yet just as Morton was lining up Hollywood nightclub bookings, Local 767 of the musicians' union shut down his band, for Morton had been using some nonunion men. He had no choice, he told Carew, because the California musicians did not know how to play his complex new tunes, while the New Orleans boys did. Unfortunately, several of the musicians from back in Louisiana had not bothered to sign up with the union, so Morton's dream band was out of business virtually before it got started.

Worse, Morton began coughing up blood shortly after Anita arrived, at the start of 1941. Too ill to get around, he moved with Anita into a white frame house at 1008 East Thirty-second Street, spending his days writing letters to Carew, whom he asked to continue copyrighting his new works, and to Mabel, to whom he sent a few dollars whenever he had it. "I haven't made any money since I've been gone, although I received the ASCAP check," he wrote to her on January 16. "But this town takes money to live, so that is about all gone." It is not known if Mabel realized that Morton was relying on Anita for sustenance and care.

Breathing was becoming increasingly difficult for Morton, and on February 13 he wrote to Carew, "I have been nearly dead, since you last heard from me. . . . There were two nights, it looked especially bad for me." Each day was becoming a battle not just for money but for life, and each day the fight weakened Morton. Yet he would not give up on his quest to return to his former position of eminence in the music world. Though he had only a few good hours a week, he used them to compose music, this time a new big-band orchestration of "Finger Breaker," the keyboard tour de force he had penned in Washington and now was rewriting as an orchestral showpiece, even as he was dying.

But writing music was about all that he could do. When offers of work finally started coming in from the movie studios, Morton was too sick to play the jobs he needed to pay for food and medicine. He was "as weak as a chicken with no energy," as he put it to Carew, and it pained him to let these jobs slip away. Finally, he realized that he had to see a doctor if he was going to live, and the X-rays the physician ordered showed that Morton's heart was dramatically enlarged. There was no comfort in this news, but to get it he found himself deeper in debt. The worry and anxiety over his health and his finances only worsened his condition, which was spiraling out of control. "My breath is very short," he wrote to Carew on May 13, "and I can't get around. I nearly smother nights trying to sleep."

Now word was starting to get out that the once brash and seemingly invincible Jelly Roll Morton was coming to the end of his torment. "Seriously ill in a little cottage just off Central Ave. lies an aging Negro musician who probably did more than any other one man to perpetuate one of America's most valuable native musical forms—the 'blues,' from which stemmed such developments as 'boogie woogie,' jazz, so-called 'modern swing,' etc.," noted *Down Beat*. "But Jelly Roll, 56 years old, sick and in financial trouble, is more angry than despairing. He's angry at the AFM [American Federation of Musicians], angry at ASCAP, angry at BMI, angry at the old pump for letting him down, when he had so much to do."

This article infuriated Morton, for he knew it was an obituary published while he still was alive. So he wrote a letter to the editors at *Down Beat*, whose solicitations had inspired numerous offers of help from Morton admirers. "It's swell to know I have friends like that," he told the paper. "Just tell 'em I appreciate the offers but don't need any help." Creole pride. Morton would sooner skip medical treatment than take a penny in charity, which is why he wrote to Carew on May 29, "I have to lay off of doctors for the time [being, on] account of finance, & I don't think the dr's were doing very much." So he turned again to homemade remedies. When an elderly woman Morton knew suggested that he chop up a few shards of raw garlic, pour them into water, boil a quart of the concoction, and drink it down, Morton held his nose and started consuming the brew—to negligible effect. Between doses of this odious beverage, he drank carrot juice, potassium broth, vegetable juice, practically any kind of health food that might restore his strength. Nothing worked. Instead, he got so weak that all he wanted to do was lie down, yet when he did, he couldn't breathe and felt as if he were being choked to death. "Unless I show better improvement . . . it will [be] harder to make ends meet," he wrote Carew, fearing for his financial state while his health slipped away, the two crises inextricably wound up with each other.

On June 19, Morton wrote to Carew in a heartbreaking, almost illegible scrawl, a terrifying line: "So sick trying to get to the hospital." But Morton knew that they wouldn't let him in without cash upfront. So he resorted to the last source of capital he had, never having imagined it would come to this. He dragged himself to the bathroom with knife in hand, flicked on the light, stood in front of the mirror, and put the blade up to the front tooth where his diamond still glittered. Though weak, he plucked the jewel out of his mouth, held it in his hand, and stared at it.

That diamond would buy at least a few days in the Los Angeles Sanitarium, at 726 East Adams Boulevard, which he knew he needed if he was going to live. As he handed the rock to Anita to pawn, it was clear that his glittering self-invention from the dawn of jazz—Jelly Roll Morton—now was dead, even as Ferd Morton breathed almost his last.

Anita gave him what she thought the diamond was worth, and at least it got him into the sanitarium, where he lay in bed, his legs so swollen he couldn't walk, and poured out his anguish to his friend, Carew. "With doctor bills & expenses, I am just about at the end of the rope," he wrote on June 21, from his bed in the sanitarium. "I pawned & borrowed money for this purpose. This spot cost me $20 a week. The Dr says I will see an improvement in about four weeks. I don't know if I will be able to stay."

The answer came soon enough, for in a few days the tests, medicines, and doctors' consultations had burned up Morton's cash, and he was asked to leave. He went back to Anita's place, but she could see that he wasn't going to survive long, so on June 28 she put a piece of paper in front of him to sign. It was a last will and testament, and Morton was so sick and weak that he could not write his signature straight. Instead, the name Ferdinand Joseph Morton slipped above and below the line designated for it, as if the signer barely could see.

Indeed, Morton did not read or understand this document, because if he had, he instantly would have spotted the laughable errors Anita had written into it. For starters, she misspelled his sister's name as Amide Colos (it was actually Colas) and bequeathed to her Morton's royalties and interests in "Temple Music Co." (the name, of course, was Tempo-Music). Anita also misspelled his other sister's name as Frances Morton (it was Mouton, her birth name) and in effect slapped Frances in the face by bequeathing to her "the sum of one dollar," for reasons unknown. Mabel Morton, who meanwhile was going broke back in New York, was not even mentioned in the will.

To herself, Anita bequeathed the biggest and best slice of Morton's life's work, and she did so in a fulsome, florid language that was the antithesis of the concise prose that distinguished Morton's letters and reaffirmed that this will was not his handiwork. "I hereby devise and bequeath all the rest and residue of my estate, whether real or personal property or mixed, to my beloved Anita Gonzales who has been my beloved comforter, companion and help-meet for many years, and whose tender care I sincerely appreciate," read the will. "This shall include all Ascap royalties, and Southern Music Co. Melrose Music Company and all property of every kind personal and otherwise wherever located."

This was quite a piece of writing, for as Morton lay dying in her home, Anita called herself his helpmate (though she hadn't seen him for the last seventeen years) and commended herself for providing tender care. Moreover, she referred to herself as Anita Gonzales, though back in Roseburg, Oregon, she was Anita Ford, wife of John F. Ford.

With the last will and testament signed, Anita arranged for Morton to be taken to Los Angeles County Hospital, the only facility that would accept ailing indigents. When Morton arrived, on June 29, he was placed in a broom closet, the only space available in the charity ward. A few days later, he was promoted to a bona fide hospital room, and those who visited him were struck by what they saw. As he had stopped shaving weeks ago, Morton's golden-skinned face now was partly covered by a black and gray beard. "He actually looked like a black Christ," noted the writer Dave Stuart, who sat at Morton's bedside but found that the composer either wouldn't or couldn't talk. Stuart simply held Morton's hand, trying to comfort a man who was well past consoling.

"I always thought he recognized me, but I couldn't be sure," said Stuart. "He would smile at me." How strange, thought Stuart, that this most loquacious of men—a fellow whose life was all about making and organizing sound—had fallen utterly silent.

At 2 P.M. on July 10, Jelly Roll Morton died in Los Angeles County Hospital, a victim of "cardiac decompensation" due to "hypertensive heart disorder," according to the death certificate, which listed his wife as "Anita Morton" and his race as "Ethio.," or Ethiopian. With Morton dead and soon to be buried, Anita was intent on being deemed his wife and on covering up his Creole race, of which she was ashamed.

In its prime, in the first decade of the twentieth century, St. Patrick's Church ranked with the most elegant shrines in Los Angeles, its triptych of Gothic towers—each topped with a stone cross—beckoning parishioners from miles away. But these three spires came tumbling down during the great earthquake of 1933, and the church—by then a haven for poor blacks who had migrated to the inner-city neighborhood surrounding Central Avenue—was too poor to replace them.

On the morning of July 16, when the casket containing Morton's body was carried inside, a church that could seat a thousand looked almost empty. Fewer than a hundred people assembled to mourn a man who had helped bring the sound of jazz to the world and, along the way, had proved that the music was not simply a background for sex but a vibrant art. Only one white face appeared among the bereaved, and it belonged to Dave Stuart, the writer who had held Morton's hand at his bedside in the county hospital a few days earlier. He brought with him Reb Spikes, who didn't have a car and wouldn't have been able to pay his respects otherwise. "Sure appreciate that," said Spikes. "Wanted to go as far as I could with Jelly." Because the casket was closed, all were spared the sight of Ferdinand Morton's dead body, a gaping hole marring the crown where a diamond used to gleam.

Conspicuous by their absence were Duke Ellington, who was playing at the Mayan Theatre in Los Angeles (and once said that "Jelly Roll Morton played piano like one of those high school teachers in Washington"), and Jimmie Lunceford, who was packing them in at the Casa Manana. Neither sent condolences. But a wreath in the shape of a lyre stood near the coffin, in front of the altar, courtesy of Local 767 of the musicians' union, which had shut down the band Morton had hoped would return him to the music business. At the time of Morton's death, his union dues were paid in full.

A priest Morton never had met performed a high requiem mass, but neither Mabel Morton nor Roy Carew—the two people closest to him—were there to hear it. Mabel could not afford the train ride back home to New Orleans, where she yearned to return with Morton, let alone the price of transportation across the country, while Carew could not get away from work. Both sent wires, however, as did Morton's sisters, Frances Oliver and Amide Colas.

One of the musicians who showed up, a trombonist named Ash Hardee, put together a brass band for the occasion, but when he suggested a second-line march to the cemetery, church officials said such a display would be undignified and didn't allow it. So when the service ended, a hearse and a few cars silently drove the six miles to Calvary Cemetery, with no one playing "Flee as a Bird to the Mountain" or any of the other old New Orleans funeral parade dirges.

The pallbearers carried Morton's casket to a hole in the ground marked Grave 4 at Section N, Lot 347, of Calvary Cemetery. Never was a group of men better chosen for such a task, for these were the same musicians who had played on the first black jazz band recording ever made, by Kid Ory's outfit of 1921, with Ory on trombone, Mutt Carey on cornet, Fred Washington on piano, and Ben Borders on drums. Two other members of Ory's old band, clarinetist Dink Johnson (Anita's brother) and bassist Ed "Montudie" Garland, also stood at the graveside. These New Orleans men had known Morton when a new music had erupted in the District, and they had been among the first to seize it, play it, and bring it to saloons and theaters and concert halls across the country. They recognized that Morton was the sole genius among them, and they grieved not only that he was the first to go but that he had had such a harsh time of it in those last humiliating years. If someone had asked them to play their horns, they would have let out an incredible noise, for they understood the significance of Morton's achievement and the price he had paid for it.

After the casket was lowered into the ground, the musicians tossed a few shovels of dirt on it, and everyone scattered.

The newspapers barely noted the passing of the first great composer in the American music the world embraced as jazz, but *Down Beat* devoted several pages to the man's demise. One headline, though, said it all: "Jelly Roll Rests His Case."

ten

THE AFTERGLOW

When he died, Ferdinand Joseph Morton owed $35 on a rented piano, $295 on his black Lincoln, and $48.69 for eleven days of anguish at Los Angeles County General Hospital. His assets amounted to $100 worth of clothing and fifty-one Victor records valuable to no one but himself. That Morton would sooner pry the diamond from his tooth than part with the old Victor disks indicated how much those 78s of his Red Hot Peppers meant to him, for they proved that he once had been important, the first and greatest composer in jazz and they were about all the proof he had.

Los Angeles County General slapped a lien on Morton's estate for the $48.69 bill, and after his property was sold and the estate tax paid, nothing was left. As for Morton's library of seminal jazz compositions, the tax man assessed its future value at $7,500, a pittance compared to the amounts others already had made from Morton's art and the millions it was yet to earn.

But there still was one item unaccounted for: the diamond that had once gleamed in Morton's smile. He had given the rock to Anita to pawn, the cash financing a few days' treatment at the Los Angeles Sanitarium. Anita Ford—who had called herself Anita Morton on the composer's death certificate—held the pawn ticket, and after his funeral she turned it in for the jewel. Then she drove Morton's Lincoln back to Roseburg, Oregon, resuming her life as the wife of John Ford and waiting for the royalty checks to start rolling in.

To Anita's chagrin, she received only a trickle, and not only because Morton's name and music had faded from American popular culture. More important, Mabel Morton filed a claim with ASCAP as the composer's widow, asserting that she was entitled to the crumbs ASCAP had been paying him. Because of Mabel Morton's claim, ASCAP held off making any payments to anyone until the matter could be resolved. So in the years after Morton's death, Anita collected only $2,996 in composer royalties from the company that had bought out Melrose Brothers Music.

During those last years of Anita Ford's life, she did not acquire a headstone for Morton's tiny plot at Calvary Cemetery, leaving his grave unmarked, an ignominious turn of events for a man who had once reveled in his celebrity. Offended by this disrespect, the Southern California Historical Jazz Society raised money in 1950 to pay for a marble plaque and permanent upkeep of Morton's untended grave. They took their plan to Anita, who was running a small motel near Malibu, but she would not allow it. Shamed by their grass-roots campaign, Anita said that she—and she alone—would be the one to arrange for a marker on Morton's grave, and eventually she did. But as she was discussing the matter with the Jazz Society one evening in a Los Angeles club, some of Morton's old friends shared a little secret with the Southern California Historical Jazz Society.

"That's not Mrs. Morton!" drummer Ram Hall said to music historian Floyd Levin of the Jazz Society. Hall had participated in Morton's last rehearsals in California and had known the man from the earliest days in New Orleans. "I used to go to her house in New York for gumbo—but that's not the same woman." Kid Ory, who had also played in Morton's last band, told Levin the same thing. "I never saw that woman before in my life," Ory said. "I know Jelly's wife very well. Why did you bring me here and introduce her as Mrs. Morton?"

Ory and Hall knew that Mabel was Morton's wife, but Mabel was having no success in persuading anyone of this fact, least of all ASCAP. Throughout the 1950s, she waged a one-woman campaign to get widow's benefits for the man she had comforted and consoled during the downward spiral of the last thirteen years of his life. In 1958, ASCAP finally ruled that Mabel was not entitled to a cent because she could not produce a marriage certificate. She argued that she and Morton had been wed in November 1928, before a Judge McGuire in Gary, Indiana, and that Morton had kept the license. But neither ASCAP personnel investigating Mabel Morton's claims nor researchers who later combed the marriage records of Lake County, Indiana, could find a trace of the elusive document.

In a more just world, however, a marriage license would have been beside the point. For if Mabel Morton had been able to afford a decent attorney, her counsel easily could have established that she was the composer's common-law wife and therefore merited full widows' benefits. The attorney could have cited letters Morton wrote addressing her as "My dearest Mabel, wife." And if Mabel Morton had known of the two-hundred-plus letters Morton had written to Carew, her case could not have failed, for throughout this correspondence Morton referred to Mabel as his wife and companion.

Like Morton, however, Mabel could not obtain decent legal representation and therefore received nothing for the years in which she and Morton had considered themselves wed. When ASCAP finally released the $12,813 it had been withholding, in 1958, Anita had been dead for six years. So the lump sum went to Anita's husband, John Ford, who boasted to friends that he also had the diamond that had once shone in Jelly Roll Morton's mouth. Morton never knew Ford, yet—as Anita's heir—Ford became the recipient of a royalty income that grew inexorably through the years. In stage plays (such as revivals of Tennessee Williams's *A Streetcar Named Desire*) and films (*The Newton Boys, Catch-22, Wild Man Blues*), Morton's music was used as the soundtrack for stories set in old New Orleans and Roaring Twenties Chicago. No modern-day composer could write scores as true to the spirit and the letter of early jazz as Morton's works, for he had witnessed and participated in the creation of this art.

When Alan Lomax turned his Library of Congress interviews with Morton into *Mister Jelly Roll*, his oral biography of Morton, the author was appalled by the insults that Walter and Lester Melrose had hurled Morton's way. "Old Jelly was a good orchestra man, but he couldn't write music," Lester Melrose told Lomax, with a straight face. "Jelly Roll wouldn't have been nothing if it hadn't been for Melrose. We made Jelly and we made all the rest of them. We made the blues. After all, we are here and where are they? Nowhere."

Walter Melrose agreed: "So far as Jelly Roll originating anything, he didn't do that. . . . We did a lot to build him up. We published the tunes. We got him a Victor contract. And he lived off his royalties."

This was more than Lomax could take. "As I listened to his sour comments," wrote Lomax of Walter Melrose's lies, "my dislike of this man grew." Lomax did not mention, however, that Morton had awaited payment after the Library of Congress dates were finished. When Morton was running out of cash in New York in 1939 and 1940, he wrote to Carew that Lomax had not yet come through with the money. "I wonder how Lomax think that I don't need money to live just the same as anyone else," wrote Morton. "I worked for months doing the (archives) & it meant nothing to me financially." When *Mister Jelly Roll* was published, years after Morton's death, Lomax did not share any of the proceeds with the composer's estate.

The book quoted Morton at length, posthumously giving him an important platform from which to be heard. But, alas, it also codified many of the myths that had long gathered around Morton's name. "Jelly Roll's whole life was constructed around his denial of his Negro status," wrote Lomax, not taking into account Morton's constant soliloquizing on the greatness of Tony Jackson, King Oliver, and Scott Joplin, all men "black as coal," as Morton once said. Nor did Lomax pay heed to his own statement that Morton, in his conversations with Lomax, "never lost sight of his main point: hot jazz was the creation of New Orleans Negroes." What's more, Lomax contended that Morton had cited 1885 as the year of his birth because it was "a date that puts him in Storyville earlier than most other jazzmen and gave him plenty of historical elbow room." But no one ever had denied or doubted that Morton was among the earliest players in the District. Moreover, Morton himself expounded at length about the great men who had played piano there before him, among them Jackson, Alfred Wilson, Albert Carroll, Buddy Carter, and Josky Adams. And both of Morton's half sisters placed his birth date somewhere in 1885 or 1886.

When Morton made the Library of Congress tapes, he said he was giving as accurate an account of events as possible, for the record. But few cared to believe him, preferring to cast the colorful composer as a self-loathing Creole genius who hated his race, lied about his age, and exaggerated his achievements. Even in death, Morton could not escape the charges of charlatanism that caricatured him in life.

In 1947, six years after Morton's death, Walter Melrose sold his Arizona ranch and moved back to Chicago, hoping to cash in on a resurgent interest in Dixieland music. Had Morton lived, he might have benefited from the Dixieland revival sweeping the nation, with New Orleans veterans such as Louis Armstrong and Sidney Bechet lionized by the media and adored by the concert-going, record-buying public. Their old-timers' New Orleans music—as exuberant and characteristically optimistic as ever—was ideally suited to a nation emerging from the dark years of World War II.

Though many of the New Orleans musicians whom Walter Melrose had published and swindled in the 1920s ended up destitute—most notably Morton and Joe "King" Oliver—Melrose now was rested, rejuvenated, and ready to conquer Chicago again. He opened an office above the Woods Theater, at 54 West Randolph Street, the same spot where Melrose's old associate, Marty Bloom, had unloaded Morton to the MCA booking agency in 1927. With a baby grand and two small desks crowded into the new Loop headquarters, Melrose was convinced he could rekindle the fun and profit of the good old days, energetically promoting the white trumpeter Muggsy Spanier, as well as a host of no-names. Unfortunately for Melrose, Jelly Roll Morton was not at his side this time, so the publisher fared no better than he had in the early 1920s, before Morton walked into the old shop at Sixty-third and Cottage Grove and turned a failing business into a fast moneymaker. After a couple of years of struggling in Chicago's Loop, Melrose retreated from the music business, moved to the affluent suburbs north of the city, and contented himself with buying and selling real estate. At his death in 1973, Melrose was worth well over half a million. Yet Melrose's death did not erase his life's work. In 1979, AS-CAP gave his widow a prestigious award in Melrose's name, citing "his outstanding composition of a country song, 'Make Love to Me.'" But "Make Love to Me" was simply an updating of "Tin Roof Blues," written by the New Orleans Rhythm Kings—Leon Rappolo, Paul Mares, George Brunes, Ben Pollack, and Mel Stitzel. Melrose had copyrighted the tune in 1923 and, as usual, added his name as lyricist, which meant that he collected 75 percent of the royalties on the song, while the five men who had created it split the remaining 25 percent. With "Tin Roof Blues" reborn in the late 1950s as "Make Love to Me," singer Jo Stafford had a major success, as did Melrose. The 1979 country recording of the tune gave Melrose a posthumous hit, a new honor from ASCAP, and a new stream of royalties that poured in to his heirs, though Melrose had had no part in writing the hit song in either its early or late incarnations.

Moreover, when Hollywood films used Morton's music, the credits that rolled at the end routinely gave Walter Melrose top billing as lyricist on Morton's hits, though none of Melrose's dreadful lyrics was used. In the 1998 film *The Newton Boys,* for instance, Melrose's name appeared above Morton's on the credits, which list Melrose as coauthor of Morton's indelible hits of the Roaring Twenties.

If Walter Melrose had dedicated his life to shunning the black music that made him rich, Lester Melrose had taken a different but equally unsavory path. Realizing that black musicians were the font of American popular music, Lester Melrose in the late 1930s began traveling the American South, pirating tunes from illiterate black musicians or paying them a pittance to purchase the copyright. Then he returned to Chicago and hired other black artists to record them, keeping the royalties for himself.

Lester Melrose proved so adept at pilfering black compositions that both RCA and Columbia hired him to run their race-music subsidiaries out of Chicago, with Melrose often bragging that he had recorded fully 90 percent of the black music urban America was dancing to in the 1930s, 1940s, and 1950s. Certainly Melrose's income suggests he was onto something, for as early as 1938—the year of Jelly Roll Morton's ill-fated attempt to retake New York—Lester Melrose grossed $139,000, his tax filings show. After making his fortune off uncounted black blues musicians, Lester Melrose retired to an orange grove in Florida, where he died in 1979.

Morton had made a mission of exposing the abuses of ASCAP. In the last years of his life, he had walked the streets of the music-publishing district, his collar turned up against the wind, condemning ASCAP to anyone who would listen, for he had figured out precisely how ASCAP earned money off every tune that the radio stations played. By excluding most black songwriters from membership, ASCAP was robbing an entire class of artists of its due. When ASCAP finally began admitting blacks, in the late 1930s, the organization classified composers and songwriters according to the artistic value of the work—as judged by ASCAP's white board members. Music by black songwriters such as Morton were judged less consequential than tunes by their white counterparts and therefore were given low ratings that resulted in puny payments. Because ASCAP held a near monopoly on licensing music to radio stations and performance venues, black composers had little recourse but to accept the pennies they were given.

In railing relentlessly against ASCAP's corrupt practices, Morton gained a reputation as a complainer at best, a crackpot at worst. Undeterred, he detailed his allegations in a series of letters to the antitrust division of the U.S. Department. of Justice, demanding an investigation and offering to testify.

In 1941, a few months after Morton's death, the United States filed a lawsuit in the Southern District Federal Court of New York, charging that the ASCAP board of directors had engineered voting rules so that major white music publishers and songwriters stayed in power (and called the shots on membership and payments), while small operators like Morton, Carew, and Tempo-Music Publishing were frozen out. The legal arguments continued for more than a decade, while the discriminatory classification system remained locked in place.

But the groundswell of complaints that Morton had helped release led to congressional hearings in 1956. And the congressman who took up the cause of disenfranchised publishers and songwriters was Representative James Roosevelt—the man to whom Morton had addressed some of his first complaints, when Roosevelt was secretary to the president of the United States, his father, Franklin Delano Roosevelt. The younger Roosevelt chaired the subcommittee of the Select Committee on Small Business that was investigating abuses by ASCAP, and his hearings dissected the operation of ASCAP, as songwriters testified about experiences nearly identical to Morton's.

These sessions won over public sentiment to the cause of exploited songwriters, but no congressional action was taken. Instead, the battle shifted to the courts, where the songwriters and their heirs told of decades of discrimination and financial chicanery. Edward Niles, attorney for the estate of Morton's old rival, W. C. Handy, spoke eloquently for all in 1959: "I say that these writers should have credit not only for the income which is directly brought in by their works, but they are entitled to even more. Their work has been getting rewritten ever since they started writing. They started styles which have increased the popularity of popular music."

Indeed, black artists such as Morton and dozens more had created America's pop music industry, asking only for the proceeds from the music they had written—and that they were denied by ASCAP. The court did not go so far as to increase rewards for jazz pioneers or compensate them for their wrongful exclusion, but, finally, in 1960—nearly two decades after Morton's death—ASCAP consented to a federal court decree that banished the rigged classification system. From this point forth, ASCAP was required to base payments on precise calculations of an individual song's commercial use. The consent decree meant that composers henceforth were to be paid by ASCAP from fees collected from broadcast stations and cabarets, based upon the frequency of the use of their music, not on the arbitrarily assigned value of their work as judged by a board of directors accountable to no one.

By documenting ASCAP's abuses, Morton helped set the stage for reforms that were nearly two decades away.

Morton's death wounded no one more than Roy Carew, who in 1938 quixotically believed he might save an aging, forgotten musician. But Carew also hoped to revisit a more heady and freewheeling moment in his own life, when he had ventured to New Orleans in 1904 and heard Morton's beguiling music wafting out of Hilma Burt's whorehouse.

Both men had gotten sidetracked in the ensuing decades, though in distinctly different ways. Morton had erred tragically in placing his trust in Walter Melrose and had been steamrolled by a burgeoning music industry that crushed the black geniuses who had invented it. Carew had settled into the comfort of a white middle-class life that bored him so badly he began to pour his money into a two-bit music-publishing company he knew had scant chance of surviving against the majors.

Yet for a brief period, from 1938 to 1941, Carew reinvigorated his life and temporarily revived Morton's hopes. Beneath all their big plans and great ambitions, perhaps the two men realized they had little chance against a crooked publisher, a monopolistic licensing organization, and the music industry at large, which was barreling ahead without them. But in their planning and letter writing, they nurtured an illusion that helped sustain each of them.

If Carew had not strolled past Hilma Burt's on that signal night in 1904, the noble failure that was Tempo-Music Publishing never would have come into being, nor would Morton have had a business partner with whom he could share his dreams and pour out his frustrations in more than two hundred letters that serve as the true last testament of a dying man. Once the letters stopped and Morton was buried in Calvary Cemetery in Los Angeles, Carew heroically continued the fight without him.

He wrote articles extolling Morton's genius in tiny record-collector magazines, he wrote threatening letters to publishers who infringed on Morton's copyrights, he sued movie studios and theatrical production companies that borrowed Morton's tunes without paying up, and he always won. In his most poignant campaign, he took on the successor firm to Melrose Brothers Music, which in 1950 put out a folio of Dixieland songs that included the 1926 hit "Sweetheart O'Mine." But Carew knew that this tune was nothing more than a steal from Morton's "Frog-I-More," the very first composition that Morton had copyrighted, in 1918. By lifting the trio of Morton's "Frog-I-More," hiring someone to adapt it, and adding his own lyrics, Walter Melrose in 1926 had hijacked yet another Morton work, with King Oliver and Louis Armstrong, among others, successfully recording the new "composition." Satchmo, in fact, achieved one of his first famous solos on this Morton tune.

Melrose's successor company rereleased the tune nearly a quarter century later as "Sweetheart O'Mine," complete with Walter Melrose's sickly, sappy lyrics. This was more than Carew could tolerate, so he went to court and succeeded in reclaiming the rights for Tempo-Music.

In a way, everything important that Carew did after Morton's death revolved around the man's music, yet it's difficult to fathom why Carew told the executor of Morton's estate, Hugh E. Macbeth, that Morton had transferred his interest in Tempo-Music to Carew to cancel outstanding debts. Perhaps Carew, knowing that Macbeth had been hired by Anita to finalize Morton's dubious last will and testament, simply did not wish to cooperate with the man. Certainly it pained him to know that Morton's posthumous royalties were going to no one connected to the composer by blood or love but, instead, to Anita's heirs. Regardless, Carew dutifully paid Morton's songwriting royalties on Tempo-Music tunes to the composer's estate, though these amounts were negligible, less than a hundred dollars per quarter.

But the portion of Morton's music that Anita had bequeathed to herself, the Melrose Brothers Music tunes of the 1920s, swelled in value after her death. By 1965, Morton's Roaring Twenties tunes had earned $115,589 for Anita's heirs, the rapidly increasing funds generated mostly by movie and stage play uses of Morton's music. With the well-documented jazz resurgence of the 1980s and 1990s, the music Morton had written for his Red Hot Peppers returned to the spotlight with an intensity perhaps no one but Morton himself might have expected. Thanks in part to performances by the Lincoln Center Jazz Orchestra in New York, the Smithsonian Jazz Masterworks Orchestra in Washington, D.C., and the Chicago Jazz Ensemble in the city where Morton achieved his greatest acclaim—as well as the movies and TV shows that used Morton's music—his oeuvre began generating a fortune in the last two decades of the twentieth century. By the year 2000, Morton's work had earned more than $1 million in royalties for the composer's estate and at least twice that much for his publishers—over $3 million in all. After Morton's death, however, his royalties did not go to his blood relations, who were cut out of the will Anita created. But Morton's true heirs, the descendants of Amide Colas and Frances Mouton, were more dismayed that they had no voice in how Morton's music was used or his image portrayed. These decisions were made, and always will be, by the heirs of Anita Ford, aka Gonzalez, aka Morton, née Johnson.

Carew lived long enough to see his friend vindicated by the court decree forcing ASCAP to change its monopolistic ways but did not witness Morton's resurgence in America's concert life. He died in 1967 at age eighty-four, knowing that he had been the confidante of the first bona fide composer of jazz, and that he had given a great American artist a reason to persevere when no others were apparent.

Better still, Carew had saved the precious correspondence that helped lay bare the true story of Morton's last years. These documents, as well as hundreds of others unearthed since, have rendered the myths and lies meaningless. Had Carew not preserved this paper trail, Morton would be fixed in history as the liar and charlatan conventional wisdom long made him out to be.

Yet it took nearly another three decades for that truth to come to light.

EPILOGUE

William Russell, who packed his French Quarter apartment with documents on the life and music of Jelly Roll Morton, did not set out to change jazz history. Indeed, armed with a diploma in violin and music history and theory from the Quincy (Illinois) Conservatory of Music, Russell already had a mission in life: He was going to become an important classical composer. He was so convinced of it, in fact, that he changed his birth name, Russell William Wagner, deciding that there wasn't room in the world of classical music for two great composers named Wagner.

But in 1929, a seemingly slight event changed the course of Russell's life and, by extension, the history of jazz. While teaching at a small college in New York, Russell noticed that a student had left on his desk a recording of Jelly Roll Morton and his Red Hot Peppers playing "Shoe Shiner's Drag." Russell took the disk home, played it, and never quite recovered. Everything about this music—its syncopated swing rhythms, its southern blues shadings, its lapidary instrumental counterpoint—turned Russell's world upside down. The strict rules of European rhythm, melody, and structure that Russell had been taught since childhood were rendered nearly obsolete by this music, which by comparison sounded free, personal, and utterly

American. Though steeped in the music of Bach, Beethoven, and
Brahms, Russell now considered jazz "the best music I had heard."

He wasted no time in pursuing his new passion, voraciously collecting jazz records, Morton's above all. Inevitably, he realized that he
had to meet the man who had changed his life, so in 1938 Russell
found Morton playing in a Washington, D.C., dive, forgotten by the
music industry world but laying plans for a grand return to New
York. The two men—one tired and sick, the other young and newly
inspired by Morton's art—met several times in Washington, and it
was to Russell that Morton made his sweeping declaration before
heading once more to New York: "Tell them to move over. The king is
coming back."

Russell met up with Morton again in Manhattan, when the composer still believed he had a fighting chance. But a few months later,
Morton was dead in Los Angeles and Russell was pursuing a radically
altered life's plan: He was going to snap up every scrap of paper, every
piece of sheet music, every interview, photo, and document on Morton and the great city of his birth.

Russell spent the next five decades building his collection of Mortoniana, which also led him to collect material on Bunk Johnson, Ma-
halia Jackson, Baby Dodds, Louis Armstrong, and anyone else re-
motely related to the origins of jazz. Along the way, he also founded
the American Music record label, contributed to the seminal book
Jazzmen (1939), revived the career of Bunk Johnson, and helped create the Archive of New Orleans Jazz (later renamed the Hogan Jazz
Archive) at Tulane University.

Yet none of these achievements matched the work Russell did in
gathering up missing documentation on the man whose music had introduced him to jazz. When Russell read in a newspaper that the state
of California was going to destroy official documents already on micro-
film, he headed west and swiped the original of Morton's death certificate, in order to save it. When Russell heard that his friend and fellow
Morton acolyte Roy Carew had died in 1967, he rushed to Washington
and discovered that Carew's widow had dumped Morton's letters to

Carew in the trash. Russell snatched them out, paid Carew's widow for them, and took them back to his already bulging apartment.

The man simply would not be denied when the subject was Jelly Roll Morton, to the consternation of jazz collectors across the country. "Whenever I went to chase down something relating to Morton," recalled Chicago jazz historian John Steiner, "Bill Russell always had gotten there first."

Perhaps only someone of Russell's determination and ingenuity could have found the most coveted items of all Mortoniana, the groundbreaking big-band works Morton had been rehearsing in Los Angeles before his heart gave out. Buster Wilson, who played piano for Morton's last rehearsal band, had held onto these precious documents for years after Morton's death, but he was the last man known to have seen them. For nearly a decade, they were stashed in Wilson's home, "in a large trunk draped with a silk shawl on which stood a tarnished brass lamp," wrote Los Angeles jazz historian Floyd Levin.

> Buster promised to sort through the trunk 'one day' and offered to give me those old manuscripts. I repeatedly reminded him of his offer, but he never managed to open the trunk. After Buster's death, I informed his widow, Carmelita, of his promise. I discreetly called her several times, but she seemed reluctant to let me have the arrangements. The phone eventually was disconnected. Carmelita moved. She apparently left the city, and I was unable to contact her again. With that I gave up all hope of ever locating these scores.

Levin needn't have bothered, for Russell, once again, had gotten there first, acquiring hundreds of pages of Morton's last music, the meticulously penned pitches and rhythms that told where the composer was taking his art in his last rush of creativity. But Russell did not share this music—or tell anyone of its existence—for the rest of his life. Instead, he kept these irreplaceable scores safely boxed and shelved in his apartment, awaiting discovery after his death.

Theatre of Quarter ? ?
the F.

A few days before Russell died in 1992, at age eighty-seven, he had completed work on a mammoth tome, *Oh, Mister Jelly: A Jelly Roll Morton Scrapbook,* a potpourri of documents, interviews, and photos. But its 720 pages, published in 1999, only hinted at the scope of the Morton material Russell had jammed into used A&P shopping bags and battered Tulane Shirt Co. boxes.

Though Russell had shared bits and pieces of this material with writers and jazz buffs who had come to visit him, no one but he understood the magnitude of the collection as a whole, for it contained hundreds of transcripts of interviews with Morton's colleagues and acquaintances; the complete Morton-Carew correspondence of the last three years of the composer's life; and the missing, long-sought scores that had been in Buster Wilson's vanished trunk.

To his eternal credit, Russell ensured that all of this material would survive him, arranging for it to be made safe after his death at the Historic New Orleans Collection, in the city's age-old French Quarter. For fully three years after Russell died, archivists filed and indexed the massive holdings, newly baptizing it the William Russell Jazz Collection.

But it was not until April 29, 1998—nearly fifty-seven years after Morton's death—that the composer's last music finally was performed, at Le Petit Théâtre du Vieux Carré (the Little Theatre of the French Quarter), under the auspices of the Historic New Orleans Collection. For three nights straight, Don Vappie and the Creole Jazz Serenaders Orchestra gave the world premiere performances of Morton's sprawling big-band scores, the pieces he had hoped might return him to glory.

The music proved not only revelatory but more radical than anyone could have imagined. These posthumous premieres revealed a composer no longer elaborating in the ornate polyphonic style that had made him famous in the 1920s, no longer relying on the two-beats-to-the-bar stomps and lazy blues dirges that epitomized New Orleans–Chicago jazz. Instead, Morton's music had become sleek and streamlined, in the style of the World War II dance bands, but it was something more as well. The start-stop rhythms and unexpected silences he had brought to his orchestration of "Mr. Joe" showed a master composer toying with listeners' expectations. The shimmering orchestral colors and aggressive swing backbeats that drove "Oh, Baby" might well have made this the hit tune Morton had been looking for.

Neither of these works, however, prepared listeners for the cryptically titled "Ganjam," the most daring work of Morton's late career and, in some ways, the most revolutionary he ever penned. Breaking from the conventions of his past, Morton had laid out "Ganjam" in the form of the first movement of a symphony, complete with multiple themes, a development section in which these themes are transformed, and a recapitulation—the same structure that everyone from Mozart to Mahler had followed for more than two hundred years. Here was the meager classical training of Morton's youth coming to the fore, in full bloom. Even more surprising, Morton in "Ganjam" had ventured into the kinds of unabashedly dissonant chords and exotic Eastern scales that were not to be heard in jazz for at least another decade, with the experiments of Charles Mingus in the 1950s.

No one familiar with Morton's work could have anticipated a piece with such strange harmonies and such long and winding melody lines. Nor could anyone have imagined that such a piece could have been written between 1938 and 1940, when even Duke Ellington still was years away from the breakthroughs of his orchestral tone poem "Black, Brown and Beige."

With "Ganjam," Morton—who had given jazz its first great artistic leap, by proving it could be written down—gave jazz yet another, pointing toward the next generation's avant-garde. As he was doing so, however, he was being laughed at by his peers, ignored by the jazz industry, and robbed by his Chicago publisher and by AS-CAP. Nevertheless, though sick and impoverished, Morton had managed to write his most innovative work, in effect charting one final advance for an art form he had helped create.

In "Ganjam" Morton affirmed in composition what he could not convey through performance or argument at the end of his life:

His ideas still were vital and fresh. Better still, with "Ganjam" Morton proved that he remained at the forefront of jazz, even if no one else realized it.

As Morton suspected, this music did indeed return him to glory, at least among the cognoscenti who crowded into Le Petit Théâtre du Vieux Carré to hear it, as well as those who savored the next round of performances, two years later in Chicago. Wherever "Ganjam" and the other last works are performed from this point forth, they will stand as Morton's last great musical statement.

Through these visionary compositions—and also through Morton's campaign to crack ASCAP's monopoly (which succeeded two decades after his death) and through his return to Catholicism—the composer sought, and perhaps achieved, a kind of redemption. But it took nearly six decades, and the revelation of William Russell's cache of documents, before anyone knew it.

NOTES ON SOURCES

CHAPTER ONE

1   "There was a sudden burst . . . looked out." R. J. Carew, New Orleans Recollections (*The Record Changer*, July 1943), p. 10.

2   "Happened to be . . . the parade." Ibid.

2   "Every Sunday . . . called it a ball." Ferdinand "Jelly Roll" Morton, interview, Library of Congress, 1939.

3   "One youngster . . . brains out." Ibid.

3   "I didn't care . . . I'd wager." Ibid.

4   "All the members . . . a stitch of velvet." *New Orleans Times-Democrat*, Sept. 8, 1904.

4   "I remember . . . .his trumpet." Louis Armstrong, taped conversations, 1968 Louis Armstrong Archives at Queens College, Flushing, NY.

5   "Below Canal street . . . entertainment." Danny Barker interview by William Russell, Aug. 1968. Historic Orleans Collection.

6   ". . . has the distinction . . . Tenderloin." Blue Book advertising directory, New Orleans, 1909.

6   "I was the first . . . wanted to hear." Kay C. Thompson, "The First Lady of Storyville," *The Record Changer*, Feb. 1951.

7   "It was always . . . music and laughter." Danny Barker interview by William Russell, Aug. 1968. Historic Orleans Collection, p. 8.

8   "There were more . . . in the country." David Stuart interview by William Russell, Hollywood, CA, July 1969.

8   "found himself . . . for life." Danny Barker, "Buddy Bolden," p. 101. Copyright 1998, Estate of Danny Barker and Alyn Shipton.

8   "a couple of evil . . . being shot." David Stuart interview by William Russell, Hollywood, CA, July 1969.

9   "Miss Burt . . . Hilma Burt." Blue Book advertising directory, New Orleans, 1909.

10 "I heard him . . . through my head." Roy Carew interview by John Steiner, June 1961, p.21.

10 "Nine o'clock . . . hair combed." Stephen Longstreet, *Sportin' House*, Sherbourne, Los Angeles, p. 170–171. Copyright Longstreet, 1965.

11 "No two girls . . . and talk." Morton letter to Earle Cornwall, April 27, 1938, p.5.

11 "It was really . . . you bitches—g'wan!'" Ibid.

12 "Any time . . . would go." Partial manuscript for Tempo Publishing Co, circa 1939, p. 5.

13 "The back room . . . till later." Morton, "Fragments of an Autobiography," *The Record Changer*, March 1944, p.16.

13 "I understand . . . terrible night." Partial manuscript for Tempo Publishing Co, circa 1939, p. 5.

15 "My godmother . . . in the cell." Morton interview transcript, Library of Congress, p.1547B.

15 "Morton's first . . . gentleman." Morton comments on "We The People" radio program broadcast, Oct. 31, 1939.

16 "Those days I belonged . . . all times." Morton interview transcript, Library of Congress, p.1682A1.

17 "In those days . . . stop eating . . ." Ibid.

18 "I claim . . . .haywire." Ibid.

18 "When I first . . . by an orchestra." Ibid.

19 "I can remember . . . the family." Francis Oliver interview by William Russell, New Orleans, May 1969.

19 "The older . . . going bad." Morton, "Fragments of an Autobiography," *The Record Changer*, March 1944, p. 5.

20 "One night . . . and played." Morton interview, Library of Congress, 1939, p. 50.

21 "You'd hear music . . . next morning." Danny Barker interview by Howard Reich, April 1991.

21 "the lowest type . . . really taken." Morton interview, Library of Congress, 1939, p. 50–52.

22 "non-experienced . . . honky-tonk music." Ibid.

23 "See, the average . . . together." Percy Humphrey interview by Howard Reich, 1991.

23 "You'd hear . . . to play." Danny Barker interview by Howard Reich, April 1991.

24 "Tony Jackson . . . he had a wonderful . . . falsetto." R. J. Carew interview by John Steiner, June 1961, p. 17–18.

24 "By going into Frenchman's . . . that time." Morton interview, Library of Congress.

25 "One night he fell . . . renting a room." Ibid.

CHAPTER TWO

27 "She didn't want . . . happen again." Notes of unrecorded portions of Morton interview, Library of Congress, 1939.

27 "She told me . . . for anything." Ibid.

28 "Whenever I'd get . . . New Orleans." Morton letter to Earle Cornwall, April 27, 1838, p. 9.

29 "After my trips . . . is all right." Notes of unrecorded portions of Morton interview, Library of Congress, 1939.

29 "Back in those days . . . all the towns." Partial manuscript for Tempo Publishing Co, circa 1939, p. 8.

30 "We played to . . . black bastards." Notes of unrecorded portions of Morton interview, Library of Congress, 1939.

31 "He was the first . . . plenty money." Ibid.

31 "I'd gone there . . . new suits every day." Ibid.

32 "The coat was split . . . friend to death." Ibid.

32 "You come . . . 100 days." Ibid.

34 "I made every pigpen . . . out of Texas." Ibid.

34 "I learned that . . . of these types." Morton letter to Robert Ripley, March 31, 1938.

37 "partially wrote . . . shoot at a guy." Notes of unrecorded portions of Morton interview in Library of Congress, 1939.

38 "and I did . . . N.O. victorious." Morton letter to Earle Cornwall, April 27, 1938, p. 2.

41 "In 1911 . . . New York entertainers." James P. Johnson interview by William Russell.

41 "You could always . . . 120 pounds." Willie "The Lion" Smith interview by William Russell, New York, Dec. 1970.

42 "I was managin' . . . He was great." Benjamin J. (Reb) Spikes, interview with Jazz Oral History Project, Institute of Jazz Studies, Rutgers University, Newark, NJ.

42 "Jelly could play . . . little dark woman." Ibid.

43 "Mr. Morton . . . without hesitating." Onah Spencer, *Down Beat*, July 1, 1940, p.5.

44 "When Jelly Roll . . . supposed to go." James Haskins, "Scott Joplin, The Man Who Made Ragtime," p. 122. Copyright Doubleday & Company, Garden City, NY. 1978. James Haskins and Charlie Thompson.

47 "More than one . . . no one better." "Jelly Roll Says He Was First to Play Jazz," *Down Beat*, Sept. 1938.

50 "There was keen . . . after a skirmish." Danny Barker, "Buddy Bolden," p. 11. Copyright 1998, Estate of Danny Barker and Alyn Shipton.

50 "very uncouth . . . facial expressions." Ibid, p. 12.

CHAPTER THREE

53   "We were there . . . and screamed." George Baquet, address before
     the New Orleans Jazz Club, April 17, 1948, The Second Line, p.
     134, New Orleans, 1985.

54   "He couldn't decide . . . to be both." Clore Bryant, *Central Avenue
     Sounds*, University of California Press, Berkeley, CA, 1999, p.5.

55   "the antiquated . . . then-modern clothes." Herman Rosenberg, Jazz
     Information, Sept. 20, 1940.

56   "I can see . . . want'a give you." Tom Stoddard, *Jazz on the Barbary
     Coast*, Heyday Books, San Francisco Jazz Foundation and Califor-
     nia Historical Society, Berkeley, CA, 1998, p. 46–47.

57   "The manuscript . . . scratched on it." Ibid, p.48.

57   "We finally figured . . . playin' ad lib." Tom Stoddard, *Jazz on the
     Barbary Coast*, Heyday Books, San Francisco Jazz Foundation and
     California Historical Society, Berkeley, CA, 1998, p. 50.

58   "My God, the bunch . . . play it for them." Ibid.

63   "The clarinet . . . it went on." Ibid.

64   "She run off . . . follow her." Reb Spikes interview by Jazz Oral His-
     tory Project, Institute of Jazz Studies, Rutgers University, Newark,
     NJ, May 1980.

68   "back in those days . . . they'd be gone!" Ibid.

69   "Fellas would . . . together on it." Ibid.

CHAPTER FOUR

75   "The music business . . . pretty rough." Lester Melrose memoirs,
     1968. Provided by his grandson, George Raidell.

76   "Business boomed . . . Cottage Grove Ave." Ibid.

78   "We were getting inquiries . . . phono records." Ibid.

78   "It was [financially] impossible . . . good material." Ibid.

79   "When they opened . . . in that band." Louis Armstrong, taped con-
     versations, 1968, Louis Armstrong Archives at Queens College,
     Flushing, NY.

80   "I saw him . . . cut you to death." Kenneth Hulsizer interview by William Russell, New Orleans Historical Collection, p. 11.

82   "One day . . . on Jelly Roll." Melrose, op cit.

88   "Often he . . . at a stretch." Volley DeFaut interview by William Russell, Chicago, Nov. 1970.

89   "He helped . . . out of the red." Melrose, op cit.

89   "I'll have to . . . produce overnight." Alan Lomax, *Mister Jelly Roll*, Pantheon Books, NY, 1950, p. 229.

89   "Melrose knew . . . Hot Breaks." Morton, letter to U.S. Justice Department, Anti Trust Division, June 28, 1940.

90   "Walter asked Jelly . . . Milenberg Joys." George Hoefer, "The Hot Box," *Downbeat*, circa 1947.

90   "I had never . . . sound like him." Laurence Bergereen, "Louis Armstrong, An Extravagant Life," Broadway Books, 1997, p. 185.

93   "He talked to me . . . some character." Lee Collins, "Oh, Didn't he Ramble" *Evergreen Review*, No. 35, March 1965, p. 67.

93   "Coming from New Orleans . . . making money." Albert Nicholas interview by William Russell, Jan. 1970, New Orleans, p. 2.

96   "Ladies and . . . hell you have!" Masters of Jazz liner notes. Roger Richard, Jelly Roll Morton, Media 7.

97   "I never really . . . went to Chicago." Francis Oliver interview by William Russell, New Orleans, 1969.

CHAPTER FIVE

101   "Jelly would not . . . have that rhythm." Preston Jackson interview by William Russell, New Orleans, 1974.

102   "Thirty-fifth . . . would play it." Eddie Condon, *We Called It Music*, H. Holt, NY, 1947.

103   "The Sunset . . . best people." Laurence Bergreen, "Louis Armstrong, an Extravagant Life," Broadway Books, 1997, p. 277–278.

103   "You could just . . . all the time." Francis Mouton Oliver interview by William Russell, New Orleans, May 1969.

104   "When the people came . . . all in rhythm." Albert Nicholas interview by William Russell, New Orleans, Jan. 1970.

105 "You had to act . . . around a teacup." Stanley Dance, *The World of Earl Hines*, Scribner, 1977.

105 "I'm tired . . . sit down, man." Ibid.

105 "Why, that man . . . laugh like that." Louis Armstrong, *New York Times*, June 18, 1950.

106 "You fellows . . . all a lesson." Preston Jackson interview by William Russell, New Orleans, 1974.

107 "sat down . . . play that!" Ibid.

107 "Jelly played it . . . piece again." Ibid.

108 "I'll be loving you. . . . always." Irving Berlin, "Always," Irving Berlin Music Publishing Co., 1925.

109 "My first knowledge . . . passed it by." Morton letter to U.S. Justice Department, Anti Trust Division, June 26, 1940, p.3.

110 "When they recorded Louis . . . out of business." George Hoefer, "The Mail Box," *Downbeat*, 1947.

111 "Actually, it was his wife . . . Armstrong was there." Doc Cheatham interview by Howard Reich.

113 "He played and played . . . Lil and Louis." Nat Shapiro and Nat Hartoff, *Hear Me Talking To Ya*, p. 94–95.

116 "Very jolly . . . they were ad lib." Omer Simeon, "Mostly About Morton," *The Jazz Record*, Oct. 1945, p. 4–6.

116 "Melrose spared . . . like a king." Ibid.

118 "Jelly marked out . . . up to us." Ibid.

120 "I had never . . . go out and get it." Ibid.

121 "I remember . . . kick out of that." Ibid.

121 "Jelly wanted it . . . and he used them." Ibid.

124 "A man making . . . like myself." Lomax, op cit., p. 247.

124 "Morton was a very . . . key changes." Floyd Leven, "Anita Gonzalez," *The Second Line*, 1982.

127 "Apparently, Morton . . . an MCA band." Karl Kramer, "Jelly Roll in Chicago," *The Second Line*, 1961, p. 6. Copyright 1962, New Orleans Jazz Club.

127 "I could deliver . . . Jelly Roll Morton." Walter Melrose letter to Steve Scholes, Feb. 21, 1950.

128 "My baby's gone . . . up in a tree." Walter Melrose and Ferdinand Morton, "Sidewalk Blues," Edwin H. Morris & Co., 1926.

128 "Walter Melrose . . . receiving [royalties]." Morton letter to U.S. Justice Department, Anti Trust Division, June 10, 1940.

129 "The few contacts . . . what pleased him." Dr. Edmond Souchon, "Doctor Bites Doctor Jazz," *The Record Changer*, v. 12, No. 2.

129 "At first . . . next few months." Kramer, op cit.

CHAPTER SIX

132 "Everybody looked . . . particular style." Tommy Benford interview by William Russell, New York City, May 1970.

132 "The Rose Danceland . . . a big name." Manzie Johnson interview by William Russell, New York City, 1969.

134 "A lot of times . . . drumsticks" Benford, op cit.

136 "He had ideas . . . laughed at him." Johnson, op cit.

136 "He had went . . . no new thing." Danny Barker interview by Howard Reich, 1991.

137 "It was pretty rough . . . broke and hungry." Paul Barnes interview by William Russell, New Orleans, Oct. 1968.

138 "Mr. Peer . . . Walter Melrose." Morton letter to U.S. Justice Department, Anti Trust Division, July 2, 1940.

140 "Chicago was . . . never caught on." Kenneth Hulsizer interview by William Russell.

141 "Who is Jelly . . . listen to this." Albert "Happy" Caldwell interview by William Russell, New York, Dec. 1970.

142 "I tried to . . . *can't* play it." Danny Barker interview by William Russell, New Orleans, 1968.

143 "I want to tell . . . five cents a dozen." Trummy Young interview by William Russell, Honolulu, Aug. 1969.

143 "He'd tell us . . . in the past." Ibid.

145   "I called for . . . causing the riot." Ross Firestone, *Swing, Swing, Swing. The Life and Times of Benny Goodman*, W. W. Norton Co., NY, 1993, p. 148.

147   "The better night clubs . . . with queers." Sidney Martin, *Down Beat*, Chicago, March 1939.

147   "I don't want . . . Yours, Ferd." Lomax, p. 230.

148   "I found the legendary . . . many that listen." James Higgins, *Down Beat*, Chicago, July 1937.

148   "They don't know . . . jazz any more" Charles Edward Smith, *The Jazz Record*, Feb. 1944, p. 8–10.

150   "I simply had . . . become of Tony." Roy Carew, "New Orleans Recollections," *The Record Changer*, Sept. 1943.

150   "The day I first . . . no one knew it." Ibid.

151   "played a long stretch . . . Hilma Burt's." Ibid.

153   "These untruthful . . . history of music." Morton letter to Robert Ripley, March 31, 1938.

153   "All the Art Tatums . . . of first place." Morton letter to Earle Cornwall, April 27, 1938.

154   "As a last resort . . . be of no use." Morton letter to Supreme Court Justice Charles Hughes, May 13, 1938.

155   "Your letter . . . and rules." Hughes letter to Morton, May 16, 1938.

156   "Mr. Handy cannot . . . would be used." *Downbeat*, Aug. 1938, p. 3.

156   "I am 65 years old . . . Duke Ellington." *Downbeat*, Sept. 1938, p. 6.

157   "The twelve bar . . . musical ideas." William C. Handy, *Father of the Blues*, Da Capo Press, NY.

158   "Replying to . . . such a claim." *Downbeat*, Sept. 1938, p.5.

159   "Old Jelly . . . take down his stuff." Lomax p. 230.

159   "During the spring . . . pleased to do it." Tempo Music files, Historic New Orleans Collection.

160   "I made a good . . . since they were babies." Carew unfinished article, "12–11 U Street N.W.," New Orleans Historic collection.

161 "Had Jelly been . . . he gained little." Ibid.

163 "When I come out . . . fellow got away." Lomax p.293.

163 "Tell them . . . coming back." Russell letter to Carew.

CHAPTER SEVEN

167 "Things were really . . . they'd drift off." Frank Amacker interview by William Russell, Dec., 1968.

169 "So the money wasn't . . . out of pawn." Morton letter to Carew, Feb. 7, 1939.

171 "Practically every night . . . did show up." Wilbur de Paris interview by William Russell, New York, July 1970.

176 "I am hoping . . . underway as yet." Morton letter to Carew, Aug. 21, 1939.

178 "He was dressed . . . dealing started." Stephen W. Smith interview by William Russell, Valley Falls. NY, Jan. 1972.

179 "Before Sidney . . . except music." Ibid.

180 "those mean old . . . when he was alive." *Oh, Mr. Jelly*, JazzMedia, Denmark, 1999, p. 500.

181 "It wasn't a dance . . . make no bad record." Ferdinand Morton, Tempo Music Co., 1939.

182 "Jelly played . . . to record them." Fred Ramsey, Jr. Interview by William Russell, 1975.

183 "the session . . . failing him." Ibid.

184 "You never really . . . going to lose." Ibid.

186 "They make you promises . . . play music." Floyd Levin, *Classic Jazz*, from notes of Rex Stewart, 1967, University of California Press, Berkeley, 2000, p. 111.

186 "Those fellows . . . and such things." George Guesnon interview by William Russell, New Orleans Historical Collection, June 1958, p. 8.

187 "The Lion . . . the left hand." Albert Nicholas, autobiographical fragments, New Orleans, Jan. 1970.

188 "That was the first . . . timed perfectly." Ibid.

CHAPTER EIGHT

195 "At Jelly's request . . . to its close." "Oh, Mister Jelly" by Charles Edward Smith, The Jazz Record, Feb. 1944, p. 8.

196 "Well, Jelly . . . just wait a minute." Notes of interview of Henry "Red" Allen by John Childen, London, Aug. 1973.

196 "We hit the thing . . . time wasting." Ibid.

197 "Gee, I'm sorry . . . poor fellows waiting." Ibid.

198 "It must have been . . . back to her." George Guesnon interview by William Russell, New Orleans Historical Collection, June 1958, p. 8.

198 "All the time . . . seen it no more." Ibid.

201 "Now I'm gonna go . . . they're playin'." Albert Nicholas, autobiographical fragments, New Orleans, Jan. 1970.

203 "Jelly, I've got . . . play no intermission." Ibid.

203 "Man, I play . . . Proud." Ibid.

203 "Jelly completely . . . answer the questions." Fred Ramsey, Jr. Interview by William Russell, 1975.

204 "If he really . . . just any program." Lawrence Lucie interview by William Russell, New York, Sept. 1971, p. 5.

205 "looking for . . . more reasonable." Steven Smith, "The 1939 RCA-Victor Recording Session," New Orleans Historical Collection, Jan. 5, 1972.

216 "I've been robbed . . . I have now." George Hoefer, *Down Beat*, Oct. 1, 1940.

217 "I asked him . . . attack worse." Lomax, op cit., p. 250–251.

217 "Father, I have just . . . by degrees. Ibid.

217 "That was . . . my husband." Ibid.

CHAPTER NINE

223 "Those arrangements . . . show them." Ed Montudie Garland interview by William Russell, Los Angeles, July 1969.

227 "Seriously ill . . . so much to do." Charlie Emge, *Down Beat*, April 1, 1941, Chicago, p.13.

227 "It's swell . . . need any help" *Down Beat*, May 1, 1941, Chicago, p. 13.

230 "He actually looked like a black Christ." David Stuart, notes for manuscript for William Russell, Hollywood, CA, July 1969.

230 "I always thought . . . utterly silent." Ibid.

231 "Sure appreciate . . . could with Jelly." Spikes Benjamin J. (Reb) Spikes interview with Jazz Oral History Project, Institute of Jazz Studies, Rutgers University, Newark, NJ.

CHAPTER TEN

234 "That's not . . . Mrs. Morton." Floyd Levin, *Classic Jazz*, University of California Press, Berkeley, CA, 2000, p. 123.

236 "Jelly Roll . . . nowhere." Lomax, op cit., p. 227.

236 "So far as . . . royalties." Ibid, p.229.

236 "Jelly Roll's . . . Negro status." Ibid, p. 263.

236 "never lost . . . Negroes." Ibid, p. 254.

240 "I say that . . . popular music." Edward Niles, testimony, U.S. District Court, Southern District, New York, 1959.

APPENDIX A

COMPOSITIONS WRITTEN BY FERDINAND "JELLY ROLL" MORTON

Sources for titles and publication dates: U.S. Copyright Office, Library of Congress and Historic New Orleans Collection.

1915

Publisher: Will Rossiter
Jelly Roll Blues

1918

Publisher: Ferdinand Morton
Frog-I-More Rag

1923

Publisher: Spikes Brothers Publishing Co.
Froggie Moore

Publisher: Smith, Lloyd
Big Foot Ham

Publisher: Melrose Bros. Music Co.
Wolverine Blues
Grandpa's Spells
London Blues
Kansas City Stomp

Publisher: Morton
Mr. Jelly Lord

1924

Publisher: Melrose
King Porter Stomp

1925

Publisher: Melrose
Midnight Mamma

Milenberg Joys
New Orleans Blues
The Pearls
Queen of Spades
Shreveport Stomps
Tom Cat Blues

1926

Publisher: Melrose
Sidewalk Blues
Black Bottom Stomp
Cannon Ball Blues
Chicago Breakdown
Dead Man Blues
Sweetheart o' Mine (Frog-I-More Rag)

Publisher: Charlie Raymond
State and Madison

1927

Publisher: Melrose
Jungle Blues
Billy Goat Stomp
Hyena Stomp
Ted Lewis Blues
Wild Man Blues

1928

Publisher: Triangle Music Publishing Co.
Ham and Eggs
Buffalo Blues

1929

Publisher: Southern Music Co.
Burnin' the Iceberg
Freakish
New Orleans Bump

Pretty Lil
Seattle Hunch
Tank Town Bump

1930

Publisher: Southern
Deep Creek
Don't Tell Me Nothin' 'Bout My Man
Fussy Mabel
Harmony Blues
I'm Looking for a Little Bluebird
Little Lawrence
Mushmouth Shuffle
Pontchartrain
Red Hot Pepper

Publisher: Morton
I Hate a Man Like You

1931

Publisher: Southern
Blue Blood Blues
Fickle Fay Creep
Frances
Pep
That'll Never Do
That's Like It Ought to Be

1932

Publisher: Southern
Strokin' Away
Crazy Chords
Each Day
Gambling Jack
If Someone Would Only Love Me
Low Gravy
Mint Julep
Oil Well

1933

Publisher: Southern
Sweet Peter
Jersey Fox-Trot

1934

Publisher: Southern
Load of Coal
Primrose Stomp
Mississippi
If You Knew How I Love You

1938

Publisher: Tempo
My Home Is a Southern Town
Why?

1939

Publisher: Tempo
Anamule Dance
The Crave
Don't You Leave Me Here
Good Old New York
I Thought I Heard Buddy Bolden Say
Mamie's Blues
Mr. Joe
Naked Dance
Sporting House Rag
Winin' Boy

Publisher: Morton
I'm Alabama Bound

Publisher: Watts, Paul
We Will Never Say Good-By

1940

Publisher: Tempo

Big Lip Blues
Dirty, Dirty, Dirty
Get the Bucket
Original Rags by Scott Joplin
Shake It
Swinging the Elks

1942

Publisher: Roy Carew
The Finger Breaker

1944

Publisher: Carew
Creepy Feeling

1948

Publisher: Estate of Ferdinand Morton
Aaron Harris
Bert Williams
Jelly Roll Morton Scat Song
LaPaloma into Blues
Spanish Swat
Sweet Jazz Music

Publisher: Tempo
Honky Tonk Music

Publisher: Smith, Harrison
Smart Set Stomp

1949

Publisher: Estate
Soap Suds
Albert Carroll's Blues
Benny Frenchy's Defeat
Boogie Woogie Blues
Game Kid Blues
Crazy Chord Rag
Buddy Bertrand's Blues

Mamanita
Buddy Carter Rag
The Perfect Rag
Muddy Water Blues
Sammy Davis Ragtime Blues
Il Trovatore (arrangement)

Publisher: Carew
Miserere

1962

Publisher: Carew
Superior Rag

1999

Publisher: Tempo (filed by His-

toric New Orleans Collection, all
with new material arranged by
Morton for big band)

Mr. Joe

Oh, Baby

Southern Town

Don't You Leave Me Here

Climax Rag

We Are Elks

If You Knew

Sweet Substitute

Why?

Mama's Got a Baby

Finger Breaker

APPENDIX B

ANNOTATED DISCOGRAPHY: MORTON PLAYS MORTON

Jelly Roll Morton's recordings of his own music have been packaged and repackaged in so many different forms that listeners are hard-pressed to avoid duplication.

To help sift through the reams of reissues, the authors have focused on the most important and comprehensive releases, all on compact disc. The authors have not included reissues that tamper with Morton's recorded work, such as *Jelly Roll Morton: The Piano Rolls, Realized by Artis Wodehouse* (1997), which distorts the original recordings.

Instead, the emphasis in this discography is on releases that are characteristic of Morton's recorded output. Still unreleased, alas, are the rediscovered compositions from late in Morton's life.

Jelly Roll Morton: Complete Edition, Media 7.

This ongoing series, which to date includes eight compact discs (spanning 1923–1934), is by far the most exhaustive and scholarly of any available. Though it may be impossible for anyone to produce a complete set of Morton's recordings (bootleg and previously unknown recordings regularly turn up among collectors), this series, when finished, stands to be as close to complete as possible. Produced by the eminent French Morton scholar Roger Richard, *Jelly Roll Morton: Complete Edition* includes obscure early-period recordings made by such long-forgotten units as Jelly Roll Morton's Steamboat Four and Jelly Roll Morton's Jazz Kids, as well as seminal recordings by Morton's Trio and His Red Hot Peppers. The accompanying booklets, with erudite commentary from Richard, are never less than illuminating. The collection breaks down the Morton recorded oeuvre this way: Vol. 1, 1923–1924; Vol. 2, 1924–1926; Vol. 3, 1926; Vol. 4, 1927–1928; Vol. 5, 1928–1929; Vol. 6, 1929; Vol. 7, 1929–1930; Vol. 8, 1930–1934. Media 7, which has been releasing the CDs as part of its Masters of Jazz series, is at 52 rue Paul Lescop, 92000 Nanterre, France; tel. 41–20–90–50; e-mail is media7@easynet.fr.

Jelly Roll Morton, JSP Records.

This five-CD boxed set, which covers the years 1926–1930, is a revelation in purely sonic terms, bringing new acoustic clarity to Morton's work with various incarnations of His Red Hot Peppers. Inner voices, rhythmic details and subtleties of color that modern-day listeners had never heard before become palpably clear on these five CDs. Though the accompanying liner note material does not compare with the aforementioned *Jelly Roll Morton: Complete Edition,* this set stands as essential listening. Without it, Morton devotees cannot claim to have heard the Red Hot Peppers in their full, contrapuntal glory. JSP Records is at P.O. Box 1584, London N3 3NW, England.

The Jelly Roll Morton Centennial: His Complete Victor Recordings, Bluebird/RCA.

Offering 5 CDs in two boxes, this is the set that led many listeners to believe that Morton's birth date had been established as Oct. 20, 1890 (the accompanying booklet reproduced a "Certificate of Baptism" that was not created at the time of Morton's birth and is riddled with errors); but the assertion of this birth date no longer can be supported (see Appendix C, Notes on Morton's elusive birth date). Despite the popularity of this "centennial" edition release, it is easily superseded by the above-mentioned JSP Records set, at least so far as the 1926–1930 recordings are concerned. Yet as a general overview of Morton's career, this set is certainly adequate and has in its favor the portion of its liner notes written by the Morton scholar James Dapogny.

Jelly Roll Morton: Last Sessions, The Complete General Recordings, Commodore/GRP.

Morton's haunting last sessions, recorded in 1939 and 1940, shatter many myths, including the well-worn assertion that the man had become an artistic anachronism toward the end of his life. In fact, it would be difficult to find more timeless blues laments than Morton achieves in "Winin' Boy Blues" and "Buddy Bolden's Blues," or more stunning keyboard virtuosity than he displays on "Naked Dance" and "King Porter Stomp." Yet there's also no mistaking the world-weariness in Morton's work, particularly in the sighs and moans that mark his vocal style.

New Orleans Rhythm Kings and Jelly Roll Morton, Milestone.

The value of this single CD is in its juxtaposition of New Orleans Rhythm Kings recordings made with and without Morton in the early 1920s. Even a casual listener can hear the band transformed—for the better—when Morton is at the keyboard.

Jelly Roll Morton: Blues and Stomps from Rare Piano Rolls, Biograph.

Because the recording of piano rolls by definition allows for ambiguities in tempo and voicing, no CD of piano rolls by Morton—or anyone else—can be regarded as a definitive document of the artist's performance. This release, however, at least avoids the overediting of the previously mentioned *Jelly Roll Morton: The Piano Rolls, Realized by Artis Wodehouse* (1997). Instead, the recording straightforwardly includes Morton piano rolls from 1924–1926, as well as two newly minted rolls replicating Morton's pianism (and labeled as such), the project overseen by the noted Morton scholar Michael Montgomery.

Jelly Roll Morton: The Library of Congress Recordings, Rounder.

As a curtain-raiser for an eventual release of Morton's entire Library of Congress interviews, Rounder released the musical selections Morton played at the piano for folklorist Alan Lomax in 1938. These snippets, which cover four compact discs, are tantalizing, but one yearns to hear the complete, unedited sessions, including Morton's conversation. Until they are released on CD, these will have to do.

Central Avenue Sounds: Jazz in Los Angeles (1921–1956), Rhino.

In addition to dispelling the broadly held belief that jazz was late in arriving on the West Coast, this sterling, four-CD boxed set includes four lucidly remastered tracks by Morton, most notably a 1923 cut by Jelly Roll Morton's Jazz Band, playing "Someday Sweetheart."

APPENDIX C

NOTES ON MORTON'S
ELUSIVE BIRTH DATE

Because no birth certificate for Ferdinand Morton is known to survive, observers long have been speculating on the exact date of Morton's birth. The composer's tendency to list different dates on different occasions only served to cloud the issue.

But the date that Morton most often cited, and the one he swore was correct in his Library of Congress interviews with Alan Lomax, was September 20, 1885. Lomax may have been the first to accuse Morton of lying about this date in order to place himself at the dawn of jazz, but Lomax certainly was not the last.

Professor Lawrence Gushee, a noted Morton researcher, located a citation in a baptismal registry at St. Joseph's Church in New Orleans listing October 20, 1890, as Morton's birth date. The church issued a certificate of baptism listing this date, and because this certificate was reproduced in the liner notes to a five-CD boxed set, *The Jelly Roll Morton Centennial: His Complete Victor Recordings*, many scholars and critics have settled on the 1890 date.

Alas, this presumption is based on faulty information, for the 1890 date cannot be proved.

First, the aforementioned certificate of baptism was issued in 1984 and does not stand as the original document that many observers have assumed it to be. Moreover, both the certificate of baptism and the entry in the baptismal registry are riddled with errors. Morton's birth name, Lamothe, is misspelled, and the name of Morton's godmother, Eulalie Hecaut, is misspelled as Haco. Gushee himself concedes that October is probably the wrong month.

Moreover, Morton's half sister, Amide Colas, told William Russell that she was born in 1897 and that Jelly was eleven years older, which makes 1885 possible, if not probable. Lomax quotes Colas as telling Lomax that Morton was born "around 1886." And Morton's other half sister, Frances, concurred to Russell that 1885 was Morton's year of birth.

Lomax himself writes in his oral Morton biography, *Mister Jelly Roll,* that "after 1904 he [Morton] was constantly on the prod, using New Orleans only as a base of operations, and nurturing ambitions mortal strange for America's first jazz composer," making Morton a rover and rising composer at the unlikely age of fourteen, if the 1890 birth date is applied. In addition, Lomax quotes Bunk Johnson as having heard Morton in the District as early as 1902, which would make Morton a working professional at age twelve (an improbability, at best), if the 1890 birth date is used.

In addition, both Lomax and ragtime expert Rudi Blesh and Harriet Janis, in their definitive book, *They All Played Ragtime* (Oak Publications, 1971), affirm that Morton had planned to partake in a piano contest at the World's Fair in St. Louis in 1904, again at the unlikely age of fourteen, if 1890 was his birth year.

Finally, Carew—a Morton contemporary and confidante, as well as an eyewitness to the dawning of jazz in New Orleans—consistently placed Morton's birth date in 1885.

When informed that all of this information strongly contradicts the now oft-cited 1890 birth date, Gushee conceded as much.

"Mind you, my little world won't come to an end should the year be 1885, 1886, 1887, etc.," Gushee wrote to the authors.

In another letter, Gushee added, "It would not astound me if we found out somehow—was there a family Bible and, if so, where is it?—that Jelly's date of birth was not exactly as stated on the baptismal certificate. But ascertaining the true state of affairs is at the moment fairly far down my to-do list."

With Gushee having retreated from his original finding, 1890 clearly has no more veracity as Morton's birth date than 1885, and perhaps less.

For despite conventional wisdom, Morton was not the compulsive liar that white scholars have made him out to be, as the preceding pages have shown. Morton's disarmingly candid correspondence with Carew—which the authors verified by corroborating every detail that could be confirmed—in fact demonstrated Morton to be scrupulously correct in reciting the details of his life.

INDEX